CINEMATIC URBANISM
A History of the Modern from Reel to Real

Cinematic Urbanism presents an urban history of modernity and postmodernity through the lens of cinema while arguing that urbanism cannot be understood outside the space of the celluloid city.

Nezar AlSayyad traces the dissolution of the boundary between real and reel through time and space via a series of films that represent different modernities. He contrasts the 'rational' European city of early twentieth-century industrial modernity as portrayed by *Berlin: Symphony of a Big City* (1927) with its American counterpart in *Modern Times* (1936). He illustrates the different forms of small town life and an urbanizing modernity across the Atlantic as exemplified by *Cinema Paradiso* (1989) and *It's a Wonderful Life* (1946). Using *Metropolis* (1927) and *Brazil* (1985), he shows how utopian ideals harbour within them their dystopian realities, while Jacques Tati's nostalgia for tradition in *Mon Oncle* (1958) and *Playtime* (1967) reveals a cynical modernity and a rebelling against its idealism.

AlSayyad argues that the postmodern city of *Blade Runner* (1982) and *Falling Down* (1993) illustrates some of the urban outcomes of a globalizing economy. Turning to spectacle and surveillance, he examines *Rear Window* (1954), *Sliver* (1993), and *The End of Violence* (1997) as a voyeuristic modernity. To understand the city experienced by individuals of different social backgrounds, he takes *Manhattan* (1979), *Annie Hall* (1977), and *Taxi Driver* (1976), while *Do the Right Thing* (1989) and *My Beautiful Laundrette* (1985) are used to explore a modernity of race and ethnicity. Finally, he uses *Pleasantville* (1998) and *The Truman Show* (1998) to unpack the hyperreality of exurban postmodernity and to demonstrate how today the real and the reel have become mutually constitutive.

By considering how the real city and the reel city reference each other in an act of mutual representation and definition, this book advances the discussion on ity.

The history of the cinematic interpretation of the city has emerged as a new field of inquiry bringing together the history of art and architecture, urban, social and cinema studies. Nezar AlSayyad has provided the most lucid and thoughtful introduction to this exciting new intellectual terrain to date.

Dietrich Neumann,
Professor for the History of Modern Architecture,
Brown University, USA

CINEMATIC URBANISM

A History of the Modern from Reel to Real

Nezar AlSayyad

Routledge
Taylor & Francis Group

NEW YORK AND LONDON

First published by Routledge, 270 Madison Avenue, New York, NY 10016

Simultaneously published in the UK
by Routledge
2 Park Square, Milton Park, Abingdon,
Oxfordshire OX14 4RN

Routledge is an imprint of the Taylor & Francis Group, an informa business

© 2006 Nezar AlSayyad

Typeset in Aldine and Swiss by PNR Design, Didcot
Printed and bound in Great Britain by TJ International Ltd, Padstow, Cornwall

The publisher makes no representation, express or implied, with regard to the accuracy of the information contained in this book and cannot accept any legal responsibility or liability for any errors or omissions that may be made.

British Library Cataloguing in Publication Data
A catalogue record of this book is available from the British Library

Library of Congress Cataloging in Publication Data
AlSayyad, Nezar
Cinematic urbanism : a history of the modern from reel to real / Nezar AlSayyad.
 p. cm.
 Includes bibliographical references and index.
 ISBN 0-415-70048-5 (hb : alk. paper)—ISBN 0–415–70049–3 (pbk : alk. paper)
  1. Cities and towns in motion pictures. 2. City and town life in motion pictures.
  I. Title

 PN1995.9.C513A47 2006
 791.43'621732'—dc22

2006007637

ISBN10: 0–415–70048–5 (hb)
ISBN10: 0–415–70049–3 (pb)
ISBN10: 0–203–41303–2 (eb)

ISBN13: 978–0–415–70048–1 (hb)
ISBN13: 978–0–415–70049–8 (pb)
ISBN13: 978–0–203–41303–6 (eb)

Contents

Nezar AlSayyad is Professor of Architecture, Planning and Urban History at the University of California at Berkeley. He is the Associate Dean for International Programs at the College of Environmental Design, and Chair of the Center for Middle Eastern Studies at Berkeley. Additionally, he is the Director of the International Association for the Study of Traditional Environments and principal editor of its journal, *Traditional Dwellings and Settlements Review.*

I Ie is the author and editor of numerous books which include: *The Streets of Islamic Cairo* (1981); *Dwellings, Settlements and Tradition* (1989); *Cities & Caliphs* (1992); *Forms of Dominance* (1993); *Consuming Tradition* (2000); *Hybrid Urbanism* (2001); *Muslim Europe/Euro Islam* (2002); *Urban Informality* (2004); *The End of Tradition* (2004); and *Making Cairo Medieval* (2005). In the field of documentary filmmaking, he has written, co-produced, and/or co-directed *Virtual Cairo* and *At Home With Mother Earth* for public television.

Preface

Ever since I can remember, I have been as interested in cities as I have been in film. As an architect, I am fascinated with what film offers through its imaginative potential and its abilities to help us generate new spaces. As a planner, I view films as an arena of discourse in which our present understanding of cities and urban experience is often challenged. And as an urban historian, I see film as a very rich medium that has documented, reflected and represented human interaction in cities in a manner that no other medium has been able to approach.

In the course of the last decade, I began translating my interest into action by embarking on writing and co-producing a documentary film for public television, *At Home with Mother Earth*. This was my first experience in filmmaking, and it convinced me of the need to use the medium more effectively in research. This engagement also later led to *Virtual Cairo* – which I wrote, produced and directed for public television – which attempted to narrate an urban history of Cairo through the use of historic maps, visual images, and advanced computer-simulation techniques. The final product – part history, part contemporary reality, and part alternative fictional narrative – was very well received. Its success led me to experiment with film in the teaching of both architectural design and urban history.

First, in my Berkeley seminar, Architectural Design Thesis Preparation, I assigned students various exercises that required them to use known films to generate an underlying narrative or proposition for their theses. Then, after trying this format for a few years, I decided, in 1999, to offer an urban history seminar, which later became a full lecture course, that would attempt to narrate the story of twentieth-century urban modernity using film as the only frame of reference. My idea was simple, and my basic challenge to my students was direct: 'Imagine if there was no real New York or real Los Angeles or no trace left of them and the only thing we have are films that depict them or use them as a backdrop for their cinematic story. What kind of history would we write?'

It is this idea of history as it appears in the seemingly reel medium that got me started on this book. However, my exposure to the work of several French cultural theorists, primarily Jean Baudrillard and Paul Virilio, soon convinced me that the distinction between the real and the reel is often elusive. This applies not only to the connection between the two, but also to how these forms of experience have become co-dependent.

In the end, this book emerges as something of a compromise. To some extent, it is not a book about film, as film serves as the raw material for the telling of an alternative urban history. It is also not a book about cities, as it often does not engage with the actual physical attributes of those cities. Instead, it is a book about the space of the in-between, more specifically the in-between of real and reel space. Whether this book is ultimately also about a new theory of urban experience will only become apparent through the judgment of time.

Rather, this book aspires to present a history of urban modernity and postmodernity in the twentieth century as it is articulated in the real/reel spaces of the cinematic realm. In this regard, the book does not accept the division of spaces into real and reel but instead proceeds with the notion that reel space ceases to be primarily representational and in fact turns generative in its potential. As such, both the real and the reel in the twentieth century become mutually constitutive to a point that renders the study of one without the other incomplete or ill-informed. A study of twentieth-century urban space requires an engagement with both the real and the reel as two sides of the same coin. This book attempts to do so but in this case, the side of the coin that is up is reel space, and hence it receives more attention.

Here I would like to recall an important personal anecdote. On a family trip to New York City in 2001, my then five-year-old nephew Ishan, who was already a Hindi film buff, excitedly looked out of the car window as we crossed the Brooklyn Bridge. He was expecting to see the Statue of Liberty at any moment. When we told him that we still had some distance to go before we would see it, Ishan objected, vehemently insisting that, 'No, it should be here'. I was initially puzzled by his insistence, but as I spoke to him, his story started to unravel. Ishan's mother, who is also a Hindi film buff, used to play the Indian film *Kal Ho Naa Ho* on their VCR at home. Shot in New York, the popular film contains a scene of the actor Shahrukh Khan dancing on the bridge with the Statue of Liberty carefully montaged into the background. When in the real New York, Ishan's only frame of reference was the reel New York he saw on film. He was rightly disappointed when reality failed to match the image presented in virtual space. Ishan's story is only one among many that stands as the perfect justification for this book.

This project has taken over five years, during which the last two have been devoted to its writing. There are many individuals to acknowledge and thank. First, I would like to thank all the students who took my 'Cinematic City' seminar at the University of California, Berkeley. I have learned much from them over the four-year period it was taught. From this particular group, I would especially like to thank Suzanne Cowan, Natasha Case, and Madhuri Desai. I was so impressed by their contributions to the seminar that I invited each of them to work with me as a research assistant on specific chapters of the book. Mrinalini Rajagopalan, who has been my principal research assistant on a variety of other activities, also joined the team for one semester working on one chapter. Ipek Tureli, who came to Berkeley to do her PhD with me on a similar subject, joined the project after I stopped teaching the seminar but worked with me for an entire year diligently putting the book together. Ipek, who was already exposed to much of the literature, was my intellectual collaborator on the project during its consolidation phase, and I owe her much gratitude for her constant questioning of my ideas, a practice which ultimately resulted in a more nuanced argument. Varun Kapur was my research assistant in charge of images and releases. He did an excellent job in assembling a great visual library from which the final figures in this book were chosen. Sylvia Nam joined the project in its final stage, and worked with me on substantial last-minute revisions and on preparing the manuscript for submission to the publisher. I am grateful for her knowledge, dedication, and attention to detail. There are also others to thank. My staff at the Center for Middle Eastern Studies at Berkeley, Lily Cooc and Amanda Leung, were helpful in managing my academic life during the time I worked on the book. At Routledge, Caroline Mallinder and at Alexandrine Press, Ann Rudkin were patient and supportive and allowed me both the time and the space to produce what I hope is a unique book. David Moffat, my trusted editor and advisor for almost two decades, went through the entire book with a magnifying lens and edited much of the text. I wish to give special acknowledgment to his contribution. Ananya Roy, my intellectual partner, also gave me valuable criticism which itself had the effect of delaying the project for six months. I am grateful for her feedback, which made this a better book.

I hope that this book will spark debate among architects, planners, historians, film critics, and the general public about the city and urban life in the increasingly virtual, globalized world of the twenty-first century.

Nezar AlSayyad
Berkeley, June 2006

Introduction: The Cinematic City and the Quest for the Modern

No medium has ever captured the city and the experience of urban modernity better than film. Indeed, the relationship between the city and the cinema, although less than a century old, is a strong and well established one. The images and sounds found in movies today routinely bring people the experience of distant cities they may never visit. Film also captures the *mentalité* of society, disclosing much about its inner as well as outer life.[1] Movies influence the way we construct images of the world, and in many instances they influence how we operate within it.

If we accept the premise that movies are an integral constituent of the urban environment, then cinematic technique and cinematic representation over time should reveal much about both urban theory and the urban condition. Has this really been the case? Or have our theories and experience of modernity and postmodernity instead influenced, and possibly limited, the way we view the city in cinema?

To examine this proposition, I will start this book examining a select group of well-known films in an attempt to define the cinematic city of the twentieth century. In doing so, I will view the cinematic city through the lens of urbanization and the tropes of a rising urbanity. I will also focus on modernism's utopian aspirations and the parameters of a subsequent postmodern urban discourse. While I will deal with both images and reality, my focus will be on how images help reconfigure reality, and vice versa.

'Image' is defined in the *Oxford English Dictionary* as a likeness, a mental impression or picture, a vivid or graphic description, or a metaphor. As such, images shape our understanding of, and reactions to, the world we live in. Images act as mental reminders, cognitive maps, suggestive impositions, and creative projections.[2] The city itself is a 'social image' that has been studied in various disciplines, including literature, sociology, geography, and anthropology.[3] The links between the 'real' city and the 'reel' city may be indirect and complex.[4] However, commentators on contemporary culture and society have often noted a convergence between what is 'real' in the everyday and how we 'image' the everyday. The French philosopher Jean Baudrillard, one of the major theorists of the image in the twentieth century, has even argued that contemporary society knows itself unreflexively, only through the reflections that flow from the camera's eye.[5]

To better understand the relation between the cinema and the city, I will focus here on films that reflect attributes of the twentieth-century philosophies of modernity and postmodernity. However, I will deal with these films as a continuum rather than as representatives of dualistic concepts. In the process, I hope to emphasize the ways in which their mutually interdependent status sheds light on the meanings and practices of the cinematic city. This city is not only that which appears on the screen, but also the mental city made by the medium of cinema, and subsequently re-experienced in the real private and public spaces of the city.[6] I accept that film is always selective and partial, enabling it to produce a variety of meanings for the same image. Therefore, it is also important to understand how images may be viewed very differently by different audiences in different places at different times.

A discussion of twentieth-century modernity necessitates a look backward. Indeed, one can find its origins in the middle of the previous century. At that time, the French poet Charles Baudelaire was among the first to capture the emerging new mode of experience. He was also among the first to link this new mode of experience to the city as an arena of social interaction and economic exchange.

A fundamental part of the project of modernity has involved the reconstruction of cities. Baudelaire's day witnessed the opening of the great boulevards of Paris by Napoleon III and his city planner, Baron Haussmann. Haussmann's modernization, in fact, consisted not only of the opening of boulevards, but also the construction of monumental buildings, parks, a public transportation system, and a modern sewer system. Indeed, his urban design programme, which lasted for two decades, aimed at creating an entirely new city, one that would allow new forms of urbanization, industrialization, and capital accumulation.

Following earlier work by Walter Benjamin, and using a Marxist lens, Marshall Berman has used Baudelaire's poems – in particular, 'The Eyes of the Poor' in *Paris Spleen* – to discuss the effect of the boulevards and their importance for understanding modernity.[7] Due to the transformations he observed in Paris, Baudelaire recognized the coming of a 'modern life', the main experience of which was transient, ephemeral and contingent. Berman has suggested that this experience emerged from the destruction brought on by the top-down modernization of the city. In 'The Eyes of the Poor', Baudelaire tells the story of two lovers confronted by a poor family while sitting in a café on one of the newly opened boulevards. While one of the lovers wants the poor removed from her sight, the other is embarrassed by his privileged position; his sense of guilt eventually creates an unbridgeable gulf of feelings between them. Berman has pointed out that it was the opening up of the boulevards that enabled such new forms of public encounter between people of different classes. In this case, one such encounter forces the lovers to confront each other's worldviews, perhaps for the first time. In 'The Eyes of the Poor', the glass that separates the bourgeois lovers in the café from the poor outside may also be considered a double screen. In this nineteenth-century setting, it allows each to view the other in much the same manner provided by the movie screen of the twentieth century.

In Berman's account, the boulevards were paradigmatic sites of modernity that, among other things, created private spaces in public view. Thus, the café where Baudelaire's lovers sat was exposed to public gaze – although it was privately owned, and hence exclusionary. This sense of spectacle along the boulevards exposed the poor to a world that was previously concealed from them. The boulevards displaced the homes of the poor but not the poor themselves; indeed they revealed as never before, the misery of many inner-city neighborhoods. The traffic the boulevards encouraged also created new conditions of anonymity, and in the words of Berman 'paradoxically enforced new modes of freedom'.[8] Walter Benjamin's analysis of Baudelaire may be more appropriate here than Berman's.[9] What is significant is the idea that Baudelaire was looking for an art form that could fully capture the experience of modernity. It took close to another half century before cinema would provide this.

The ability of this new medium to capture images, process them, and then project them to the public contributed substantially to the making of the modern. In the process, cinema became engaged with the city, and vice versa, synchronizing its narrative and representational techniques with the emergence of radically new modern urban conditions. Thus, through most of the twentieth century, modernism was both depicted in and delivered from the screen to the city, defined in architectural styles and urban sociological profiles. At the end of the century, however, postmodern cinema, as a mode of representation and creative narrative, emerged to challenge this dynamic. Based on the same philosophical positions as postmodern literature and postmodern architecture, it sought either to recognize the inherent nature of fragmented realities or to deliberately project fragmentation so as to unsettle stable beliefs. It is this parallel relationship, or lack of it, between the real city and the reel city, which this book will employ as the framework on which to construct an urban history of modernity and postmodernity. Its underlying assumption is that the boundaries between the real and the reel are no longer useful to maintain.

Existing literature on cinema and the city, and the city in cinema – even when well researched – does not demonstrate a deep engagement with urban space.[10] Books by David Clarke, Dietrich Neumann, Francois Penz and Maureen Thomas, Mark Shiel and Tony Fitzmaurice, and bell hooks have laid the foundations for this exploration in cinematic space.[11] But it is my hope that this book will contribute two additional dimensions to this exploration: to make the urban a fundamental part of cinematic discourse and to raise film to its proper status as an analytical tool of urban discourse. The premise of this book then is that urban theory and theories of modernity may be greatly enhanced by using cinema as a critical medium of experience. In one sense, this project is not only about analysing cities as they appear on film, or understanding the difference between the reel and the real; it is also about new theories of the urban that emerge from cinematic space. In this sense, the project might alternatively be titled 'A Cinematic Epistemology of the City'. More particularly, however, it attempts to offer a history of modernity and postmodernity by focusing on the city in cinema as the primary medium of investigation. In this regard, cinematic space is employed both as an analytical tool and an object of critique: the city, real and reel, experienced and perceived, is both the medium and the subject of the book.

Another way of thinking about this project is that *Cinematic Urbanism* attempts to study modernity using film in the same way that Berman and T.J. Clark have used literature and painting in *All That is Solid Melts Into Air* and *The Painting of Modern Life*, respectively.[12] As in these two books, this one will also use primarily European and American examples. This is not done to locate modernity in the West, or suggest that it belongs to it. Instead, the choice to limit the parameters of discussion was made in order to understand the roots of modernity by focusing on its birthplace. No doubt, modernity was also shaped in the encounter between the West and its colonial subjects and territories, and alternative forms of modernity have arisen. One can learn as much by looking at the mid-century films of Satyajit Ray in India, Akira Kurosawa in Japan, or Youssef Chahine in Egypt. However, this is beyond the scope of this book, but I hope that some day studies of these other works will provide a logical extension of the ideas I present here.

Unlike other works which may deal with cinema, movies and cinematic concerns, it is also important to reiterate that I pursue this discourse not to learn about cinema itself, or about the cities that cinema has captured, represented and generated, but to learn about the built spaces of twentieth-century modern and postmodern society. The discourse about modern society and space has led to many distinctions in theory between modernity and postmodernity; but this book is not primarily about these discourses either. Instead it attempts to understand the actual reality and virtuality that inspired them in the first place. Recognizing that the line between the real and the virtual has fundamentally eroded, and that the two have become mutually constitutive, this book is an attempt to tell a history of the built environment in the twentieth century that is situated within this paradigm of a real–virtual continuum. The idea is that this couple of complementary parts – real–virtual – which first emerged when film started to influence and shape urban life, is not only an appropriate arena for understanding urban development in the twentieth century, but it is also a prerequisite for interpreting the socio-spatial changes that occurred during this time.

Urbanization, Industrialization and Modernity

In the early chapters of this book, I will examine a select group of films that are set in specific real or imagined cities and that illustrate the creation of modern cinematic urbanism. I will present these in a more or less chronological order when reasonable, following not only a cinematographic chronology, but also a historical timeframe of events. In later chapters, I will then examine a second set of films that construct a counterargument that highlights a break with this modernity. In the process, I hope to expose a cinematic postmodern urbanism that can be deciphered and linked to the discourse of postmodern urban space.

The first few chapters are organized as a history of the first half of the twentieth century. They are based on analysis of several films that reflect how the urbanism of traditional towns was rendered obsolete by new technologies, industrialization, and population growths, and modern ways of life.

The focus of the first chapter is the industrial modern city, particularly Berlin and New York, as depicted in *Berlin: Symphony of a Big City* (1927) and *Modern Times* (1936). Among other things, both films seek to come to grips with new Taylorist modes of production, Fordist modes of consumption, and a dramatic acceleration of life.

Walter Ruttmann's *Berlin* is among the first depictions of a rising modernity in film. It documents a typical day in the life of that city in 1927. When it appeared, it belonged to the modernist *avant garde* through its depiction of urban space and street life.[13] However, it also demonstrated how 'the general precondition for an assemblage of disparate images being viewed as having narrative meaning' relied on the 'stabilization of any number of possibly imaginable symbolic spatialities into one'.[14] In this sense, an appropriate analogy for *Berlin* may be cinema as a form of writing.

The character most easily associated with the experience of modernity is the *flâneur*.[15] Secure in his distance from the scenes he observes, and empowered by his ability to penetrate the 'labyrinthine' spaces of the city, he weaves an inevitably modernist narrative.[16] Berlin shows how the arrival of the cinema meant the return of *flânerie* – as in wandering around the city-spectacle – suggesting the confluence of 'a privileged mode of specularity and its newest mode of recording'.[17] In *Berlin*, the *flâneur* is represented by the camera, and many of its street scenes are presented with a Baudelairian flair.

Whereas *Berlin* aestheticized the new modes of production in the modern industrial city, Charles Chaplin's *Modern Times* provided an acerbic critique of these forces. The notion of Taylorist efficiency is central to both these films – particularly as it was synonymous at the time with specialization of labour and repetition in production. *Modern Times*, however, satirized factory conditions in the city. Chaplin's view was that Taylorism dehumanized workers by reducing their worth to their ability to perform mechanical tasks in the most efficient manner. In particular, the Taylorist method specified not only what a worker should do, but also how it should be done and the exact amount of time allowed for doing it, leaving no room for individual expression or innovation.

Berlin and *Modern Times* also resonated with prevailing moral views of the city in America and Europe. Many people, particularly in nineteenth-century Europe and early-twentieth-century America, considered cities to be dirty, unhealthy, dangerous, and even immoral places.[18] Many of America's best-known early thinkers, like Jefferson, Poe, Hawthorne, Emerson, and even architect Frank Lloyd Wright, expressed great hostility towards the city and urban life in general. The films, therefore, were able to tap into an existing moral dichotomy. Interestingly, this could be used not only to encompass the contrast between city and country, but between different parts of the same city – the city of affluence and capital versus the city of the working poor.

What emerges from these cultural views as a trope of industrial modernity is the character of the naïf struggling to understand his position in society. Benjamin cited just such a character when he invoked Edgar Allen Poe's short story 'Man of the Crowd', to describe the changing relationship between the modern metropolis and the practice of urban spectatorship.[19] However, unlike the *flâneur*, whose mode of observation was detached and leisurely, Benjamin argued that the man in the crowd, the badaud, was motivated by a desire to join the urban masses and immerse himself in the experience of the city.[20]

But the experience of the city here should not be isolated from its surroundings. Throughout the nineteenth century, debate raged over the merits of city versus country, drawing upon romantic traditions of the pastoral.[21] In particular, defenders of the new industrial order equated the urban with the artistic as well as the domestic.[22] In their view, the new industrial city would emancipate the working class and allow women to uphold and contribute to bourgeois domestic ideals. Given the overcrowding of cities, many reformers also actively tried to bring country life to the city.[23] Many others believed the ideal antidote to the horrors of the city was a quasi-rural/suburban retreat, accompanied by the withdrawal of women from commerce and employment. Indeed such a vision provided basis for late nineteenth-century Utopia Victoriana as portrayed in works such as Edward Bellamy's *Looking Backward* (1888), which imagined that rosy family values were preserved and held together by saccharine male–female relations.[24]

In the context of such disdain for the city, images of small-town life inevitably rose to prominence. In the second chapter, I use *Cinema Paradiso* (1989) and *It's a Wonderful Life* (1946) to understand the pressures of urbanization on small towns during the 1930s and 1940s. The films portray life in two towns, one on each side of the Atlantic, during this early modern era – which also corresponds to the introduction of cinema and other forms of mass communication.

It's a Wonderful Life remains an enduring icon of post-World War II American culture and modernity. It represents a reappearance of Victorian visions of small-town morality. Midway through the film, its setting, the small town of Bedford Falls, is contrasted in a nightmare sequence to the wild urban world of Pottersville, a dystopic place centred around a neon-lit Main Street of strip joints, pawnshops and bars. The particular Americanness of this ideal can be better understood in comparison to the similar, yet paradigmatically European, setting of *Cinema Paradiso*. Here the little Sicilian town of Giancaldo is made to conform to the nostalgic memory of the narrator, who spent his childhood there before rising to big city importance. The film describes the introduction of modernity through the evolution of cinema and its relationship with the audience, as well as its impact on the thoughts and lifestyles of the town's residents.

The trope that emerges from the experience of small-town life is one of the *blasé*, a person who becomes indifferent to the brutal conditions of everyday life in the city. Under metropolitan conditions, he has become a consumer who equally retreats, avoids, and confronts its many unpleasant encounters. The rendezvous emerges as an important compensatory social activity that signifies both the encounter with what is desired as well as its location in space.

Another response to the modern city came in the form of science-fiction depictions of dystopias. Chapter 3 uses *Metropolis* (1927) and *Brazil* (1985) to reflect on both the utopian and dystopian tendencies of this 'city of the future'. Since there is no utopian city without a dystopian vision, positive and negative images of the city in film are inextricably intertwined. It is well understood how utopias, when pushed to their logical conclusion, become dystopic; and, conversely, how all dystopias have embedded within them a utopian dream. Hence, the modern city cannot be understood apart from the embedded traditions it seems to have unsettled, and a postmodern urbanism is only possible as a reaction to or a rejection of an entrenched modernity.

Metropolis was the first futuristic movie to be shot on a studio set. It was also one of the first films to make literal the social division between an idle aristocracy of capitalists and their dehumanized labourers.[25] Here, the city of labourers is shown as existing deep underground, where it is dominated by machinery and Taylorist time-management apparatus. Meanwhile, the owning elite occupy a sunlit landscape of towering skyscrapers. When *Metropolis* was first screened it unsettled the nascent movie industry. Here was a film with a political outlook, one that could be interpreted as both strongly anti-capitalist and anti-urban, but also as anti-Nazi in particular or anti-fascist in general.

Metropolis dealt with a large number of issues that had broad contemporary relevance. It addressed problems pertaining to the urban poor and social unrest, generational conflicts, the vices and virtues of technology, and contemporary doubts about the redeeming power of religion. However the film was predominantly concerned with the city itself, and its maker, Fritz Lang, admitted that his fascination with the skyscrapers of New York had been the principal catalyst for its imagery.[26]

An understanding of the city of the future in cinema must be placed in the context of cinema's treatment of the city in general.[27] Throughout its early history, cinema shared the bias against the city that marked contemporary literature and the arts, and it espoused the widely held view that large cities were alienating and hostile places.[28] But it is also important to note that, '*Metropolis* was less a prediction of the world of 2000 AD than it was a model of the 1920s scaled up to nightmare proportions and overlain with a pastiche of the latest that New York could offer'.[29]

By contrast *Brazil* offers a postmodern portrayal of the experience of modernity as articulated by the state. The protagonist, in this filmic dystopia, is part of a bureaucratic apparatus that runs the city, who relies primarily on fantasy to escape his daily urban routine. Meanwhile the actual city he lives in is dominated by elements of panoptic surveillance, because (the film suggests) a perfect modernist city with a Fordist economy requires (or results in) total control of the inhabitants by the state. In some ways, the dystopic city in *Brazil* is spatially reminiscent of East European public housing projects in the 1950s, where the government presence was ubiquitous, inefficient and cumbersome. The dream world on the other hand, in both *Metropolis* and *Brazil*, is one of billowing clouds and rolling green hills.

The trope of the Orwellian modernity frequently present in cinema's future cities is the mechanized man – of human beings turned into machines by an omniscient bureaucracy. Robot-like, individuals must accept the roles assigned to them by the social welfare state in order to enhance Fordist modes of production.

Using two French films *Mon Oncle* (1958) and *Playtime* (1967), the fourth chapter presents another distinct view of the modernist city, one that I call 'cynical modernity'. In addition to building on earlier critiques of labour conditions, scientific rationalism, control, standardization and discipline, these films focus directly on disillusion with the physical outcome of modern architecture and urbanism. In the 1960s a general disenchantment with modernist cities began to set in, aided in both the United States and Europe by the ills wrought by urban renewal which often involved the demolition of large parts of traditional urban cores and their replacement with faceless, uniform, blocks of public, council, or social housing.

While everything around him is changing, the romantic protagonist in *Mon Oncle* continues to live in a traditional city block. His brother-in-law, by contrast, runs a plastics factory and lives in a modern Cubist villa. Through a story about the clash of these two worlds, the old and the new, the film critiques the marriage between urban renewal as a policy and modernism as an architectural ideology. *Playtime* further explores the banality of the modern city. In the film, the only time a well-known Parisian monument is seen is when a glass door opens to reveal the Eiffel Tower in ephemeral reflection. The residents of this Paris are instead portrayed as watching television, and living on top of one another, in glass apartment buildings that themselves resemble stacks of television sets.

The implied context here is the Americanization of Europe (and later, the rest of the world), which affects everything from household appliances to movies. As this passes through architecture and urbanism, it engenders a certain alienation. In these two films, the somewhat apolitical middle-class male protagonist strolls through a city, which is becoming increasingly undifferentiated from other cities. The trope of this modernity is the cynic whose experience has made him part *flâneur*, part *blasé*, and part tramp, and who is unable to relate to his modern surroundings.

Flexibility, Fragmentation, and Postmodernity

Postmodernism, in its broader scope, involves a crisis of knowledge and representation. Modernism allowed the image to become reality and the photograph to become history. Postmodernism emerged based on the recognition that there was no longer a stable, neutral, outside place, and that it was often no longer possible to differentiate between the real and the simulated. The shattering of the modernist Archimedean point of view, which had previously offered the possibility of viewing the city as panorama, gave way to a frantic montage of images.[30] Such fragmentation meant it was only possible to know the world in disjointed and chaotic ways. Unlike older media, film has been able to depict powerfully this postmodern crisis. As an art form it has been particularly successful both with its usage of images and its ability to cut back and forth across time and space, as well as being able to handle intertwining and fragmented themes simultaneously.[31] Indeed, as a medium, film is a reflection of postmodernity as an experience.

Architectural and urbanistic postmodernity can be dated, at least in America, to the early 1970s. After the 1973 recession, American cities became stages for a new type of economic arrangement in which labour, consumption and production followed new patterns of flexible accumulation. These new social relations of capitalism defined new spatial arrangements, which in turn, resulted in a recalibration of the concept of class. In this new world, the poor were left with little or no control over space. Meanwhile, the upper classes came to define their sense and access to the community less through spatial boundaries than through reaffirmations of identity based on the production of 'symbolic capital'.[32] The postmodern city embodies this compression of space and time, as well as the fragmentation of reality and the privatization of public life and space.

Using *Blade Runner* (1982) and *Falling Down* (1993), and focusing on Los Angeles, Chapter 5 attempts to tell the story of the ultimate postmodern city, where utopian aspirations have turned into a dystopic hell. These two films echo Mike Davis's writings in the *City of Quartz* on the paranoid fortress mentality in cities like Los Angeles. Such a mentality destroys any possibility of creating public space; takes class separation to architectural and spatial extremes; and turns the city into a series of prison-like commercial and private structures, in which protection is achieved through integrated electronic surveillance, and the exclusion of undesirable influences. This is the city of defensible spaces, fear and distrust, where the boundaries between creative destruction and destructive creation are no longer clear, and no longer relevant.[33]

Blade Runner is set in an apocalyptic Los Angeles of the year 2019. The film represents the city as spatially and politically fragmented, no longer organized or controlled in the comprehensive way of the modernist *Brazil*. In this city, flexible accumulation of capital has been rendered visible, and with their tremendous power corporations can hire entire ethnic communities to manufacture parts of a larger system of whose overall purpose is never revealed to them. Likewise, many goods are so highly priced that their producers no longer even contemplate the chance to buy them.

The city of the future is depicted as a montage of the most sordid physical aspects of the urban present. This is the city as a Third World bazaar, where the language in the streets has devolved into a strange, immigrant, 'city-speak'. While the masses struggle, the elite live in luxurious multi-storeyed, pyramidal structures.

The main characters of the film are a gang of escaped replicants, and its protagonist is a 'blade runner', a type of policeman, whose mission is to track them down and 'retire' them. The search for the replicants depends upon a certain technique of interrogation, which relies on the fact that they have no real history since they were genetically created as full adults and lack the experience of childhood or other processes of socialization.[34] The blade runner's relationship to the replicants, however, is rightly ambiguous, since they are both his prey and his kin and they share with him the condition of being controlled and enslaved by a powerful corporation.[35]

Falling Down uses present-day Los Angeles as its setting. The film charts the journey of two male characters, an out-of-work engineer and a retiring police officer, both of whom are trying to reach 'home'. The engineer represents an obsolete, universal 'everyman'. He traverses a landscape that he constructs as fragmented, hostile, violent, unreadable – and therefore out of control.[36]

The trope of the postmodern, postindustrial condition portrayed in these films is the cyborg or replicant. As a slave, bred to have advanced technical skills, the cyborg has been designed to replace the everyman in a new world of socio-economic fragmentation and outsourcing. But he also replaces the colonized Third World man, who is likewise becoming a slave to the new global economic order, despite living in countries with seemingly independent political status.

Using the films *Rear Window* (1954), *Sliver* (1993), and *The End of Violence* (1997), Chapter 6, next moves the discussion to the voyeuristic city. The protagonist of Hitchcock's *Rear Window* is a modern urban personification of the *voyeur* who observes the dystopic qualities of urban life from the safety of his own private realm. Constrained by physical immobility, watching becomes for him the central act of engagement with the world – to a point where it almost becomes more important than his own life.

In *Sliver*, the same figure reappears in a high-tech guise, setting up a sophisticated surveillance system to observe his neighbours' lives. When the main female character discovers her boyfriend's voyeurism, she too engages in these activities, despite having been their victim earlier, and experiences a complex mix of pleasure and guilt. The film explores the loss of innocence that is involved with becoming a *voyeur*. The French philosopher Paul Virilio has defined this moment as that when the only thing that seems to separate one space from an other is a depthless surface, an *interface*. Under these conditions, the concepts of here and now are no longer meaningful, and chronological or historical time is replaced by a time that exposes itself instantaneously.[37] This is the moment when the city becomes exposed in all its vulnerability, and the eye can see it all. This is the particular moment that connects modernity to postmodernity.

In *The End of Violence*, a secret project of surveillance to eliminate crime proves so successful that it destroys urban life altogether. One protagonist in this film is a state employee who runs this system of panoptic surveillance. The other is a powerful Hollywood producer who can only recover his life by escaping it.

As a trope for this modernity of surveillance, the figure of the invisible *voyeur* is empowered by technology but also seduced by access to the private space of others. However there is a shift in the ends to which voyeurism is put over these three films. Increasingly, voyeuristic power is seen as consolidating state power through images.

Class, Race, and Exurbanity

The last section of the book examines the modernity of class and race and its articulation in exurban space. Chapter 7 uses three films set in New York – Woody Allen's *Manhattan* (1979) and *Annie Hall* (1977), and Martin Scorsese's *Taxi Driver* (1976) – to explore the modernity of class, and to examine how the city may be imagined and reinterpreted by individuals of different social backgrounds. For years, New York has served as the quintessential metropolis, the cinematic city *par excellence*. However, these films present it through very different eyes. To create such subjective portrayals, the filmmakers recast the geographies of the city through the manipulation of light and sound, the selection of shooting locations, and the creation of narrative spaces that reflect the characters' moods. In the case of the Woody Allen films, these techniques create a sense of sophistication and privilege. In the case of *Taxi Driver*, they show the visual chaos, violence and fear that accompany the violence and fears of the urban underclass.[38]

In *Manhattan*, the city is presented as an ultimate space of consumption, where the service and the culture industries primarily exist to support a sophisticated urban lifestyle. The skyline acts as the frame of reference in the film, and the choice of the camera location often highlights the presence of important cultural institutions.

In *Annie Hall*, the protagonist is a quintessential New Yorker who embodies the elite intellectual postmodern *flâneur*. The image of his city is, however, cast in opposition to that of Los Angeles, a reputed utopian alternative for those who want to escape the truly urban. Without getting personally involved in the fragmentation of Los Angeles' urban life, the protagonist is able to use his privileged position as *flâneur* to observe, consume and critique it.

In *Taxi Driver*, New York is presented through a jittery camera positioned on the cab's front bumper, or through the eyes of its driver, a Vietnam War veteran. While driving his cab through the red-light districts of the city, the protagonist witnesses a dark, raw and violent city. At first he adopts a *blasé* attitude towards what he sees. But he later goes on a mission to wash it clean of all he categorizes as filth. In the end, this leads to an act of horrific violence.

The contrast between these two New Yorks suggests the emergence of a different form of *flânerie* in the second half of the twentieth century. Unlike the Baudelairian *flânerie* of mid-nineteenth-century Paris, this new modernity is devoid of class encounter; instead each class has created its own city within a city.

Chapter 8 next shows how the use of race and ethnicity as a lens to understand the city further complicates this picture. It explores these views using the films *Do the Right Thing* (1989) and *My Beautiful Laundrette* (1985). In *My Beautiful Laundrette*, problems of race and ethnicity get tied up with larger imaginaries of nation and identity. The film addresses questions of legitimation and authenticity in contemporary multicultural British urban society, where the idea of otherness is constantly defined and redefined. The evolving relationship between the two main protagonists, a White working-class youth and the son of a Pakistani immigrant, crosses boundaries of class, race and sexuality. Within the neighbourhood they reside in, fighting provides a forum of person validation and a test of masculinity. But they become, in succession, friends, lovers, and finally employer and employee in a reversal of ethnic roles.

The film shows how White, working-class boys are able to reaffirm their own identity through their sense of superiority over girls and members of ethnic minority groups. However, the multicultural condition of the city they inhabit also implies the notion of a multiracial subject. Still, racial friction and violence define specific economies of class and race.

Similarly, *Do the Right Thing* is about a deeply fragmented city and society, where social interaction implies a continuous struggle to appropriate space along racial lines. The multiethnic community portrayed in the film consists of African, Italian, Asian, and Hispanic Americans. But its apparent balance is shattered by a confrontation over who should be represented on the walls of a neighbourhood pizzeria: Italian-American or Black celebrities.

Two years after *Do the Right Thing* appeared, the LA riots were triggered by the verdict in the Rodney King beating case. At that time, the popular media focused on issues of community breakdown in an attempt to explain the breakout of urban mayhem. But Mike Davis has suggested that the real cause of the race riots in Los Angeles was underlying fictional views of race. He has further contended that our gleeful response to the fictional destruction of Los Angeles in films reflects our ongoing desire not only to isolate ourselves from, but also to destroy, the 'other'.[39] This is a modernity of race where the city is not only divided into ethnic neighbourhoods whose ethnic mix creates and recreates unresolved encounters on the streets, but also a modernity where the race of the observer and the observed often redefine the nature and meaning of the encounter itself.

This leads us to the cinematic city of the 1990s, where ultimate scopic control and paranoid security necessitate ideal, anti-urban environments which double as stage sets. In Chapter 9, I move the discussion of the postmodern city back to the small town of *It's a Wonderful Life* – but this time in the form of a manicured postmodern New Urbanism as represented in *The Truman Show* (1998) and *Pleasantville* (1998).

The protagonist of *The Truman Show* is a character in a reality TV show, whose entire life is manipulated and manufactured around him. As the audience begins to identify with the protagonist, the film calls into question our own definition of reality by highlighting the virtues of the virtual city. Here, TV supplants the real and the boundaries between the real and the staged disappear, until the protagonist reaches the very edges of his fake town and discovers that he is being watched. In his desire to free himself, he discovers that he has been the prisoner in an inverted panopticon. But he eventually realizes that, as the subject of voyeurism by an entire society of virtual *flâneurs*, he can control those who surveil him as much as they control him.

Pleasantville also concerns a TV show about a perfect town. But the *status quo* here is constantly reaffirmed by clearly defined gender roles. With no possibility of difference or conflict breaking through the perfect equilibrium, reality has become a homogeneous, orderly, harmonious, and literally black-and-white experience. Pleasantville's leader is not a mayor but the head of the chamber of commerce, life seems under control, and entertainment and leisure happen following the script of commercial advertisements. However the inability of town residents to represent places denies them their own existence, an existence confined to undisturbed and predictable acts. It is only through the introduction of knowledge from outside, by means of newcomers transposed from real life into the TV show, that authenticity and freedom can burst out. Colour becomes the metaphor in the film for real and differentiated experiences, and an awakening to the unpredictability of life.

The trope of the postmodern exurban condition is thus a panopticon. Unlike the traditional panopticon, however, this device is inverted, allowing the prisoners to view a central space over which they have some control. This is a new world where the reel has become the real, and where the observed have entered the camera itself, to be reprojected not as themselves but as places that transcend the spatial-virtual divide.

Faced with the paralysis of the postmodern cinematic city, we are inevitably confronted with questions of apprehension: 'Where do we go from here?' What could exist after the Los Angeles of *Blade Runner*, *The*

Truman Show's Sea Haven, or *Pleasantville*?[40] How can we ameliorate the alienation of the individual? In *Lisbon Story* (1994), the director Wim Wenders offers an answer. It tells of a filmmaker who is paralyzed by the realization that the city he captures on film is not the 'real' city. Hoping to explore this dilemma, he lets the camera roll behind his back capturing images that his eye does not see. The protagonist is a soundman who wanders about recording an alternative narrative composed solely of sound. The soundman finally confronts the filmmaker, reminding him that the magic of cinema is this very act of looking and representing. It is this confrontation that makes both the real and the reel meaningful.

As this short synopsis indicates, the films I discuss here either reveal the dystopic potential of modernist utopias, or present a postmodernist fragmentation that cannot be understood without the embedded assumption of modernist desires. I have increasingly come to believe that our understanding of the city cannot be viewed independently of the cinematic experience. Baudrillard's much-quoted notion of starting from the screen and moving to the city accepts a duality between the real city and the reel city that no longer exists.[41] I propose instead that to understand this relationship better, we should start not from one and move to the other, but engage both simultaneously. In what Baudrillard calls the 'collapse of metaphor … the obscenity of obviousness … our chasms of affectation', culture keeps imitating and duplicating itself in a delirious self-referentiality. In a pervasive game of mirrors reflecting each other, art imitates life, life imitates art, art imitates art, and life imitates life.[42]

Starting with traditional towns and moving to big cities, this book analyses the changes that time and history have imprinted on our imagination of them and the way these changes have been represented in cinema. Here, the real city and the reel city reference each other simultaneously, in an act of mutual representation and definition. The relationship between modernity and postmodernity is further intertwined when we accept that every moment of utopian modernity contains within it the entropic possibility of becoming a dystopia. Likewise, postmodern fragmentation is facilitated by such modernist inventions as the compression of time and space, the flexible accumulation of capital, and the dissolution of the individual under regimes of surveillance and hyper-reality. In other words, postmodernity is graspable only in terms of the modernist parameters that lie at its core.

Today's cinematic city often reflects the nostalgic desires of postmodernity that translate in acts of replication and self-representation – as attempts to go back to the lost village, the family, and the community. The modern Baudelairian *flâneur* of the streets has become the postmodern virtual *voyeur* staring at himself – or at himself trapped in a panopticon where the observer and the observed are no longer relevant to the operation of that whole. The inevitable result of all this is that the beginning becomes the end, and the end meets the beginning.

In this same manner, we come full circle following the path cities have taken in cinematic and urban history: from tradition and the modernist utopias and dystopias, to the anguish of postmodern fragmentation, and finally to the only thing that is left to desire – to go back.

Films

Annie Hall (1977) directed by Woody Allen

Berlin: Symphony of a Big City [*Berlin: die Die Sinfonie der Großstadt*] (1927) directed by Walter Ruttmann

Blade Runner (1982) directed by Ridley Scott

Brazil (1985) directed by Terry Gilliam

Cinema Paradiso (1989) directed by Giuseppe Tornatore

Do the Right Thing (1989) directed by Spike Lee

Falling Down (1993) directed by Joel Schumacher

It's a Wonderful Life (1946) directed by Frank Capra

Manhattan (1979) directed by Woody Allen

Metropolis (1927) directed by Fritz Lang

Modern Times (1936) directed by Charles Chaplin

Mon Oncle (1958) directed by Jacques Tati

My Beautiful Laundrette (1985) directed by Stephen Frears

Playtime (1967) directed by Jacques Tati

Pleasantville (1998) directed by Garry Ross

Rear Window (1954) directed by Alfred Hitchcock

Sliver (1993) directed by Phillip Noyce

Taxi Driver (1976) directed by Martin Scorsese

The End of Violence (1997) directed by Wim Wenders

The Truman Show (1998) directed by Peter Weir

Notes

1   A. Schlesinger Jr., 'Forward'. in J.E. O'Connor and M. Jackson (eds.) *American History/American Film: Interpreting the Hollywood Image*. New York: Frederick Unger, 1979, p. xi.

2   G. Suttles, *The Social Construction of Communities*. Chicago: University of Chicago Press, 1972.

3   B. Pike, *The Image of the City in Modern Literature*. Princeton: Princeton University Press, 1980; R. Park and E. Burgess, *The City*. Chicago, University of Chicago Press, 1967 (1925).

4   S. Aitken and L. Zonn, 'Representing the Place Pastiche', in S. Aitken and L. Zonn (eds.) *Place, Power and Spectacle*. Lanham, MD: Rowman and Littlefield, 1994, p. 5; D. Muzzio, '"Decent People Shouldn't Live Here Anymore": The American City in Cinema', *Journal of Urban Affairs*, vol.1, no. 18, p. 194.

5   J. Baudrillard, 'Astral America', in C. Turner (trans.), *America*. London: Verso, 1988.

6   D. Clarke (ed.), *The Cinematic City*. London: Routledge, 1997.

7   M. Berman, 'Baudelaire: Modernism in the Streets', in *All That is Solid Melts Into Air: The Experience of Modernity*. New York: Simon and Schuster, 1982, pp. 131–171.

8   *Ibid.*, p. 159.

9   W. Benjamin, 'The Paris of the Second Empire in Baudelaire', and 'Some Motifs in Baudelaire', in *Charles Baudelaire: A Lyric Poet in the Era of High Capitalism*, H. Zohn (trans.). London: Verso, 1983.

10 While there are other books with similar titles, there is no comparable, competitive book that takes one step further into a larger picture of contextualizing cinema in historic urbanism.

11 D. Clarke (ed.), *The Cinematic City*; D. Neumann (ed.), *Film Architecture: Set Designs From Metropolis to Blade Runner*. Munich: Prestel, 1996; F. Penz and M. Thomas (eds.), *Cinema & Architecture: Méliès, Mallet-Stevens, Multimedia*. London: British Film Institute, 1997; M. Shiel and T. Fitzmaurice (eds.), *Cinema and the City: Film and Urban Societies in a Global Contex*. Oxford: Blackwell, 2001; and bell hooks, *Reel to Real: Race, Sex, and Class at the Movies*. New York: Routledge, 1996.

12 M. Berman, *All That is Solid Melts Into Air*, pp. 72–89; T.J. Clark, *The Painting of Modern Life: Paris in the Art of Manet and His Followers*. Princeton, NJ: Princeton University Press, 1984.

13 W. Natter, 'The City as Cinematic Space: Modernism and Place in *Berlin: Symphony of a City*', *Place, Power and Spectacle*, p. 204.

14 *Ibid.*, p. 203

15 E. Wilson, 'The Invisible *Flâneur*', in S. Watson and K. Gibson (eds.), *Postmodern Cities and Spaces*. Oxford: Blackwell, 1995, pp. 59–79. The reference is from page 61.

16 R. Williams, *The Country and the City*. New York: Oxford University Press, 1973, p. 227.

17 W. Natter, 'The City as Cinematic Space…', pp. 204–208.

18 D. Muzzio, '"Decent People Shouldn't Live Here Anymore"…' p. 190.

19 W. Benjamin, 'The Paris of the Second Empire in Baudelaire', and 'Some Motifs in Baudelaire'.

20 T. Gunning, 'From Kaleidoscope to the X-Ray: Urban Spectatorship, Poe, Benjamin and *Traffic in Souls* (1913)', *Wide Angle*, vol. 19, no. 4, 1997, pp. 25–63.

21 Raymond Williams's literary exploration on the 'the country and the city' also allows us to explore the notion of the stranger in the city. In R. Williams, *The Country and the City*. New York: Oxford University Press, 1973.

22 E. Wilson, *The Sphinx in the City: Urban Life, the Control of Disorder, and Women*. Los Angeles: University of California Press, 1992.

23 *Ibid.*

24 Utopia derives from '*u-topos*' meaning no-place/*eu-topia*, good place/ *ude-topia*, never-land.

25 N.G. Leigh, and J. Kenny, 'The City of Cinema: Interpreting Urban Images on Film', *Journal of Planning Education and Research*, no. 16, 1996, p. 52.

26 N. Dietrich, 'Before and after Metropolis,' in *Film Architecture*, p. 34.

27 J. Gold, 'From "Metropolis" to the "City": Film Visions of the Future City, 1919–39', in J. Gold and J. Burgess (eds.) *Geography, the Media and Popular Culture*. London: Croom Helm, 1985, p. 125.

28 *Ibid.*

29 *Ibid.*

30 E. Soja, *Postmodern Geographies: The Reassertion of Space in Critical Social Theory*. London:Verso, 1989; E. Mahoney, '"The people in parentheses": Space Under Pressure in the Postmodern City', in *The Cinematic City*, p. 169.

31 For more on this, refer to D. Harvey, *The Condition of Postmodernity: An Enquiry into the Origins of Cultural Change*. Oxford: Basil Blackwell, 1989, p. 308.

32 D. Harvey, *The Condition of Postmodernity*. Also, see F. Jameson, *Postmodernism, or, The Cultural Logic of Late Capitalism*. Durham, NC: Duke University Press, 1991.

33 *Ibid.*, pp. 311–313; M. Davis, 'Fortress Los Angeles: The Militarization of Urban Space', *City of Quartz: Excavating the Future in Los Angeles*, London, Verso, 1990, pp. 221–264.

34 D. Harvey, *The Condition of Postmodernity*, pp. 311–313.

35 *Ibid.*

36 E. Mahoney, '"The People in Parentheses"…', p. 174.

37 P. Virilio, 'The Overexposed City', in N. Leach (ed.) *Rethinking Architecture: A Reader in Cultural Theory*. London: Routledge, 1997, pp. 382–383.

38 P. Kruth, 'The Colour of New York: Places and Spaces in the Spaces of Martin Scorsese and Woody Allen', *Cinema & Architecture: Méliès, Mallet-Stevens, Multimedia*, pp. 70–80. The reference is from page 73.

39 M. Davis, *Ecology of Fear: Los Angeles and the Imagination of Disaster*. New York: Metropolitan Books, 1998, p. 282.

40 D. Harvey, *The Condition of Postmodernity*.

41 Baudrillard argued that the city seems to have stepped out of the movies: 'To grasp its secret, you should not then begin with the city and move inwards towards a screen, you should begin with a screen and move outwards toward the city'. J. Baudrillard, 'Astral America'. Literature on film and the city has been much inspired by Baudrillard's work. For instance, David Clarke's introduction to *The Cinematic City* starts with Baudrillard's understanding of the relation of city and cinema.

42 J. Baudrillard, 'Astral America', p. 27.

Chapter 1

Industrial Modernity:
The *Flâneur* and the Tramp in
the Early Twentieth-Century City

Thus, the metropolitan type of man – which of course exists in a thousand individual variants – develops an organ protecting him against the currents and discrepancies of his external environment which would uproot him.[1]

Although the rise of the city in the twentieth century is closely allied to the experience of modernity, many theorists have distinguished between the experience of urban modernity and the larger processes of modernization. In these accounts, the experience of urban modernity is often based on Charles Baudelaire's encounters in the context of Haussmann's Paris.[2] Paris coalesced many of the images, marvels and regrets associated with a modern urban landscape – an amalgam of pleasure, guilt and detachment.[3] In general, a sense of detachment emerged in response to the sheer sensory experience characteristic of the modern city. But that sense of detachment and blaséness, which has its roots in the Baudelairian modernity of encounter in the mid-nineteenth century, was a more complex attitude that increased substantially.

Sociologists Georg Simmel and Louis Wirth were among the first to theorize the relationship between the individual and the modern city in the context of the rapidly industrializing world of the early twentieth century.[4] Simmel, the seminal theorist of modernity in Weimar Germany, had a 'unique position as a historically and geographically located cultural commentator on the urban modernity of his time'.[5] In a famous 1903 essay, 'The Metropolis and Mental Life', he identified the city in terms of its urban personality, which he believed was markedly different from that of small-town and rural life.[6] In a departure from earlier analyses, Simmel's essay was grounded in sociological analysis rather than an aesthetic response to the city. In particular, he used Baudelaire's trope of the gazing *flâneur* as a point of departure, and proceeded to describe the psychological effects of industrial capitalism on the individual city dweller.

In the modern city, Simmel suggested, there was an excess of sensory stimuli, against which modern man had to adopt a 'blasé attitude', or an incapacity to react. In Simmel's model, reactions were determined by intellect and calculation rather than by intuition and feelings. Driven by intellect, and protecting himself with a blasé attitude, the modern big-city resident became indifferent to 'genuine individuality' because it could not be easily explained in terms of economics. In the big city, individuality and difference were sought only if they pertained to a marketing strategy. Specialization and the division of labour in the big city also discouraged self-employment, leading Simmel's urban personality to feel socially freer – but economically dependent and hence vulnerable.[7]

Recently, Mark Gottdiener identified seven traits of Simmel's urbanite, an imaginary person he names 'Hans'.[8] In addition to acquiring a blasé attitude toward society at large, Hans's relationship to his work would be reduced to quantity rather than quality. In his relationship to his employers, he would experience impersonality due to monetary exchange. Outside work, he would turn into an anonymous consumer of a mass spectacle of consumption. Hans would attain skills of rational calculation. He would start experiencing time as schedule and space as construct. Yet, against all these disorienting developments, in the city Hans would be freed from the restrictions of the tightly knit community which he had in his Bavarian village. This last factor, then, would enable him to develop his individuality.[9] All of these are attributes which may be observed to different degrees in the protagonists of the films discussed in this book.

A contemporary of Simmel, the American sociologist Louis Wirth also pointed to the lack of personal communication among urbanites before World War II, and argued that existing theories of urbanism were not adequate to explain the complexities and social characteristics of cities.[10] Among other things, Wirth suggested that density, heterogeneity, and size of population should become bases of observation and research. Size enabled freedom, but also brought forth superficial, transitory encounters. Density prioritized visual communication in place of physical, social and verbal contact. Heterogeneity broke down and complicated class structure, replacing it with status group affiliation, which enabled social mobility but hindered individual self-expression. In addition, Wirth believed that age, sex, race and ethnicity were diversified in the city.[11]

Some fifty years later, the urban geographer David Harvey analysed 'the project of modernity' as an effort, beginning with the Enlightenment of the eighteenth century, to develop objectivity, universal morality, and law. Specifically, as time and space became sources of social power, the compression of time–space resulted in the rise of modernism as a cultural force. Driven by the impetus to create a new world, an essential part of this process was a project of 'creative destruction'. In order for a new world to be created, the existing one had to be destroyed.[12]

> Yet we are forced, if we strive for the eternal and immutable, to try and put our stamp upon the chaotic, the ephemeral, and the fragmentary. The Nietzschian image of creative destruction and destructive creation bridges the two sides of Baudelaire's formulation in a new way.[13]

Drawing on the work of Harvey, Bjorn Wittrock has suggested that the 'condition of modernity' implies certain cultural and institutional shifts in a society. For a society to be modern, Wittrock believes, there has to be some involvement of institutions in the form of large corporations or the state. These institutions are bound to fulfil the hopes and expectations that people necessarily have in a modern society.[14]

The city of the early twentieth century cannot be viewed independently of the process of industrialization; a dialectical relationship. As urban workers began to become consumers, and a range of new business, service, trade, construction, and transportation professional occupations came into being, urban populations provided an internal market for manufactured products, consumer goods, and services. Technology was a further important facilitator of this process. For instance, the development of rail transport and new manufacturing technology created many new skilled, unskilled and managerial jobs.[15] New forms of transportation also allowed for the emergence of a new form of suburban living. Mass entertainment was another integral part of the modern industrial city. Indeed, cinema itself was a significant new way for sensory experience to be consumed on a large scale. As a medium, cinema also began to express the city. The result was a new kind of urbanite whose dreams and aspirations were shaped by Taylorist production techniques and Fordist practices.

This chapter is an exploration of the different trajectories that these developments took in European and American cities as they appear in the two films, *Berlin: Symphony of a Big City* (1927) and *Modern Times* (1936). Using these two films, the chapter attempts to relate early theories of urban sociology developed by Simmel, Wirth, and others to the trope of the blasé to understand the transformations of the city in this newly industrializing era. Another equally significant variable, which will also be discussed, is the role of the state in regulating and maintaining the emerging urban order of the times. In some sense, industrial modernity is the subject of our analysis in this chapter; the invocation of the blasé is our main analytical tool; the relationships between production and consumption, state and market, is our spatial context; and, literally, the two films provide our main field of evidence.

Time, Mechanization and Urban Expansion

The dialectical relationship between the city of industrial modernity and the process of suburbanization was closely allied to developments in transportation. As industrialization progressed, revolution in mass transit changed the urban landscape, as well as the lives of its inhabitants, by obviating previous geographic limitations.[16] The pre-industrial city of the eighteenth and early nineteenth centuries had been a city of pedestrians and horse-drawn transport, and its limited physical size had created a certain degree of social integration, which shaped the options of both rich and poor.

As Europe and America became industrialized in the nineteenth century, the city's manufacturing, commercial, cultural and entertainment functions came to be concentrated in urban cores. However, innovations in mass transit allowed cities to spread over a larger geographical area, creating sharper class divisions. Privately operated omnibuses, street car lines, cable cars, and commuter railways enabled the more affluent to abandon the city centre in favour of peripheral suburbs, leaving the centre to the working poor and to immigrants.[17] Meanwhile in England, the process of suburbanization was aided by new transportation infrastructure. A general increase in income levels also made commuting affordable to greater numbers of people.[18]

Consciousness of time also became a structuring force in industrial society. For instance, when the New York City subway opened in 1904, the New York Times declared, that 'in modern city life, distance is measured in time'.[19] Since the clock and the daily schedule were paramount, it was important not to waste time in unproductive activities such as the daily commute. Faster transportation implied time saved. And since punctuality was now an obligation, trains could no longer be run in an ad hoc manner.[20]

Over the course of the nineteenth century, employers had already begun to exercise increased control over employees' work habits. In many cases this involved drawing up strict timetables for employee conduct. One reason for this increased regulatory control was the process of mechanization itself; when employers had to make large capital investments in machinery, they did not want to see it lying idle. Eventually, discipline became internalized. For instance, in the 1880s Beatrice Webb, a social activist and a leader in the Fabian Society, found that textile workers at a Lancashire town accepted the regular work habits required of them for better efficiency.[21] Time as a structuring factor in the lives of people also implied an increased schism between work and leisure. Free time came to be viewed as a reward, in opposition to time at work. As if to emphasize this new regime, many countries abolished religious holidays and replaced them with national holidays instituted by law.[22]

In America one of the most important figures of this new age was F.W. Taylor who sought to reform the inefficient and wasteful production processes of the American factory. Taylor's time-and-motion studies tried to account for every small operation and movement so as to establish the most efficient way to perform a task. The intent was to set new production standards that would prevent factory workers from 'loafing' on the job. To accomplish this, Taylor timed each activity with a stopwatch and then established certain speeds at which workers were expected to perform. The moving assembly line, first introduced in meat-packing plants and automobile factories was the ideal device to regulate such outputs. It demanded perfect timing from workers, since it was inflexible to the vagaries of the individual.[23] This was a society of the survival of the fittest and the most obedient. It was argued that hard work would bring a sense of high morality and well being. Bonuses and wage increases were also to be meted out to those who were capable of a productive consumption of time.

Industrial modernity thus meant that workers were increasingly regulated by the clock. As E.P. Thompson wrote:

> By the 1830s and 1840s it was commonly observed that the English industrial worker was marked off from his fellow Irish worker, not by a greater capacity for hard work, but by his regularity, his methodological paying-out of energy, and perhaps also by a repression, not of enjoyments, but of the capacity to relax in the old, uninhibited ways.[24]

Though well established as theory, and useful in leading to more careful study of production problems, Taylorist management techniques failed to produce labour harmony. A number of managers refused to install the system completely. There was no place within the Taylor system for unionism. And to workers, scientific management signified greater speed, less pay, and the breakdown of collective bargaining. As a result, they set their faces against it.[25] Nevertheless the major components of the industrial city, such as the streetcar, the factory whistle, and the railroad timetable, all bespoke a new era of personal discipline and social control. And, in the suburb of Pullman, outside Chicago, George Pullman erected a bell tower 'as a reminder of the discipline demanded by the new factory system'.[26]

Another great figure of the new industrial age was the auto-industry mogul, Henry Ford. Within the tenets of Fordism, a worker's reward for being subject to new forms of control was adequate income and hence the ability to consume the goods he produced. In this society, 'nice housing in the manner of Pullman, or uplifting leisure activities' would be provided to all workers.[27] They would even be able to purchase one of Ford's own Model-T cars.

Such a Fordist utopia remained elusive however. Welfare schemes for

Modern Times (1936). Film poster.

workers often failed and ran out of steam. The workers also soon found that profit-sharing and special rewards were often accompanied by wage and benefit cuts. And better factories, houses, and sanitation were likely to be accompanied by increased surveillance. Often, when employees were offered stock in a company, they found it also bound them to that company. Overall, the result of such schemes was to make workers ever more suspicious of new management techniques.[28]

Both the Taylorist and the Fordist dimensions of the modern industrial city were captured, narrated and critiqued in films made during the early part of the twentieth century. Today, these films serve not only as representation of this time, but as an arena which allows us to observe the different forces behind this modernity.

Berlin and New York: Cinematic Cities of the Modern Industrial Age

Industrial modernity could be distinguished from earlier forms of modernity

Berlin: Symphony of a Big City (1927). The collage represents the city.

by its categorical acceptance of mechanization and consumption of industrial products. The industrial modern city was one of mechanized, Taylorist production, with the average worker a slave to the accelerated rhythms of the assembly line. The Fordist side of this city was the simultaneous development of a consumer culture. Thus, efficiency at the factory was coupled with financing structures to allow workers to consume the goods they produce. The cities of Berlin and New York, as depicted in the films *Berlin: Symphony of a Big City* and *Modern Times* were both capitals of this new urban modernity.

Directed and edited by Walter Ruttmann in 1927, Berlin attempted to present an objective record of the activities of the city on a typical late spring day.[29] The narrative brings the viewer into Berlin by train as day breaks, and then follows the life of its citizens as they go to work and pursue various

Berlin: Symphony of a Big City. The train arrives in the city.

forms of entertainment until dusk, when the same train takes the viewer out of the city.[30] Photographed by Reimar Kuntze, Robert Baberske, and Laszlo Shaffer using hidden camera techniques, the film is essentially a series of seamlessly edited documentary vignettes.[31] *Berlin*'s main protagonist is the city itself.

Berlin was produced in five *akts*, which correspond to certain times of the day. Repeated shots of a large clock emphasize the new awareness of time, which is now an inextricable aspect of urban modernity. The clock breaks time into hours, minutes and seconds, just as Taylorism breaks production into discrete tasks. The film is a 'symphony' because it is so precisely timed.

As the first act begins, the film shows a long-distance train approaching the city, rushing through its suburbs toward its industrial and commercial centre. As day breaks, people begin to appear in the streets there. In a sense, the city is preparing to receive the train. Gradually, crowds of people gather, and workers are 'herded' into factories like cattle.

The second act corresponds with early morning. It is eight o'clock and the full variety of the city's residents rise to go about their day. The elite prepare to go riding in the park, children go to school, the streets are cleaned, and people leave their apartments to shop for groceries. As the third act begins, the film rises toward the 'crescendo'[32] of mid-morning life. The film highlights stations, factories, road junctions, apartments, and houses, providing glimpses of public and private lives.

The fourth act begins at noon. As the machines stop whirling the entire city goes to lunch. Here, the film focuses on all classes of Berliners, juxtaposing the lives of workers and the wealthy. For instance, a series of shots of the rich and the poor at their respective lunches are interspersed with shots of lions tearing up raw meat. The latter half of this act depicts late afternoon leisure activities. People go boating, racing, golfing, play polo, or go for a stroll in the park.

The fifth and final act begins as the sun sets. Lights go on in building windows, and vehicles turn on their headlights. The city is now one of consumption and leisure. The camera shows theatre and circus performances, casinos with gamblers, and restaurants with dancers.

Berlin was part of the Weimar discourse on urban modernity and it expressed a celebratory view of the modern metropolis. This attitude becomes clear when it is contrasted with the views of industrial modernity in America as seen in *Modern Times*. Set in the 1930s, during the Great Depression, *Modern Times* was directed and produced by Charlie Chaplin.[33] It depicts New York as a modern city of industrial Taylorist production and Fordist consumption. The film itself declares, that it is about industry, individual enterprise, and the pursuit of happiness.

As the film begins, the setting is the Electro Steel Corporation, an industrial enterprise run by a big brother-like manager, who spies on all

Berlin: Symphony of a Big City. Morning scene. A shopkeeper cleans up before the beginning of the day.

Berlin: Symphony of a Big City. A restaurant during weekday lunchtime.

parts of the factory through a panoptic device, a two-way television screen. Production at the factory is based on an assembly line where movements are precisely timed, and each worker performs the same task repeatedly. The absolute tyranny of the assembly line is such that during a short break, the tramp, the film's protagonist (and Chaplin's stock-in-trade) cannot stop his jerky, rhythmic, nut-tightening movements. Mechanization is taken to further extremes when management attempts to feed workers with an automatic feeder that is intended to eliminate the workers' lunch hour. The device features a revolving table, an automated soup plate, an automatic food pusher, a revolving corncob feeder, and last but not least, a sterilized mouth wipe.[34] After lunch, the president of the company decides to enhance efficiency by speeding up the conveyor belt so the workers are forced to move faster. The tramp makes a heroic effort to keep up, but goes berserk under the strain of the job, and is quite literally dragged into the machinery. A series of nightmarish experiences have now driven him insane, and he is carted away to a psychiatric ward. The sphere of work in *Modern Times* is ruled by a dystopic relationship between the protagonist and the assembly line, a metaphor for all aspects of industrial production.

Released from the hospital, the tramp joins a large number of unemployed people. On the streets, he picks up and waves a red flag that has fallen off a truck, only to be mistaken for the leader of a group of Communist agitators and imprisoned. In jail, however, he is rewarded with his own private cell when he inadvertently averts a breakout. Perversely, it is only in jail that he can experience the comforts of a modern home. When he is granted a pardon and released, he requests: 'Can't I stay a little longer? I'm so happy here'.[35]

The gamine, a mischievous street-smart girl (played by Paulette Goddard), who has been stealing food to feed her family, is arrested and placed under the childcare authorities. On the run after stealing a loaf of bread, she bumps into the tramp, who is trying to get arrested so he can go back to prison. The tramp attempts to take the blame for her crime, but is unsuccessful. He then enjoys a large meal at a cafeteria that he is unable to pay for. As he is carted off to prison, he meets the gamine again in the police wagon. The tramp is only able to parody a consumer in his attempts to be arrested; he is never able to be a real consumer himself.

The tramp and the gamine escape together when a fortuitous accident occurs, and they reach the suburban edge of the city. In contrast to the European industrial modernity of Berlin, the city of *Modern Times* is surrounded by residential suburbs – havens of Fordist consumption. The city dweller's identity is split between town and country. The split between town and country is stark: the city is a place of industrial mechanization, bourgeois consumption, and hedonistic entertainment; the suburbs are places where the husband goes off to work and the wife stays behind to

Berlin: Symphony of a Big City. Pedestrians, cars and trams share the streets.

Modern Times. The Capitalist behind the production line.

maintain a supposedly blissful domesticity. By nature, the tramp possesses a certain degree of freedom unknown to the people portrayed in *Berlin*. In Ruttmann's film, every body, thing and function has a designated place and time. But the tramp of *Modern Times* resists being placed in one or the other category. Unfortunately, his freedom means he is forever without a home, unable to fulfil the desires the industrial modern city inculcates.

The film next goes into a dream sequence in which the tramp and the gamine pursue an ideal. A bright cheery home, a steak cooking on the stove, trees laden with fruit, and a cow ready to be milked are some of the elements of this paradise. However, when the two return to reality, they find themselves back in the city. Needing to make some money, the tramp next gets a job as night watchman at a department store. Seeing no harm in it, he lets the gamine in, helps her to food, and tucks her to sleep in one of the beds. But this solution to the dilemma proves too good to be true and the tramp is again arrested when he sympathizes with the plight of some burglars and helps them steal food.

When the tramp is released from prison this time, the gamine takes him to a shack on the outskirts of the city, a ramshackle 'suburban paradise'. There, they live out a parody of a suburban existence, where the food is tough and tasteless and the rafters constantly fall on their heads. Their attempt to realize modernity's promise on the suburban fringe satirizes the idea of Fordist consumption as both a spatially-based and class-specific privilege.

At last, however, they are successful at holding down jobs – as entertainers at a restaurant. But the system eventually catches up with them here too as the authorities take the gamine away under charges of vagrancy. At the end of the film, the tramp and the gamine escape one last time, walking away optimistically into a sunrise on a country road.[36]

The Industrial City and Cinematic Space

These two films provide us a glimpse into the cinematic spaces of industrial modernity. Although replete with scenes of urban mass transportation, *Berlin* represents a European industrial modernity, where the suburb is not yet a dominant phenomenon. It also presents a largely celebratory (although in parts mildly sarcastic) picture of a city of industrial modernity.

This was but one view of the modern industrial city at the time however. Social theorists, like Simmel, were deeply concerned with the effects of industrial capitalism on the morality and psyche of the individual, and they worried that such environments alienated the individual from his own moral core.[37] For Simmel, the trouble with the city of industrial modernity was that it was shaped by a consumer society that promoted an objective culture. In particular, his writings emphasized the changes that individuals went through as a result of hard qualities of the capitalist economy and new gender divisions between 'objective male and subjective female culture'.[38] For Simmel, the division of labour brought by modern industrial production

Modern Times. Chaplin shows 'scientific management' as applied to eating.

Modern Times. The tramp as part of the machinery of production.

was essentially male in nature. He reasoned that the housewife had more 'natural' characteristics.[39] We see very specific traces of this position in the gender roles of *Modern Times*.

Simmel's 'The Metropolis and Mental Life' was published simultaneously with two of his other pieces: 'On the Spatial Projection of Social Forms' and 'The Sociology of Space'.[40] The three essays together demonstrated Simmel's interest in the metropolis as a site for the making of the modern individual. In this work, Simmel was concerned about excessive social control over the individual and the imposition of an unnatural degree of order.

If, as Simmel proposed, the industrial city divided the individual from himself, it also divided urban life into unnecessarily separate spheres of production and consumption, home, work and leisure. Nevertheless in *Berlin*, the general population is shown as having access to almost all of the city's functions and activities. In the film, we observe factories, schools, public parks and beaches, cinema houses, theatres, and restaurants. The streets of the city are crowded with people, and the city is at once a place of work, play and residence. A viewer of *Berlin* gets an impression of land being at a premium. We see repeated shots of apartment houses, with only an occasional glimpse of a 'single-family home'. In actuality, Berlin was severely congested, its basic unit of development a five-storey 'rental barracks' planned around a narrow courtyard. Patrick Abercrombie, the British planner, observed that the outskirts of Berlin then were not comprised of straggling suburbs; rather, its dense pattern of buildings along wide streets pushed out into the countryside. This was unlike the case in the US where Fordist consumption meant that the personal automobile was increasingly accessible to large portions of the population.[41] There was no spatial transition from sparse countryside, to denser suburb, to a very dense city centre in Berlin. There was only a direct contrast between full-blown city and countryside.[42]

In the US, the city of industrial modernity was a very different place, characterized by a tension between centrifugal and centripetal forces. While there was a desire to gravitate to the centre for work and leisure, there was a corresponding desire to escape this centre for a semi-rural domesticity in the city's suburbs. In *Modern Times*, we observe this tension at play.

Indeed, in both *Berlin* and *Modern Times*, law-enforcement agencies are ever present. They parade in the streets of the city of Berlin, and they directly affect the lives of the tramp and the gamine. Both films imply that for industrial modernity to be successful, a certain degree of urban order is imperative. The industrial city is a place where diverse people come together to work and play. Some friction is inevitable, and both films imply that if disparate peoples are to occupy the same spaces, rules of conduct must be laid down. Ruttmann is mildly sarcastic about these conditions. But for Chaplin, this sense of order has a topsy-turvy insanity about it. An institution committed to handing out punishment to wrongdoers is the only place the tramp is at peace. He is a law-abiding citizen in jail, but a thieving disaster in spaces, such as the department store, where the law expects him to be a capable consumer. Had the tramp not met the gamine and dreamt of suburban domestic bliss, he would have preferred to stay in jail.

This difference indicates a more general difference in the point of view between the two films. For example, by depicting the sequence of the automatic feeder, Chaplin in *Modern Times* is mocking the insanity of the drive for efficiency and the extreme tyranny of the modern system. The device itself is sold by a mechanical salesman; and needless to say, it also goes haywire – a case of Taylorism gone berserk. By contrast, *Berlin* seeks primarily to record life in a larger modern metropolis. Mechanization increasingly pervades all aspects of life, but the film takes no position on this issue. Instead, the camera experiences simple voyeur-like fascination with its processes.

In *Modern Times*, the centre of the city is attractive for its employment opportunities both in production (the assembly line) and consumerism (the department store). The desirable place to live, however, is on the periphery. And this was where divisions on the lines of class have set in. The tramp and the gamine are clearly not of the same economic class as the couple they observe living such an idyllic suburban existence.

A society of industrial modernity was necessarily one in flux. As Berman has pointed out, one experience of the condition of modernity has been a sense that people, relationships and institutions do not remain the same for long.[43] In the face of constant change, governments and institutions could only respond by trying to establish order and control. Accordingly, mass demonstrations and strikes were often dealt with through police intervention, penal institutions and even military force.[44] The other prong of societal control involved state-sponsored welfare activities that sought to reorder the lives of the vagrant and the poor. Thus, in *Modern Times*, it is the state that decides the fate of the gamine and her siblings, and it is the state that steps in when the tramp is caught in a rally, supposedly demonstrating against its authority.[45]

On the other hand, *Berlin*'s neutral commentary and disengagement with these issues has caused many commentators to be severely critical of the film. For example, the film has been critiqued by some as a selective representation of the city as various contemporaries recognized enough of 'their' Berlin in Ruttmann's film to decry the absence of those other parts that 'should' have been included. But here, critiques of *Berlin* also serve our attempt to understand industrial modernity. It is important to recall that the film's depiction of an actual place at a specific time in its history coincided with an intense debate on the ethical values of urban life in Weimar Germany.[46] The industrial city is then seen as the site of all the contradictions, conflicts and tensions associated with this transition to an industrial age. Later, as Berlin grew into a twentieth-century metropolis, it also drew many of the criticisms targeted toward the industrial city. In particular, as Nazism and Fascism took hold, the city was associated with the twin symbols of luxury and effeminacy and became a sexualized symbol of the 'evils of modernity'.[47] With its celebratory attitude toward industrial modernity, *Berlin* also succeeded in confirming the fears of critics of modern urban life who were nostalgic for a more agrarian lifestyle.[48]

Although we can view it as a historical snapshot today, *Berlin* also gives us an inherently ahistorical view of the city's life by subsuming any latent conflict within the larger whole of the urban entity itself. In a sense, the film can be read as a generic portrayal of a large metropolis through the specific case and living patterns of this particular city. Another criticism of the film, thus, is that it aestheticized the experience of the city. Aesthetically, Berlin's modernity was the product of a new experience of space, time and motion by which it had become characterized.[49] The street itself became one such site, connecting places, events and activities, and providing a dynamic, collective understanding of place.

But the film also became caught up in the larger contemporary critique of the 'beautiful documentary film'. Allan James Thomas, for example, cites an article written in the 1930s by John Grierson that employs *Berlin* as an instance of what a documentary should not be:

> For all its ado of workmen and factories and swirl and swing of a great city, Berlin created nothing. Or if it created something, it was that shower of rain in the afternoon… The people of the city got up splendidly, they tumbled through their five million hoops impressively, they turned in; and no other issue of God or man emerged than that sudden besmattering spilling of wet on people and pavements.[50]

One may argue that *Berlin* does not attempt any didactic function; that it expresses no opinion on the condition of modernity or the lives of the city's inhabitants. Its techniques of montage thus leave issues open-ended, and it is up to the viewer to interpret its relatively optimistic message. At times, Ruttmann also produces cynical remarks about urban society through cross-cutting shots. For instance, a courting couple is paired with mechanized dolls in a store window, and workers entering a factory are juxtaposed with cattle grazing in a field. However, one can argue that this sarcasm does not challenge the *status quo*. Rather, it implies that the camera is the only institution through which the city is seen, and that the act of seeing is itself mechanized. Similarly, in *Modern Times*, there is a degree of cynicism both in the story line and in its depiction in cinematic space, and the machine is also seen to prevail. But, the two films exhibit fundamentally different attitudes towards a modernity they accept. Indeed, the use of the machine to control human beings is never questioned in *Berlin*.

However, in *Modern Times*, the machine is overpowering and swallows the tramp. His comical resistance underscores his inability to find a space within this new world – either to earn a livelihood, or to enjoy his environment, as the citizens of *Berlin* clearly seem to be doing. In the end, the machine 'vomits' the human protagonist. But, by mocking it, *Modern Times* rejects the machine. In Berlin, the machine finds a kind of harmony. In one scene that links the two films, Ruttmann takes his camera inside a cinema and we glimpse the feet of Chaplin's tramp on the screen.

In *Berlin* then, the classic trope of modernity, the *flâneur*, is personified by the camera, which travels through the city, providing a detached and aestheticized view of differences of social class, the increasingly hectic urban life, and a new interconnectedness of people and places. The advent of cinema itself has enabled 'a new mode of *flânerie*', a wandering around the city and a new ability to conceive of it as a spectacle and a source of sensory experience.[51]

By contrast, the trope in *Modern Times* is that of the tramp. Unlike the literate and bourgeois *flâneur*, the tramp is an indigent, with no steady job or home. Despite these obvious distinctions however, the two might have more in common than previously imagined. Elizabeth Wilson has suggested that the trope of the male *flâneur* obscures the real marginal and vulnerable existence it supposedly represents.[52] In that regard, the tramp may be a vulnerable version of the *flâneur*, lost not in the encounter of the newly opened streets of Paris, but in the maze of a new city as machine.

In *Modern Times*, the tramp's experiences are the real historical events of the Great Depression and an inability to adjust to the control demanded by an industrial modernity. His defence lies in a caustic critique of this condition. *Modern Times* depicts an industrial modernity that overwhelms its protagonists. Its mechanized workplaces are inhuman in scale, and its places of consumption lie beyond the reach of the working classes, who have desires but lack the means to fulfil them. Unable to work or exist within the relentless and unforgiving assembly line, the two creative protagonists, the tramp and the gamine, finally find work 'playing the fool'. They become tertiary entertainers themselves, since they are unable to be primary producers.

Home and Work: The Industrial Cinematic City

The redefined relationship between home and work is also an important product of industrial modernity. If home and work were often connected and undelineated spaces in premodern times, the separation between them that occurred in the early twentieth century irrevocably changed this relationship and the ensuing nature of urban communities, and was facilitated by new modes of movement and transport.

Modern Times and *Berlin* both deal with issues of community, home and work. In *Berlin*, modernity is defined through the power of the moment and the creation of fleeting communities. These are communities of factory people, people at lunch, and people at play. Although the factory people are monitored, they are still a community; and although these groups of people come together only fleetingly, they still form communities.

In *Modern Times*, on the other hand, there is no community. The tramp is presented as having nothing in common with the workers on either side of him on the assembly line. This difference could possibly be explained in terms of the differences in social relations between the European and the American context. On the other hand, connections through a deliberate rendezvous (when the tramp meets the gamine), or casual encounters (when he catches his assembly line co-worker in the act of burgling the department store) define the extent of the tramp's interpersonal relationships. While spaces for socializing exist, they are sites of entertainment, and not of community.

In relation to such meanings in social interaction, the rendezvous, or the meeting of two people, is an important trope to invoke in analysing the spatial experiences of the city of industrial modernity.[53] As Dorothy Rowe has pointed out, Simmel had a great interest in understanding the urban phenomenon of the rendezvous. He understood it as a 'specifically sociological form whose spatial determinacy is characterized linguistically through the ambiguity of the word: it signifies both the encounter and its location'.[54] Thus, the rendezvous is located in 'the tension between the necessity for punctuality, and its fleeting quality on the one hand, and its temporal and spatial fixity on the other'.[55] In Simmel's sociology, the rendezvous was a source of spatial and emotional experience, one possibly enhanced by this new form of industrial modernity.

In both films, the space of 'home' is also defined by recognizing different spheres of life that are divided both spatially and temporally and also along lines of gender. In *Modern Times*, the sense of home is depicted as a life in the suburbs – thus allying the issue of suburbanization with the expectation of modernity. When the tramp and gamine desire a home, it is framed within a certain articulation of consumer desire – to own a house in the suburbs with conveniences and appliances handy. Perhaps, more importantly, home involves a distinction of gender roles with the husband going into 'the city' to work and the wife and home-maker staying behind. Walter Ruttmann also recognizes the space of home as a space of feminized domesticity and an entire *akt* in the film is devoted to it. In an industrial modernity in the European context, these different spheres of life are shown to operate according to different temporal and spatial fixities highlighted by the ticking of the clock. As shown in *Berlin*, when it ticks, men go to work. When it ticks again, women perform domestic activities.

Although the spheres of work and home are spatially segregated in the industrial modern city, the two are part of the same system, driven by consumption as well as production. The ability to be a consumer is predicated on the ability to be also a producer. In *Modern Times*, the tramp is unable to be a producer, and so he is denied the privilege of being a consumer. When he accidentally stumbles into the sphere of consumption, the department store, he knows his time there is limited, and there is something essentially self-destructive in his actions.

The spheres of work and home in the two films can be understood within the context of Taylorism and Fordism. In *Berlin*, all production processes are mechanized (and one suspects, Taylorist). And although Fordist expectations are not articulated in terms of a suburban home or car, they are latently present in the city's ability to consume what it produces. *Berlin* portrays a city where the spheres of home and work are spatially and temporally separate. And yet, the two are interdependent. The feminine domestic sphere is sustained economically through the work that the man puts in within the sphere of production. On the other hand, the sustenance of this domesticity is what lends moral legitimacy to a man's efforts. In other words, the ability to be a successful producer within the largely Taylorist assembly line allows access to Fordist systems of consumption. In *Modern Times*, however, the tramp's dysfunctional relationship with the Taylorist assembly line is obvious, but he is equally dogged by his inability to consume properly the goods he produces. Thus, although he can visit the sites of Fordist reward, such as the suburbs and the department stores, these are clearly aspects of urban modernity that are beyond his reach, just like sitting in the café was beyond the reach of the poor in Baudelaire's mid-nineteenth century Paris.

Functions and Locations:
The City of Production and Consumption

In the city of industrial modernity, a further separation clearly exists between work and leisure. In *Berlin*, every aspect of leisure, from food to recreation, involves an act of consumption. When the inhabitants of the city, workers and businessmen, are at lunch, all classes of Berliners are depicted, and they are shown to resemble wild beasts attacking flesh in their respective acts of consumption. Ruttmann is ambivalent about particular city dwellers' ability to be consumers. He presents consumption as an aspect of city life in general rather than as a segment of any particular individual's existence.

In *Berlin*, the city is also clearly distinguished from the countryside in much the same way that a medieval city formed an island by virtue of its walls and gates. In this case, the railway station takes the place of city gates, and gives city dwellers an identity that sets them apart. Such an identity was predicated on permutations of fast motion.[56] Such aspects of modernization have distressed critics of industrial urban life who see them as indicative of a machine myth that for some assumes the pose of an eternal truth.[57] Harvey has characterized such a view as typical of a 'heroic' modernism of the interwar years. Dogged by disaster, it was eventually replaced by a more 'hegemonic' modernism that had a more 'comfortable relation to the dominant power centers in society'.[58]

One consequence of this heroic view is that it allows the classes seemingly to occupy the same space: the city itself.

> For all of the juxtapositions of rich and poor and their respective lifestyles we find in Berlin, the ultimate effect is not to oppose the two in a dialectic of class struggle, but to suggest their ultimate unity as differentiated parts unified by their common membership of the same organic whole, that is to say, itself. [59]

Anton Kaes has pointed out how *Berlin* was criticized for not addressing class conflict.[60] The day ends for *Berlin*, the city, in a grand finale of fireworks. Afterwards, the train which rushed into the city at dawn rushes out again at night, emphasizing the importance of a single centre – the heart of the modernist metropolis.

Ruttmann's film also stresses the interconnectedness of places within the city via networks of transportation, communication, circulation and exchange. In this sense, the street more than any other privileged middle-class interiority serves as an important connection of places, events and activities, providing a perspective on the city that refutes any static or privatized understanding of place.[61]

The world expositions also played a role in this industrial modernity. Cities, engaged in the act of exhibition, became spectacles unto themselves. As symbols of modernity, they were remade through exhibitions; a necessity then for global positioning. From London's Crystal Palace, the Exposition Universelle in 1855, which set the urban landscape of Baudelaire's Paris, to the Columbian Exposition of 1893 in Chicago, industrial modernity was forged in the compacted time and space made possible through Taylorist production, Fordist consumption, and urban spectacle. As already mentioned, one of the major aesthetic features of Berlin's modernity at the time was the new experience of space, time and motion. Contemporary descriptions of the city, such as catalogues for the 1896 Berlin Trade Exhibition, focused on these characteristics and attempted to establish Berlin's claim to the status of a *Weltstadt* (world city). Critical responses to Berlin's rapid elevation to this status – in particular, Simmel's – allow us today to examine Berlin's self-conscious positioning in relation to its European rivals, mainly Paris and London.[62] The text of the exhibition catalogue was also representative of responses to Berlin's rapidly developing modernity.[63] It avoided idealizing the city excessively, yet guided readers through the city's zoological garden, new museums and monuments, transport system, banking quarter and stock exchange, hospitals, and military quarters.[64] Its primary focus was to stress Berlin's rise from its humble origins as a fishing village, and its ability to compete with other European cities.

Another picture of Berlin was drawn by the architect August Endell in his 1908 book *The Beauty of the Big City*.[65] While recognizing the social deprivation in the metropolis, Endell managed to aestheticize it by taking a 'metaphorical stroll through the "landscape" of Berlin'. In the same manner as a *flâneur*, Endell made the eye of the beholder the repository of all urban beauty. In this activity, he was as fascinated with scenes of urban poverty, sickness and deprivation, as he was with the rhythms and mechanics of industrial machinery. In the end, he was able to abstract and extract aesthetic pleasure from both kinds of scenes.

In his analysis of the Berlin Trade Exhibition, as in his other writings, Simmel was principally concerned with the effects of the city on the individual. After paying their entry fees, he pointed out how individuals were increasingly alienated from objective culture and forced to develop an amused, dulled response to the exhibition displays. His observations once again describe the trope of the blasé mentality that emerged. Even at this event, supposedly heralding Berlin's arrival on the world stage, individuals had to measure social relations in terms of monetary interactions rather than emotional ones.

The modernity of the American city, by contrast, manifested itself in the pace with which the morphology of the city was being transformed, according to some of its observers, even faster than the likes of its inhabitants.[66] Characterized by rampant growth and property development, the American city had aroused mostly negative sentiments throughout the nineteenth century.[67] By the 1920s however, the visionary imaginary of the skyscraper became the new representation of a modernity specific to America. Hugh Ferris's *The Metropolis of Tomorrow* (1929) is perhaps the most well-known publication describing the skyscraper city as conceived during the decade.

According to architectural historian Carol Willis, it was New York's zoning law of 1916 that stimulated the transformation of views among American designers toward cities.[68] The law was introduced to counteract the tendency of developers to crowd giant buildings on small lots. Instead of allowing buildings to tower uniformly along the contours of a site, it formulated a setback formula that came, eventually, to generate a new aesthetic for the American city. Since high-rise buildings on small lots were no longer profitable, developers now had to combine smaller lots and build on whole blocks, or even create super blocks. Standing on their own, tall towers now had to be designed as three-dimensional forms in space rather than tall façades with ornament. Willis has argued that the impact of the zoning law was multifaceted – not only did it change developers' practices, transform property markets, and challenge the way architects thought but it gave new importance to planning.[69] It was in this milieu that 'a new era in American urbanism' opened.[70]

In general, the height restrictions limited the construction of skyscrapers in Europe. But this did not prevent an architectural debate around the city of the future.[71] In Europe, Berlin was both celebrated and condemned as the most American(ized) city.[72] It was relatively new in comparison to other European capitals, and it had come to industrialization late so that the effects of industrial modernity were experienced simultaneously with that of mass consumerism. Interestingly, Berlin was also not compared to New York but to Chicago in terms of its newness and position as Germany's leading industrial metropolis.[73]

Both *Berlin* and *Modern Times* take issue with the growth of the industrial city and its dependency on a simultaneous growth of mass consumerism.[74] In *Modern Times*, the tramp is unable to regulate his behaviour according to the demands of either the clock or the assembly line. He possesses the ability to be uninhibited in his enjoyment of life, but there is no room for such displays. The film also establishes a tie between the centralizing tendency of American industry and the emergence of the private corporation. The corporation was an innovative form of organization based on new methods of structuring and managing labour and capital. Its emergence was also encouraged by government agencies that allowed it ease of access to public land and natural resources.[75] By contrast, in *Berlin* acts of consumption and leisure still take place in the public spaces of the city, such as parks and the riverbank, indicating the contrived presence of genuine public life. While more exclusive acts of consumption can and did occur in more private places such as clubs, the theatre, cinema, restaurants and casinos provided additional opportunities for public awareness. Nevertheless, it is obvious that one needed a high income to partake of these pleasures, and the film is ambivalent about which classes in the city could afford them.

The emergence of mass markets on both sides of the Atlantic at the beginning of the twentieth century stimulated the mechanization of production. Cities became centres for wholesale and retail business as well as for manufacture. The city emerged as a hub for the production, as well as a centre for the advertising, marketing, and the sale of consumer goods. Thus, the city of industrial modernity was not only allied with the city of consumption, it was simultaneously a consumption-driven production centre. The cinematic city of industrial modernity both represented and contributed to rising feelings of alienation and blaséness that accompanied this growth of industrial capitalism. On the one hand, the industrial city of the early twentieth century was seen as an emancipator from the repression of earlier forms of urbanization associated with feudalism. But on the other, the modernity of this industrial city involved a compromise, balancing between freedoms gained from the anonymity of the metropolis and the isolation of the new urban lifestyle. The spatial patterns that resulted express the political economy of the city of industrial modernity, just as much as the parody of *Modern Times* and the aesthetic of *Berlin* articulate specific manifestations on both sides of the Atlantic.

Notes

1   G. Simmel, 'The Metropolis and Mental Life', in D. Frisby and M. Featherstone (eds.) *Simmel on Culture. Selected Writings*. London, Sage, 1997.
2   For example, drawing on Charles Baudelaire's poem 'Eyes of the Poor' in *Paris Spleen*, Marshall Berman makes such a distinction. M. Berman, 'Baudelaire: Modernism in the Streets', in *All that is Solid Melts into Air: The Experience of Modernity*, London: Verso, 1983.
3   L. Benovolo, *The European City*, C. Ipsen (trans.). Oxford: Blackwell, 1993, p. 171.
4   G. Simmel, 'The Metropolis and Mental Life'. L. Wirth, 'Urbanism as a Way of Life', *American Journal of Sociology*, vol. 38, 1938, pp. 60–83.

5   D. Rowe, *Representing Berlin, Sexuality and the City in Imperial and Weimar Germany*. Aldershot: Ashgate, 2003, p. 4.

6   G. Simmel, 'The Metropolis and Mental Life', in *Simmel on Culture*.

7   *Ibid.*

8   M. Gottdiener, *The New Urban Sociology*. New York: McGraw Hill, 1994, pp. 103–105.

9   *Ibid.*

10 L. Wirth, 'Urbanism as a Way of Life', p. 67.

11 *Ibid.*

12 D. Harvey, 'Modernity and Modernism', *The Condition of Postmodernity*. Oxford: Basil Blackwell, 1989, p. 16.

13 *Ibid.*, p. 17.

14 B. Wittrock, 'Modernity: One, None, or Many? European Origins and Modernity as a Global Condition', in S.N. Eisenstadt (ed.), *Multiple Modernities*. New Brunswick and London, Transaction Publishers, 2002, pp. 53–55.

15 R.A. Mohl, *The New City: Urban America in the Industrial Age, 1860–1920*, Arlington Heights, IL: Harlan Davidson, 1985, p. 55.

16 R.A. Mohl, *The New City*, pp. 28–29.

17 *Ibid.*, p. 27-52.

18 C. More, *The Industrial Age: Economy and Society in Britain 1750–1985*. London, Longman, 1989, pp. 285–286.

19 Cited in R. A. Mohl, *The New City*, p.65.

20 G.J. Whitrow, *Time in History*. Oxford: Oxford University Press, 1989, pp. 160–161.

21 C. More, *The Industrial Age: Economy and society in Britain, 1750–1995*, p. 182.

22 G.J. Whitrow, *Time in History*, pp. 162–163.

23 R.A. Mohl, *The New City*, p. 65.

24 E.P. Thompson, 'Time-work Discipline and Industrial Capitalism', in *Past & Present*, vol. 38, 1967, pp. 56–97.

25 T.C. Cochran and W. Miller, *The Age of Enterprise: A Social History of Industrial America*, rev. ed. New York: Harper and Row, 1961, p. 244.

26 R.A. Mohl, *The New City*, pp. 64–65.

27 S. Kostof, *America by Design*. Oxford: Oxford University Press, 1987, p. 104.

28 T.C. Cochran and W. Miller, *The Age of Enterprise*, p. 247.

29 Walter Ruttmann was born in Frankfurt in 1887. He lived and produced films in a milieu in which artists were trying to transgress traditional media and to explore the potentials of new media. In his film making practice, he drew from his background in painting and music. Before *Berlin*, he had already made abstract animated films. R. Russett and C. Starr, 'Walter Ruttmann', in *Experimental Animation*. New York: Da Capo Press, 1976, pp. 40–42.

30 A.J. Thomas, 'Berlin: Symphony of a City', *Senses of Cinema*, April 2000. Viewed on 17 February 2004, at http://www.sensesofcinema.com.

31 Viewed on 17 February 2004, at http://www.german-cinema.com.

32 Viewed on 17 February 2004, at http://www.lib.unc.edu/house/mrc/films.

33 Charlie Chaplin was born in London, England in 1889 to parents in theatre. As a teenager, he started acting as a comedian in vaudeville, which led him to the US in 1910. His success on stage brought him motion picture contracts in the US. Upon the expiration of his acting contract in 1917, he started producing and directing his own films. D. Robinson, *Chaplin, His Life and Art*. New York: McGraw-Hill, 1985.

34 *Modern Times*, 1936, Charles Chaplin (dir.).

35 *Ibid.*

36 Viewed on 17 February 2004, at http://www.moderntimes.com/palace/chaplin/film.htm.

37 D. Rowe, *Representing Berlin*, p. 19.

38   *Ibid.*, p.65.

39   *Ibid.,* p.66.

40   G. Simmel, *Simmel on Culture*, pp. 255–258.

41   D. Harvey, *The Condition of Postmodernity*.

42   P. Hall, *Cities of Tomorrow: An Intellectual History of Urban Planning and Design in the Twentieth Century*, 3rd ed. Oxford: Blackwell, 2002, p. 33.

43   M. Berman, *All that is Solid Melts into Air: The Experience of Modernity*. London: Verso, 1983.

44   R.A. Mohl, *The New City*, pp. 154–155.

45   M. Foucault. *Discipline and Punish*.

46   W. Natter, 'The City as Cinematic Space', pp. 214–219.

47   D. Rowe, *Representing Berlin*, p. 11.

48   W. Natter, 'The City as Cinematic Space', p. 222.

49   *Ibid.*, p. 12.

50   J. Grierson quoted in A.J. Thomas, 'Berlin: Symphony of a City'. John Grierson, 'First Principles of Documentary', in Kevin Macdonald and Mark Cousins (eds.) *Imagining Reality: The Faber Book of Documentary*. London: Faber and Faber, 1996.

51   W. Natter, 'The City as Cinematic Space'. The usage of the term 'city of spectacle' is not to be confused with the notion of the 'society of the spectacle' as proposed by Guy Debord. For Debord, there is a power relationship embedded within the notion of the spectacle. It has been designed by the bureaucratic apparatus as a means of managing and controlling human beings, and it is directed by the logics of capital. The term 'spectacle' as used in this essay implies merely a feast for the eyes. While Debord's notion is not alien to Ruttmann's *Berlin*, the camera here, merely enjoys the city.

52   E. Wilson, 'The Invisible *Flâneur*', *New Left Review*, no.191, February 1992.

53   G. Simmel, 'Sociology of Space', in *Simmel on Culture*, pp. 137–169.

54   D. Rowe, *Representing Berlin*, p. 74.

55   *Ibid.*

56   W. Natter, 'The City as Cinematic Space', p. 219.

57   *Ibid.*, p. 214.

58   D. Harvey, 'Modernity and Modernism', in *The Condition of Postmodernity*, p. 35.

59   A.J. Thomas, 'Berlin: Symphony of a City'.

60   A. Kaes, 'Leaving Home: Film, Migration and the Urban Experience', *New German Critique*, no. 74, 1998, p. 188.

61   W. Natter, 'The City as Cinematic Space', p. 218.

62   G. Simmel, 'The Berlin Trade Exhibition', in *Simmel on Culture*, pp. 255–258.

63   D. Rowe, *Representing Berlin*, p. 13.

64   *Ibid.*

65   A. Endell, *Die Schonheit Der Grossen Stadt*. Stuttgart: Berlag von Streder and Schroder, 1908. Also in D. Rowe, *Representing Berlin*, p. 15.

66   J.P. Sartre quoted in A. Krieger, 'The American City: Ideal and Mythic Aspects of a Reinvented Urbanism', *Assemblage*, no. 3, July 1987, pp. 38–59. The quote is on page 41.

67   A. Krieger, 'The American City', p. 40.

68   C. Willis, 'Zoning and Zeitgeist: The Skyscraper City in the 1920s', *Journal of the Society of Architectural Historians*, no. XLV, March 1986, pp. 47–59.

69   *Ibid.*

70   Willis challenges what she sees as the standard argument in American architectural history that dates the 1922 Chicago Tribune Tower Competition and with it the influence of European modernism as the starting point in innovative skyscraper architecture in the US. C. Willis, 'Zoning and Zeitgeist', p. 53.

71   F. Passani, 'The Skyscrapers of the Ville Contemporaine', *Assemblage,* no. 4, 1987,

pp. 52–65. Auguste Perret, Le Corbusier, Mies van der Rohe designed controversial schemes with skyscrapers for European cities.

72 K. Scheffler (1910) quoted in D. Jazbinsek, B. Joerges, and R. Thies, 'The Berlin "Grossstadt-Dokumente": A Forgotten Precursor of the Chicago School of Sociology'. Viewed on July 13, 2005, on http://skylla.wz-berlin.de/pdf/2001/ii01-502.pdf.

73 D. Jazbinsek, B.Joerges, and R. Thies, 'The Berlin "Grossstadt-Dokumente"'.

74 R.A. Mohl, *The New City*, p. 61.

75 *Ibid.*, p. 57.

Chapter 2

Urbanizing Modernity: The Traditional Cinematic Small Town

Urban discourse has always viewed the small town as distinct from the big city. Dichotomies such as distance versus proximity, individual versus community, community versus society, stability versus change, public versus private, integration versus isolation, and sacred versus profane have long been used to substantiate this difference.[1] But are small towns or big cities definable entities? Are they different urbanistically? And if so, how?

At the beginning of the twentieth century, many small towns underwent a dramatic transformation that brought changes to both their economic life and physical environment. These changes had a deep impact on the lived experiences of their residents. Before and immediately after World War II, transformations became more evident, emerging as a central theme in scholarship and leading to the emergence of the field of urban sociology and the study of urbanism on both sides of the Atlantic.

Louis Wirth defined urbanism as 'that complex of traits, which makes up the characteristic mode of life in the cities'.[2] Viewed, thus, as the form and culture of urban societies, urbanism emerged (or re-emerged) as an important research topic only at the beginning of the twentieth century. Ultimately, what caused this rise of interest was population shifts from rural to urban that were by-products of industrialization that happened within a single generation in some nations. Wirth understood that urbanization could not be assumed to be solely a product of , or a parallel to, industrialization. Cities, as hubs of governance, barter and exchange, had existed long before industrialization. Yet, he argued that what distinguished contemporary civilization from its predecessors was that it was predominantly urban. According to Wirth, contemporary civilization was modern (novel, new) with regard to the growth of its cities. Urbanization, which to him, denoted 'the development and extension of these factors [of urbanism]', could also be held responsible for major psychological and social transformations and the loss of tradition that had occurred in many societies.[3] While early sociology tried to disassociate itself from nostalgia by pinning down the characteristics of the urban and the rural as rivals, Max Weber, the father of urban sociology, emphasized community as a variable quality that could exist both in the village and the city.[4] As Dorothy Rowe has noted,

> It must have been quite clear to many of those familiar with urban sociology at this time that Weber's approach to *The City* was a new way of addressing the familiar dichotomy between *Gemeinschaft und Gesellschaft* which stood at the heart of contemporary dissatisfaction with the modern alienating metropolis. Weber's concept of a 'full urban community' was part of the contemporary discourse of urban modernity that was motivated by the need to address the perceived crisis of modern city life in order to stem the threat of revolutionary rebellion.[5]

This focus on the experience of the city was motivated in part by the view that migrants to the city became free 'individuals' with the potential of 'revolutionary rebellion'. Tradition, found in the village or the small town, no longer bound them together. In contrast to the big city, then, the small town was seen as traditional because of its perceived sedentary character – which, ironically, was one factor that caused some of its inhabitants to want to move to the city.

Rowe has suggested that the dichotomy of town and big city has been a principal issue in the discourse of modernity, 'which has as its end product a peculiarly German as opposed to a Parisian paradigmatic model'.[6] She further suggested that it was the German sociologist Ferdinand Tönnies's work from which other urban theorists of the Weimar Period 'forged many of their ideological positions' regarding the urban–rural continuum.[7] As early as 1887, Tönnies made the distinction between the social lives of the town and city:

> The town is the highest, viz., the most complex form of social life. Its local character in common with that of the village, contrasts with the family character of the house; the village retains more, the town less. Only when the town develops into the city are these characteristics almost entirely lost.[8]

In Tönnies's explanation, the village and the small town were typical of natural will and community (*Gemeinschaft*), while the city, with its division of labour, mass production, and commercial value system, was typical of rational will and society (*Gesellschaft*).[9] According to Tönnies, the town was the highest form of social life because it was based on tradition. It was when the town grew into a city that organizing principles became commercial and tradition was lost.

In his 'Metropolis' essay, also discussed in Chapter 1, Georg Simmel attempted to comprehend the ways in which the experience of modern life affected the individual.[10] Similar to Tönnies, Simmel argued that the criterion of intellect was established in the city by the monetary economy. According to Simmel, modern man had been freed from the constraints of the village or small town, but in the process he had been thrust into a (spiritually hollow) urban world where differences and individuality were flattened to monetary value, and where qualitative aspects of life had been replaced by quantitative ones.

These views of Simmel and Wirth are relevant as we look at the cinematic urbanism of the interwar years in both America and Europe. At that time, the introduction of modernity into small-town and rural communities allowed mass media to gain an unprecedented significance in the lives and views of their residents. This caused the previous social solidarity – that sense of kinship and community in the village or the small town that resulted from day-to-day experiences – to be called into question. Italo Calvino may be an appropriate commentator on this subject. The imaginary small town of Giancaldo in the film *Cinema Paradiso* may also be an appropriate example to make this point.

In his essay 'The Cinema-Goer Autobiography', Calvino professed to present 'cinema as another dimension of the world'.[11] But the cinema he is referring to comprises films he saw in his youth in his provincial hometown. In this regard, Calvino distinguishes between two modes of cinema-going: that of his youth and that of the present. The small-town experience was a cinema of distance and the modern one is a cinema of proximity, and of intellectual scrutiny. In reference to himself and to Federico Fellini's autobiographical work, Calvino explains that 'the lives of idle young boys were pretty similar' in the provincial seaside towns of Italy during the 1940s and 1950s. In Fellini's films, he recognizes:

> … the unsatisfied youth of the cinema-goer, of a provincial world that judges itself in relation to the cinema, in a constant comparison between itself and that other world that is the cinema… His young man leaves the provinces, goes to Rome and crosses over to the other side of the screen, making films, becoming himself the cinema… The provinces acquire meaning by being remembered in Rome. Rome acquires meaning having arrived from the provinces.[12]

The distinction Calvino makes between modes of cinema-going correlates to a major shift following World War II in both the histories of cinema and urbanism, and it legitimizes the small town and the big city as linked categories. The supposed dissolution of traditions and the advent of modernization in the small town thus becomes a process that is important to reflect upon. Here, tradition and modernity, either in real or cinematic cities, are and will always be independent. Hence, in theorizing cinema and the city, we should not look at these media as distinct entities, but as complementary realms that shape the cinema-goer's perception, or as urban tropes that help us understand the world.

In the American context, the story may be a little different. The small town has long been a prevalent type in the US to the extent of constituting a genre in cinema as well as in other forms of cultural production such as literature and theatre.[13] Regarding the small town as the 'focal point' of American identity, many writers have argued that close examination of the portrayal of small towns in Hollywood films reveals the characteristics of this identity.[14] For example, in his study of the American small-town genre in film, MacKinnon concluded that the small town represents quintessential American values and captures the true American identity. The small-town movie, hence, serves to point to the potential good and promise of perfect happiness in the small town, and then to justify and restore its qualities to heal the present social malfunction. Through the pain of the characters, old-time 'values are retrieved and made credible once more, at the points where they seem most threatened'.[15]

To discern what is particularly unique about the American and European contexts, this chapter will compare two cinematic small towns: Bedford Falls in Frank Capra's *It's a Wonderful Life* (1946),[16] and Giancaldo in Giuseppe Tornatore's *Cinema Paradiso* (1989).[17] This comparison will also allow us to distinguish the spatial traits of urbanization in the two contexts.

I believe we do not learn as much by looking at the entire genre of films as we do by examining in detail two selected films that capture the nature of the transformation in two cinematic small towns, one on either side of the Atlantic. One reason is that in small-town films, it is more the idea of the small town, and not its particularity that is emphasized – as opposed to the portrayal of big cities in which, generally, the city is clearly identified as New York, Los Angeles or London. 'As in literature, it is frequently the case that one small town, albeit geographically located, stands for all small towns, or the small-town mentality in general'.[18]

Thus, Bedford Falls in *It's a Wonderful Life* and Giancaldo in *Cinema Paradiso* are not unique. In fact, they are both (cinematically) designed to embody the typical characteristics of the small towns of the US and Italy, respectively, during the war and the immediate postwar period. It is also frequently the case that a cinematic small town is shot in several small towns. Moreover, the definition of the small town does not have to do with size or population, but with specific relationships within the town and the relationship of the town to the outside.[19] Using these films, we will be telling an urban history of small towns and their transformations on both sides of the Atlantic during the early modern era, which corresponded to the introduction of cinema and other forms of mass communication. Our focus will be on understanding the urbanization process of small towns during the 1930s, 1940s, and 1950s. At a time when many small-town communities were major consumers of Hollywood films, these communities began to find similarities between the cinematic space on the screen and their actual social experiences.

The European Small Town

In Giuseppe Tornatore's *Cinema Paradiso*, the Sicilian town of Giancaldo echoes the descriptions of the principal town in Italo Calvino's *The Road to San Giovanni*.[20] In the film, Giancaldo is presented in nostalgic flashbacks from the memory of its main character, Salvatore di Vita, known as 'Toto' as a youth (played by Salvatore Cascio, Marco Leonardi and Jacques Perrin for childhood, adolescence and adulthood). In later life, Salvatore becomes a well-established director, and as such, he is Tornatore's screen *alter ego*. In

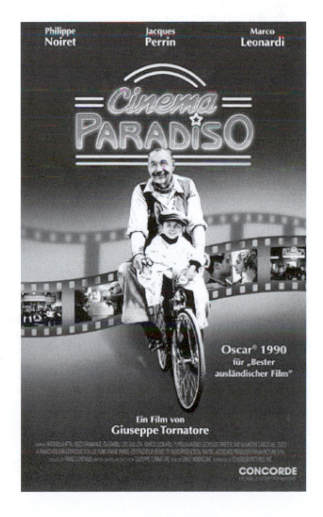

Cinema Paradiso (1989).
Film poster.

his journey into the past, Salvatore encounters his authentic self, which is presented through his re-encounter with the town in which he grew up – the traditional values, close social networks and rhythms of which were often dictated by religion. The narrative of the film shows the introduction of modernity through the evolution of cinema, its relationship with its audience, and the impact of this new social force on the life expectations of town residents.

'Cinema Paradiso' is the name of the only film theatre in the town. The fact that it is also the name of the film indicates the centrality of the theatre to the life of this small town during and immediately after World War II. At the beginning of the film, Salvatore has just heard the news of the death of his friend, Cinema Paradiso's projectionist Alfredo (played by Philippe Noiret). Although Giancaldo is only an hour away by plane from Rome, Salvatore has never returned since leaving there as a young man. However, when he does finally return to attend the funeral, he finds the town transformed, and the theatre itself in derelict shape, awaiting demolition.

On his return, Salvatore also discovers a box of old film clips saved by Alfredo. The clips contain all the kisses removed by the censor – also the town's priest – from movies shown at the theatre during its early years. The kisses, edited together, embody Salvatore's nostalgia for the postwar town of his youth. Overall, *Cinema Paradiso* is thus also eulogy to the history of cinema.

The film illustrates the transformative power of cinema, particularly in two scenes involving instances when films are projected out of doors. The first occurs when Alfredo is able to calm down a disorderly crowd unable to get into an already-full theatre by projecting the film everyone wants to

Cinema Paradiso. Giancaldo's main square becomes animated with cinema-goers.

Cinema Paradiso. The main square from the projection booth.

see onto the wall of a house across the town square from the theatre. When the crowd asks for sound, however, the managers demand payment. In the midst of the dispute, the theatre catches on fire. The second scene is a long take that pans from fishermen's vessels, to cinema seats, to the image on the screen. The film being shown is about primitive life and the heroic struggle of humankind with nature.

In general terms, the film's flashbacks trace Salvatore's youth. After losing his father in the war, Toto becomes fascinated with films and the space of the theatre itself. Toto is not alone in this passion. Going to the theatre is

Cinema Paradiso. Alfredo projects the film onto the façade of a building across the square.

a favourite pastime for the whole town, even for its priest who must also censor what the Church may consider inappropriate from its films. Toto divides his time between home, church, school and cinema. At home, he is irresponsible. He lives with his younger sister and his mother, who is obstinately and futilely awaiting the return of her soldier husband. Although they are very poor, Toto is obsessed with the cinema. He spends his milk money on film tickets, and he nearly causes his house to burn down when the celluloid scraps he keeps under his bed catch fire. In church, he is a bored altar boy; in school, he is a bright but disinterested student. But in the theatre, he is an attentive, gifted and devoted apprentice to Alfredo, to the point of saving the projectionist's life in the conflagration that begins on the night of the outdoor projection.

Eventually, the film relates how a new theatre, the Nuovo Cinema Paradiso replaces the old one. A state-of-the-art facility with neon lights is built by a lottery-winning Neapolitan, who lives in Giancaldo. The films shown in the new theatre are no longer censored. And Salvatore, now a teenager, becomes the projectionist, replacing Alfredo, who has lost his eyesight. However, Alfredo keeps on coming to the projection room and continues being his guardian angel. Soon, Salvatore falls in love with a middle-class teenager named Elena. Guided by Alfredo, he pursues his love doggedly. Elena reciprocates his love, but her disapproving parents take her away, leaving Salvatore heartbroken. Salvatore is then called for military service, and on his return, he decides to leave Giancaldo permanently for Rome.

As the story evolves, the relationship between Salvatore and his mentor, guardian, and surrogate father Alfredo becomes even more important. Alfredo has little education other than the diverse experiences he has seen on film. In fact, Alfredo is illiterate (he needs Toto's help to pass his literacy exam). But on each important occasion, he comes up with wise quotes, which are actually parts of scripts he has memorized from films over the years.

Lamenting the passage of life, Alfredo urges Toto to leave the small town. This is a specific moment of modernity in which a decision is made to leave one's traditional life behind. But the capacity to be modern is also seen to depend here on the ability to engage the creation of nostalgia. Alfredo's advice thus makes the conditions under which Toto can later create his own sense of nostalgia. Ironically, Alfredo advises him to never come back because 'Life is harder than the movies'.[21]

In the cinematic space of the town, it is significant that the theatre is situated on the town square across from the church. Indeed, the townspeople's fascination with the moving image eventually transforms the physical reality of the space of the theatre into a new social institution that eclipses the functions of the town square and the church.

Cinema Paradiso. The town's crowd waits for the demolition of Cinema Paradiso.

As portrayed in *Cinema Paradiso*, the cinema-goers of the 1940s and 1950s do not watch films passively, nor silently. And just as the theatre is inclusive of men and women of all classes and ages, so is the audience receptive to all kinds of films, from Hollywood melodramas to Italian comedies and neo-realist social critiques. The theatre shows such diverse films as *Gone with the Wind, Stage Coach, Modern Times, Blue Angel, Fury, Ulysses, The Lower Depths, Seven Brides for Seven Brothers, Dr. Jekyll and Mr. Hyde, Casablanca* and *La Terra Trema*. There is, however, a strong 'parallel drawn between the evolution of cinema, through the selection of cinema films, and the experiential growth of the characters in the film, but this relationship is neither chronological nor systematic.[22]

Cinema as experienced in Cinema Paradiso provides a basis of social solidarity and reference. As the new 'paradise', it takes over many of the social and theological functions of the church. In a way, the demise of Cinema Paradiso as a theatre is an allegory for the end of the paradise of Toto's childhood and the dissolution of the close-knit world of the small town.

The American Small Town

The reality of life in Giancaldo describes a condition that applies only to the European small town. In America, the small-town community did not exist as such, but rather remained a 'collective fantasy'.[23] This can be seen in Capra's *It's a Wonderful Life* in which the utopian representation of a postwar American town is used to portray the reality of Victorian family values and gender roles. In the film, George Bailey (played by James Stewart) is mysteriously given the responsibility of saving Bedford Falls, a traditional

It's a Wonderful Life (1946). Film poster.

Middle-American town, from becoming Pottersville, a dystopic big city. The latter is portrayed as the epitome of a corrupt, vulgarized, mercenary world, full of blaséness – in short, the opposite of warm, caring Bedford Falls.

The film starts on a Christmas Eve when celestial narrators reveal that George Bailey is broke and suicidal over a misplaced loan. Clarence Oddbody, a second-rate angel, is to guard him. The senior angels narrate George Bailey's life story as one of sacrifices. He partially lost his hearing while saving his younger brother from drowning. He endured a beating to save the life of both the pharmacist, Mr. Gower, and a sick boy by refusing to deliver the wrong medicine. He gave up his plans to travel upon the unexpected death of his father, because he felt obligated to prevent Bailey Building and Loan from collapse and the greedy businessman, Mr. Potter, from taking control of the town. Instead of going to college himself, he used his own savings to send his brother Harry. And, he gave up his honeymoon to prevent a financial crisis in his company.

When Clarence meets George, George impulsively wishes that he were unborn. He is unaware of the importance of his deeds, or of his significance

It's a Wonderful Life. The Bailey Building and Loan's motto: 'Own your own home'.

to those around him. To convince him of his worth, however, Clarence takes George on a journey across Pottersville, the city that the idyllic Bedford Falls would have become if George had not been born. Afterwards, George realizes that, despite it all, he has a 'wonderful life' and he decides to embrace it as it is. Finally, the tight community that George derided, but also supported throughout his life, turns out to support him, and saves his business and reputation by collecting the missing sum.

It's a Wonderful Life. A suburban development like Bailey Park, built by Bailey Building and Loan – a place for families and children.

The plot revolves around George Bailey's lifelong unfulfilled desire to escape Bedford Falls. As a young man, however, he fails at this and he turns his frustration into an effort to re-make Bedford Falls by 'building'. First, he wants to become an architect and 'build things, design new buildings, plan modern cities'.[24] This desire, however, denotes not just nostalgia for the past but also for a particular future, remade in the image of the past. But just as he cannot travel, George Bailey also cannot attend college and become an architect. And while he detests Bedford Falls, he is only able to initiate the suburban Bailey Park project through the family business, Bailey Building and Loan. By mid-life, he finds himself still trapped, married with children, living in the old, dilapidated mansion at 320 Sycamore, at the sight of which, in his younger days he had announced his desire 'to shake off the dust of this crummy little town' and 'see the world'.

For narrative purposes, the film also places two pairs of characters in opposition to each other: Mr. Potter (played by Lionel Barrymore) and George's father, and Violet and George's wife Mary (played by Donna Reed). The former wrestle for the same business, Bailey Building and Loan, while the latter compete for the same man, George. According to Randall Fallows, within the political context of the film, Uncle Billy is also opposed to Mr. Potter.[25] With his impotency and absentmindedness, Uncle Billy represents the progressive, while the cruel Mr. Potter represents the conservative. '... Capra characterize[s] the political Right as placing greed over morality, money over physical needs, fascist ideas over democratic values'.[26] It is Peter Bailey, George's father, who maintains a position in-between these two extremes. A successful man, Peter Bailey is aware of the community, unlike Uncle Billy. But unlike Potter, he wants to help it, as opposed to exploiting it.

Initially, George sets out to emulate his father: 'Ask Dad. He knows'.[27] But when his father is no longer there to guide him, he is fortunate that Clarence comes from Heaven to mentor him. The story is hinged around the relationship between Angel Clarence and George. Clarence needs to save George to earn his wings. To do so, he constructs a nostalgia of invented tradition to convince him of how ugly the entire life of the town would have been if he had never been born. Clarence tells George that he cannot leave.[28] In the end, the integrity and cohesiveness of the community are maintained. It is only Clarence and George who are deeply transformed. Clarence gets his wings with the help of George, and George comes to appreciate and accept his life with the help of Clarence.

As the film progresses, the alternate worlds that Clarence shows George highlight the discrepancy between tradition and modernity. Without George in the world, the pharmacist (Mr. Gower) becomes a panhandler; the happy wife with kids (Mary) becomes a librarian; the seductress (Violet) becomes a prostitute; the respectable lady (Ms. Bailey) becomes a boarding house

It's a Wonderful Life. Bailey Park's antithesis is 'Pottersville'.

keeper; the businessman (Uncle Billy) becomes a lunatic in an asylum; and the national heroes (brother Harry Bailey, the cab driver Ernie, and the police officer Bert) are either dead, insignificant or abusive people.

In its representation of small-town American values, it is significant that social life takes place predominantly during the daytime in Bedford Falls, and in the numerous small shops on the Main Street. Among these shops, the pharmacy has a special place. As a youth, George made his earnings there, and those earnings enabled him to help his family and community. The pharmacy is important also as a community shop, and it sells consumables like ice cream that bring children and adults together. It also brings the children into the adult world. Mary and Violet first experience an attraction for George at the pharmacy and they first compete for him there. In general, children have a strong presence in Bedford Falls because they assure the continuity of community and there is little that is hidden from them. As a child, George has access to all of the town's establishments including his father's Bailey Building and Loan.

Connection to the past is equally important. In Bedford Falls, aging street trees have the capacity to connect residents to their ancestors. All across the town, residents also know each other by the name. Porches provide intermediate spaces between the public and the private, facilitating interaction. The cab and the police car regularly watch over the streets. The cabby and the policeman are also George's friends, and they help Mary turn the Granville House into an exotic honeymoon hotel. Not only are the townspeople caring, but they are also imaginative. At night, an immigrant Italian's venue, Martini's, helps alleviate residents' problems with its music and warmth.

Its traditional physical fabric helps Bedford Falls maintain a strong sense of community. However, immediately following World War II, a decision is made to extend the town through the development of Bailey Park. Bailey Park is a suburban settlement that George envisions will empower the people of Bedford Falls by giving them a way to own homes. But in contrast to Bedford Falls, there is no street life in Bailey Park. There are no trees, only lawns; no porches, only private back patios. Moreover, it is constructed on what was once the cemetery, thereby erasing traces of lineage and history. However, this is also where Martini, an Italian immigrant, will be able to consolidate a new, American life. In contrast to such newcomers, the Bailey family, Mary's family, and (when they are married) George and Mary continue to live in the old part of the town, making it new by rebuilding and repairing it.

Bedford Falls is connected to the outside world physically by a bridge, which features both at the beginning and end of the film. At the beginning, it is the site of George Bailey's suicide attempt. At the end, it is the site of his redemption. Angel Clarence meets George only at the bridge to take him to the future. The bridge is a metaphor for the state of limbo that Bedford Falls is in, between inside and outside, present and future, small town and big city, community and society, tradition and modernity.

Transformations of Spaces and Institutions in an Urbanizing Modernity

What these two films indicate is how the arrival of modernity acted differently on the spaces and institutions of European and American small towns. The differing effects of urbanizing modernity can be seen by examining its impact on the three social worlds: home, business/work, and community.

The idea of home as family hearth is central to American identity. In this regard, it differs significantly from the European sense of home, which is more diffused, and, often associated with a village, town, or particular geography, i.e., 'homeland'. At the beginning of *It's a Wonderful Life*, George does not understand why Mary tries to prevent him from throwing a rock at the old Granville house at 320 Sycamore. He understands even less why she would want to live there. Even when they get married and start living there, George's feelings do not change.

Although George has doubts about living in the old house, as well as having a family and children, Mary has no problems coming back to Bedford

Falls after college, marrying her childhood love, living in a dilapidated old house, or having children. Portrayed in soft focus, the lovely, intelligent, creative, hard-working and well-educated Mary stands for the ideal homemaker and nation-builder. She throws her energy into rebuilding the Granville House, and volunteers for the army during the war. George, too, is a homemaker in his own right. Through Bailey Building and Loan, he sets out to build homes in Bailey Park that will allow a new generation of town residents to set down roots in traditional Bedford Falls.

In contrast, *Cinema Paradiso*'s protagonist Salvatore has no ambitions of 'building' in his hometown. Instead, he only sends money to repair a home he has abandoned. Indeed, the opening shot of *Cinema Paradiso* zooms in from the sea to the interior of a mansion where Salvatore's mother is trying to reach her son in Rome by phone. Salvatore is next pictured as having just returned from work to a comfortable residence he shares with a female partner. From the brief conversation Salvatore has with his companion about his mother's call, it is inferred that he is not committed to anyone. Thus, the film implies that this is not his 'real' home. Home was the single room he shared with his mother and younger sister in his childhood. There, the only precious asset was the box of family photographs later destroyed in a fire caused by his own collection of film strips. When Salvatore returns to Giancaldo after many years, he finds this family home has grown from a simple room into a seaside mansion as a result of his financial contributions, while the few belongings he left have been turned into a room-museum.

The second important sphere of small-town life, business/work, is where its relative isolation allows it to connect to the world outside. In *It's a Wonderful Life*, the institution of Bailey Building and Loan represents a form of shared socio-economic responsibility unique to the small town. As a family business, it is contrasted with the modern institution of the bank in its function and spatial organization. The Bailey Company is a living place, whose success benefits the entire community. A bank, on the other hand, is a sterile environment, whose activities are focused only on monetary profit. In one sequence when depositors make a 'run' on his company to pull out their money, George pleads with them to stick to the community as opposed to pursuing their individual benefits. He points out that the holding of one deposit builds a home for another. In the following sequences, George is tempted by Potter's lush job offer, but refuses for the good of the community, just as his father did before him. The Baileys never seem to be able to make large sums of money for themselves, since money is never their priority.

Similarly, in the year immediately after World War II, business is not solely pursued for profit in Giancaldo. Early in the film, Alfredo returns the milk money that Toto spends to enter the theatre when he hears his mother is in need. But gradually, money becomes a more important concern in the town. First, in the outdoor projection sequence, the theatre claims the public square, and the crowd there is asked for payment. Then, the censorship dictated by the Church is eliminated. Later, the restrooms are used as a brothel. Finally, projections are made mobile, to increase profits.

Community and social relationships constitute the third social entity through which it is possible to discern the effects of urbanizing modernity. In *Cinema Paradiso*, the physical spaces of the church, school, theatre, and the town square double as social institutions and spaces. Regardless of whether they are public or private, they are transformed by modernity. The theatre is first demolished in the 1950s by a fire and then again in the 1980s for a multi-storey car park. The town square, once the centre of everyday social encounter, is invaded by cars. As the residents of Giancaldo in the 1980s explain, the new technologies of TV and VCR render such places of public life redundant.

In *It's a Wonderful Life*, the physical space of Bedford Falls embodies both the traditional town and its opposite, Pottersville. In the nightmare sequence, Clarence shows George how the Bailey family and its supportive environment cannot exist in the world of Pottersville. Clarence takes him first to Bailey Building and Loan, which has turned into 'Welcome Jitterbugs', a sleazy night venue; second, to his own home, which is a ruin without family and children; third, to his parents' house, which has turned into a boarding house with his mother as the keeper; fourth, to the cemetery in which Harry lies; and finally, to the library where Mary is working as a librarian. Since Mary cannot marry and raise children, lineage – thus, continuity and tradition – are endangered.

Symbolically, it is important that in contrast to Bedford Falls where Main Street comes alive during the day, Main Street in Pottersville is experienced at night as a menacing conglomeration of bars and night clubs. Martini's convivial Italian atmosphere is replaced by Nick's hard-drinking bar, from which not only the panhandler but also George and Angel Clarence are excluded. Pottersville represents the much-feared big city alternative to the town. It is 'a nightmare vision of modern America, a vision of the noir city in which the spectacle of urban degeneracy signifies a corruption of the social body, which the film links to the "crippled" body of Potter himself'.[29] Whereas Bedford Falls is associated with transparency and inclusiveness, Pottersville is a non-productive town in which the primary functions are consumption and leisure, and in which the inhabitants are shaped by commerce.[30] Frank Krutnik suggests that:

> The folk community of Bedford Falls resembles Thomas Jefferson's pastoral ideal, a realm of localized Americanism protected from the pestilence of urbanity. And Pottersville is a corrupted city of strangers that has betrayed the Edenic promise of

America – a world in which consensual social bonds have been obliterated under the pressures of unchecked capitalism.[31]

By virtue of being opposites, Bedford Falls and Pottersville define each other, with the latter giving meaning and legitimacy to the former. There is nothing special about Bedford Falls; nothing that would tie one to it – one reason why George wants to escape. Yet during the course of the film, Bedford Falls is turned into utopia by the countervailing presentation of a dystopic Pottersville. Bedford Falls is the only alternative to this dystopia. It is the fear of dystopia/Pottersville that frames the understanding of utopia/Bedford Falls.

The narrative in *Cinema Paradiso* spans the period between 1940 and 1980, while *It's a Wonderful Life* spans between 1919 and 1946. The 1940s – the war and immediate postwar years – were perceived as an important turning point for the small town by both directors. Yet they portray their concerns in distinctly different ways. Giancaldo is assembled as a collage of different Italian small towns. Indeed, *Cinema Paradiso* was shot on location in the Palermo province of Sicily, in Tornatore's hometown of Bagheria (a coastal town of 50,000), in Palazzo Adriano (an inland city of 2500), and in several other towns.[32] By contrast, Bedford Falls was shot on a studio set that comprised '75 stores and buildings, main street, factory district and a large residential and slum area'; it was constructed, in 1946, for the three-month duration of the shooting, on a ranch in Encino, California.[33] Only the Charleston contest scene, with the floor opening to reveal the swimming pool underneath, was shot on location at the newly built Beverly Hills High School gymnasium.[34] Meanwhile, it is important to also note that although Bedford Falls was an entirely fictional town, its name alludes to the prosperous suburban settlement of Bedford Hills in Westchester County, NY.

It's a Wonderful Life never seeks to portray Bedford Falls specifically, but only as an idea. We are never sure of its layout or its size; instead, orientation is maintained by emphasizing certain houses and institutions. This lack of completeness serves to invest individual houses and locations with important social meaning. Such fragmentation also visualizes the archetypical antithesis that underlies the genre of the small-town film: 'Old time idealism versus present malfunction'.[35] Indeed, MacKinnon has suggested that:

> … particularization of a locale might be fatal, since a movie about 'every American' loses much of its point if there can be comfortable responses to the problems posed by it, such as that these social attitudes and conflicts are peculiar to the big city.[36]

The difference between Tornatore and Capra's choices of shooting locations is a reflection of their philosophies.[37] That difference may speak to a fundamental difference between European and American modernity. Both cinematic towns are equally invented: Bedford Falls is about a past whose particular intent is to imagine the future; Giancaldo's past is one that cannot be reclaimed – a mournful nostalgia that does not have any projections towards the future. Thus, American modernity cannot imagine a future independent of its short history, and hence uses nostalgia to create its future. European modernity is more accepting of the passage of time. Even if nostalgia is not needed to create a future, it is needed to justify actions of the present.

Tradition and Modernity

Both Giancaldo and Bedford Falls establish a clear demarcation between the traditional and the modern. To understand how, it is first necessary to delineate what tradition is and how it changes. While there is no consensus on the definition of tradition, in earlier works I have discerned three prevalent conceptions of it. The first view is that tradition is about the absence of choice: in this sense, it denotes constraint and stands as the antithesis of modernity.[38] The second view emphasizes the process of handing down – transmission – as opposed to the material culture of the handed-down products.[39] The third view treats the concept as one of degrees – an attribute – which can be called 'traditional-ity', by which a given environment can be evaluated.[40]

In *Cinema Paradiso*, modernity is portrayed through the demolition of the theatre while in *It's a Wonderful Life* it appears through the nightmarish dystopia of Pottersville. As modernity arrives, the protagonists of both films strive to break free from the limitations of the small town. Salvatore leaves Giancaldo without looking back. And even if George never manages to leave Bedford Falls, he does not understand the necessity of tradition as continuity. His sin is so great that celestial powers must be summoned to bring the idea of continuity to him by means of the contrasting vision of Pottersville.

In Pottersville, the break between the traditional and the modern is characterized by George's attempt to assume the old degree of familiarity and camaraderie in the old Martini's – which has become 'Nick's Bar'. In the process, he annoys Nick by referring to him by his first name; likewise, a client is hostile to the panhandler-turned-pharmacist, Mr. Gower. While Pottersville suggests the triumph of monopoly capitalism, it is also a powerful warning against the dissolution of social consciousness that results from a purely monetary society.

In *Cinema Paradiso*, modernity triumphs at the moment when films no longer have to be censored by the priest. The movie theatre is no longer owned by a native Sicilian, who conforms to the traditional values of the small town and the Church, but by a Neapolitan who is able to transform its socio-spatial institutions. The change is well received in the community and the first kiss on screen is met with applause from the audience. However, this exchange is also a moment of commerce; a triumph of consumerism over other social institutions.

As the theatre represents the town in *Cinema Paradiso*, social intercourse – growing up, love, sex, friendship, marriage, learning, curiosity, otherness, etc. – are all exercised in its space. As a result, life on the theatre screen becomes the life of the citizens. Modernity is introduced to the town through the cinema. But it eventually thrives independently of this virtual world. Thus, the death of the cinema as a social institution (following the introduction of newer forms of mass communication) and as a physical place (following the demolition of the theatre) does not signify the death of modernity, but rather its articulation of different directions.

An Urbanizing Modernity

These films remind us of Wirth's dictum that urbanism has become 'a way of life' – a new way that has displayed, in a single generation, the idea of the small town as the world. Whereas the older generation was not aware, or interested in the outside world (Alfredo never plans leaving, nor does George's father) – the new generation has to leave. Thus, the family of Toto's classmate, Peppino, leaves Giancaldo to find work in Germany; and he, himself, leaves to become someone people talk about. Sam Wainwright, George's brother Harry, and even Violet have to leave Bedford Falls to seize opportunities elsewhere. It is through mass communication and cinema – through Salvatore's films and George's copies of *National Geographic* and travel brochures – that distant lands gain place in the imaginary of the new generation.

Neither Giancaldo nor Bedford Falls are industrial centres, but they are both modern since they experience the effects of modernity. As a result of World War II, both towns went through physical and social transformations that are unique to their contexts. Emanuel Levy has suggested that Hollywood movies of the 1940s pursued a post-Depression faith in Americanism as manifest in the small town.[41] He explains, 'The threat of totalitarianism and World War II itself necessitated reaffirmation of traditional values: family love, commitment to the land and defense of the country'.[42] Accordingly, Bedford Falls celebrates its war heroes. But *It's a Wonderful Life* is also concerned with the ideas of opportunism and conservatism that threaten small-town way of life. According to MacKinnon:

> [T]he wider message [of the genre of small town movies] seems to be that, at times
> when it loses confidence in Americanism, the American people should have the faith

in itself and its institutions to see beyond the failures and compromises to the reality of an ideal which may still be effective, given the commitment of all to it.[43]

The small town's set of values comprises egalitarianism, decency and 'fairness, equality before the law; respect for family life and the traditional role of the sexes, together with a generalized good will' as archetypes of Americanism.[44] In a sense, American national identity is firmly connected to the idea of the small town, just as small-town movies serve to point to the potential good, the promise of perfect happiness, and to justify and restore the present metropolis of malfunction. Through the pain of the characters, old time 'values are retrieved and made credible once more, at the points where they seem most threatened'.[45] In this way, Hollywood has contributed to the making of a unique modernity based on the myth of the small town.

In contrast to Bedford Falls, on the other side of the Atlantic, Giancaldo has to mourn its dead. *Cinema Paradiso*, while romanticizing the small-town life, also problematizes the socio-economic limitations of the idyllic small town that characterized prewar Italy. In the postwar period, Italy, as a defeated nation, had to accept and embrace change. In Giancaldo, first religion, then cinema cease to be guiding principles, to be replaced by capital profit. Those physical and social spaces that gave Giancaldo its prewar small-town character are transformed to hold new functions.

Unlike Giancaldo, Bedford Falls manages to avoid transformation. It is shown to expand economically and physically through the new economic possibilities while maintaining the physical and social aspects of its small-town character. The trope of an urbanizing small-town modernity in *It's a Wonderful Life* is Bailey Building and Loan. Although it is a corporation, it is portrayed as a community-based institution handed down from generation to generation. Yet, for it to endure, sacrifices have to be made and struggles need to be won. In *Cinema Paradiso*, the trope is the theatre. Like Bailey Building and Loan, the theatre is both a business and a social institution. All stages of life are experienced within it and all types of personalities gather there. Meanwhile, the changing patterns of seating and audience conduct reflect changes in the social structure of the town. By virtue of its physical limitations, the theatre as the town heightens the effect of distance between the town and the metropolis. Its replacement by a multi-storey car park also stands as a metaphor for socio-economic transformation throughout Europe in the 1980s. However, in the American context, Bailey Building and Loan, hence the small town itself, is saved with the help of its constituents.

Through these cases, we can discern how the small town does not always develop into a big city, but still experiences the effects of urbanization and modernity. Yet these films also convey how different the moments of modernity were in Europe and America, and they express, as well, the variations in the continuum between tradition and modernity. Capra's film involves a moralistic modernity rooted in libertarian American values. It is a modernism related to, or a product of, the New Deal policies which made its housing environments possible in the first place.[46] Housing, here, is seen as involving something more than a collection of houses, as a house is not necessarily a home and the process of making a home is the first act of dwelling in space. On the other hand, housing, as a term, refers to an entire programme of dwelling in space and colonizing land. One of the consequences of the modernization of small-town life was a subtle shift in the importance of the house from being an almost primordial constituent of the American landscape to something bigger, something more organized, and state sponsored. This housing environment was made possible by savings-and-loan associations like the one run by George Bailey.

In the European context, the tradition – modern continuum involves a fragmentation of time. Social entities of family and community are hollowed out and deprived of their traditional functions of maintaining continuity. In Tornatore's film, it is *time* that defines the relationship between the individual and the society. As G.J. Whitrow suggested, 'for many people today, time has become so fragmented that only the present appears to be significant while the past is regarded "out of date" and therefore useless'.[47] For Salvatore, the famous film director, the death of his mentor Alfredo is only significant in relation to that past. However, again, according to Whitrow: 'the past "is being ground to pieces" by the mill of inexorable, incomprehensible change', and hence, the 'out-of-date' film theatre is allowed to be 'ground to pieces'.[48]

In the context of American and European cities, the fundamental transformation around World War II involved the birth of a new modernity associated with a unique form of urbanization. It is not the modernity of Simmel, of blaséness or of encounter. And it is not the modernity that comes with industrialization, or one propelled by fundamental changes in consumption and production. It is, instead, a modernity fuelled outside cultural influences. This modernity can be seen as intruding into the life of the supposedly insular small town or village. As such, it is a modernity that is comfortable with small scale and low density. These outside influences are presented through the medium of cinema in Giancaldo, and through economic institutions like the Building and Loan and the bank in Bedford Falls. Here, the urbanizing modernity of Europe seems more resilient to the forces of disintegration than its American equivalent. This fragility may be reflected in the nightmare scene, as the entire town is transformed by outside economic forces and where its values have given way completely to those of the big city. The irony here is that 'nightmarish' places, such as X-rated movie theatres, did start to appear in small-town America following the recession of the 1980s. The nightmare of Bedford turning into Pottersville seems to have happened in many small towns in the US today. The fact that this transformation is depicted in film before it occurs in real life supports the idea that the real and the reel have become mutually constitutive.

While public space is the site of urban vitality in Giancaldo, it is the home that serves a similar function in Bedford Falls. George's business provides the opportunity for people to have homes. And George and Mary's ability to fix up an old house and turn it into a successful home remains the unique American experience of an urbanizing modernity. But equally important is the fact that the fixing of the house is what allows it to be accepted by the community, which later comes to Bailey's aid in his hour of need. Even though it is a physical structure, the home here is not about material physicality; it is about what the Building and Loan as an institution allows people to achieve.

The idea of home in Giancaldo does not seem as complex. Here, home involves the entirety of a small, somewhat insular town. In the age of urbanization, one fundamental difference between the American and the European cases lies in where modernity is spatialized or where it resides. In the premodern European context, meaning resides in public space, while in the American context, it resides within the space of the home.

The failures of the New York Stock Exchange, the collapse of the national economy, and the ensuing Depression of the 1930s are depicted in *It's A Wonderful Life* as the failure of Bedford Falls. It is an outcome Bedford Falls cannot escape. Giancaldo, as presented in *Cinema Paradiso*, is more romanticized as a self-contained economy.[49] Tornatore's coverage of its economy is minimal. It is not clear what jobs the audience at the movie theatre have; we get only a few glimpses of their means of livelihood. Clearly, they are not farmers, as we see no one working the land. And aside from the priest and several teachers, the theatre's employees are the only ones presented as working hard, even as they lose their sight or their loved ones. A few people seem to be self-employed, like the women who dye and dry their fabrics on the public square, but clearly Toto's mother does not have a job. There is almost no economy except for an implied bank where Elena's father, who comes from the outside, works. Tornatore's romanticization of Sicilian urban life inadvertently and unfortunately subscribes to the common notion that small-town folk in places like Sicily lead idle and possibly lazy lives.

Both Giancaldo and Bedford Falls are presented as inevitably coming under the spell of the big city. What Capra and Tornatore seem to have in common is a desire to escape an urbanizing modernity. But this cannot be stopped by reverting to the pastoral experience that formerly embodies small-town life. There is one final factor that stands out in our attempt to understand the cinematic city of the postwar period. The urbanizing modernity of the small town, in both Europe and America, was fundamentally related to, and possibly a product of, a nostalgia. In the European case, it was nostalgia for an imagined idyllic, peaceful and pre-industrial condition of lower density and community. In the American case, it was a utopian nostalgia for a past that never was.

Notes

1   E. Levy, *Small-Town America in Film: The Decline of Community*. New York: Continuum, 1991, pp. 24–25.
2   L. Wirth, 'Urbanism as a Way of Life', *American Journal of Sociology*, 1938, p. 66.
3   *Ibid.*
4   M. Weber, *The City*. New York: Free Press, 1956 (1921).
5   D. Rowe, *Representing Berlin, Sexuality and the City in Imperial and Weimar Germany*. Aldershot: Ashgate, 2003, p. 23.
6   *Ibid.*, p. 4.
7   Rowe has pointed out that 'The ideal of community living was a particularly strong feature of urban sociology in Germany and was fostered especially by Ferdinand Tönnies in his text *Gemeinschaft und Gesellschaft* (Community and Society), published in 1887. The widespread influence of Tönnies's work on the development of urban theory in Germany during and after the nineteenth century renders it worth considering in more detail as part of the more general context from which theorists of Berlin during the Imperial era forged many of their ideological positions'. *Ibid.*, p. 18.
8   F. Tönnies, *Community and Society*, C. P. Loomis (ed., trans.). New York: Evanston; London: Harper & Row, 1963. Original as *Gemeinschaft und Gesellschaft*, 1887, p. 226.
9   Rowe has suggested that 'In Tönnies's distinction between *Gemeinschaft und Gesellschaft*, *Gemeinschaft* was understood to refer to the notion of a small town or rural community based upon generational ties and traditional values whilst *Gesellschaft* was used to define a society that was much more broadly based and, at its highest and most impersonal level was represented by the state'. D. Rowe, *Representing Berlin*, p. 18.
10 G. Simmel, 'The Metropolis and Mental Life', in D. Frisby and M. Featherstone (eds.) *Simmel on Culture. Selected Writings*. London: Sage, 1997.
11 I. Calvino, 'The Cinema-Goer Autobiography', *The Road to San Giovanni*, Tim Parks (trans.). New York: Pantheon Books, 1993, p. 54.
12 *Ibid.*, p. 65.
13 E. Levy, *Small-Town America in Film*, p. 16.
14 See K. MacKinnon, *Hollywood's Small Towns: An Introduction to the American Small-Town Movie*. Metuchen, NJ: The Scarecrow Press, 1984, p. 45.
15 *Ibid.*
16 Frank Capra (1897–1991) is an American film director. Capra's family emigrated from Italy to California when he was a child. He studied at CalTech to become an army-engineering instructor. He started directing films in 1921 as well as writing and editing. In 1928, he began his association with Columbia Pictures, for which he produced very popular, financially successful, and prestigious feature films through the 1930s. Capra is known for his patriotism and belief in American values. But his patriotism is not blind; in his films, he persistently examined the American system. When World War II started, Capra enlisted in the army and served in the Signal Corps, where he made documentaries. His first postwar film was *It's a Wonderful Life* (1946). Although not a success in the year of its release, after the expiry of its copyright in the 1970s, it became a TV hit and a classic. Capra made other films after *It's a Wonderful Life,* but his prewar success was not revived.

17 Many reviews have considered Giuseppe Tornatore's *Cinema Paradiso* as an 'autobiographical work'. Tornatore is an Italian photographer, director and writer. He was born in 1956 in Bagheria near Palermo in Sicily. As a photographer, he won many prizes in Italy. He made his first short film when he was sixteen. Because of his success, RAI Television commissioned him to do numerous TV films. He won a prize for Best Documentary in 1982 at the Salerno Film Festival for 'Ethnic Minorities in Sicily'. Indeed, Sicily has been a predominant theme in his work. *Cinema Paradiso,* his second feature film, brought him awards – a Cannes award in 1989 and an Oscar in 1990 – and international recognition.

18 K. MacKinnon, *Hollywood's Small Towns*, p. 18.

19 *Ibid.*

20 I. Calvino, *The Road to San Giovanni*. New York: Pantheon Books, 1993.

21 The following conversation takes place between them:
    Alfredo: Toto! Go away! This land is cursed. When you're here every day you feel like you're at the center of the universe, it seems like nothing ever changes. Then you go away, one year, two... And when you come back, everything's different. The thread has broken. You don't find those you were looking for, your things no longer exist. Isn't that the case?... You've got to go away a long time, for many, many years, before coming back and finding your people again, the land where you were born...But not now, it's impossible. Now you're blinder than I am.
    Salvatore: Who said that? Gary Cooper, James Stewart, Henry Fonda? Huh?
    Alfredo: No, Toto, nobody said it. I say it! Life's not like how you saw it in the movies. Life ... is harder.

22 M. Frontier, 'Cinema Paradiso'. Retrieved on 22 June 2003, http://www.reel.com/.

23 K. MacKinnon, *Hollywood's Small Towns,* p. 8.

24 *It's a Wonderful Life Final Script*. Retrieved on 21 June 2003, http://geocities.com/classicmoviescripts/script/itsawonderfullife.txt

25 R. Fallows, 'George Bailey in the Vital Center: Postwar Liberal Politics and *It's a Wonderful Life* (A Comparison of Frank Capra's Movie and Arthur Schlesinger's Political Book)', *Journal of Popular Film and Television*, Vol. 25, No. 2, 1997, p. 53.

26 *Ibid.*
    Fallows, following Raymond Carney, has argued that Capra's films are 'politically unclassifiable and ideologically elusive'. However, as Fallows suggests, although Capra evades 'neat ideological classification', through an analysis of contemporaneous politics and history, 'we can partially explain why the film took the shape it did'. Instead of viewing Capra's political stances in film as, according to Fallows, 'unclassifiable', it is in fact more appropriate to see them as commercially savvy. He clearly defends socialist values and maintains his political stance. At the same time, he recognizes that the New Deal had its opponents. By presenting all sides, Capra avoids criticism for explicit misrepresentation.

    Fallows's political and historical analysis of the film's circumstances leads him 'to discern the qualities that make George's life wonderful from those which make it regretful'. He suggests that political and cultural positions as portrayed in the film are limited and there is not much we would 'want to believe in' as other critics have defended. When we look at the two worlds of Bedford Falls and Pottersville, as existing simultaneously rather than being incommensurately supplanting each other, we can – through George's eyes – understand that the qualities that make George's life wonderful are the ones that make American modernity unique.

27 While working in the pharmacy as a child, George is confronted with the dilemma of delivering wrong medicine. He does not know what to do. He sees a Sweet Caporals ad, which, in capitals, reads: 'ASK DAD HE KNOWS'. Upon seeing it, he rushes off to his father's workplace to do just that.

28 Clarence says, '[At the toll keeper's] So you still think killing yourself would make

everyone feel happier, eh? … [upon George's wish to be unborn] Oh, you mustn't say things like that... [After George meets Ms. Bailey in the unborn sequence] Strange, isn't it? Each man's life touches so many other lives, and when he isn't around he leaves an awful hole, doesn't he?'
It's a Wonderful Life Final Script. Retrieved on 21 June 2003.
http://geocities.com/classicmoviescripts/.

29   F. Krutnik, 'Something More than Night: Tales of the Noir City', in *The Cinematic City*, David Clarke (ed.), London: Routledge, 1997, p. 86.
30   *It's a Wonderful Life Final Script.* Retrieved on June 21, 2003.
     http://geocities.com/classicmoviescripts/.
31   F. Krutnik, 'Something More than Night', p. 87.
32   J. Bernard, 'Cinema Paradiso', *New York Post*, 2 February, 1990, p. 23.
     A search in Google for 'Palazzo+Adriano+cinema+paradiso' generated 797 pages. Retrieved 15 September 2003. Examples include:
     http:// www.palermo-sicilia.it/english/palazzo_adriano.htm. And:
     http:// sicilia.indettaglio.it/eng/comuni/pa/ palazzoadriano/palazzoadriano.html
     http:// www.arbitalia.it/katundet/palazzo/ palazzo.monumenti.htm
     http:// www.guzzardi.it/arberia/mappa/sicilia/ palazzoadriano/pagine/monumenti.htm
     http:// www.sizilien-rad.de/infos/cinema.htm
33   Retrieved 11 June 2003.
     http://www.geocities.com/Hollywood/Makeup/8156/iawlmoviefacts.htm
34   American Film Institute records. Retrieved on 11 June 2003.
     http://afi.chadwyck.com/cgi/full_rec
35   K. MacKinnon, *Hollywood's Small Towns*, p. 30.
36   *Ibid.*, p. 74.
37   Tornatore accepts the inevitability of moving on in allowing the theatre to be destroyed. He is nostalgic for what is lost with modernity's advent into the small town, but also, he holds equal faith in the capacity to find resolution within modernity.
         Cinema Paradiso's original version was not well received by Italian audiences. The edited version, however, made the film an international hit. In *Small-Town America in Film,* Levy argues that 'the mythology of the small town is a distinctly American creation, hence the concept of Small-Town America exists in contrast to the mythology of the Big City'; a construct shared in many Western societies. He adds that the 'activation of specific (and not others) Small Town and Big City myths at certain (and not others) historical times calls for an explanation'. Accordingly in the 1980s, while comedy was the main genre of films featuring small towns in the US, in Italy, a sentimental examination of the 1940s and 1950s small town was made popular.
         In the 2002 unabridged and fully restored version, *Nuovo Cinema Paradiso*, distributed as the Director's Cut, Salvatore goes home where he finds Elena and clarifies their unresolved affair. Nostalgia is reconciled through closure; made possible by facing the past. While, for Tornatore, the small town, as it was, is no longer viable; for Capra, it bears promise. Capra has faith in the possibility of redemption within the small town. Therefore, he invents a small town to fulfil his nostalgia with an 'imagined myth'.
38   Y. Tuan, 'Traditional: What Does It Mean?', in N. AlSayyad and J. Bourdier (eds.) *Dwellings, Settlements, and Tradition*. Lanham, MD: University Press of America, 1989, pp. 27–34.
39   P. Oliver, 'Handed Down Architecture', in *Dwellings, Settlements, and Tradition*, pp. 53–76.
40   A. Rapoport, 'On the Attributes of Tradition', in *Dwellings, Settlements, and Tradition*, pp. 77–105.
41   E. Levy, *Small-Town America in Film*, p. 71.
42   *Ibid.*

43 K. MacKinnon, *Hollywood's Small Towns,* p. 45.

44 *Ibid.*, p. 59

45 *Ibid.*, p. 45.

46 The National Housing Act created the Federal Housing Administration in 1934, which oversaw and encouraged banks and other loan institutions to lend to low-income families.

47 G. J. Whitrow, *Time in History: Views of Time from Pre-History to the Present Day.* Oxford: Oxford University Press, 1989, p. 183.

48 *Ibid.* (Hans Meyerhoff's remark)

49 Giancaldo is a collage of several small towns, and being so, it displays the cinematic limitation of capturing an urbanizing modernity.

Chapter 3

Orwellian Modernity: Utopia/Dystopia and the City of the Future Past

Thomas More is credited with coining the term 'utopia' in the sixteenth century, but More's utopia was by no means the first. Utopias are as old as the history of humankind. In his 1939 lecture titled 'Utopia', H.G. Wells argued that utopias are historically situated, and that they reflect 'our stresses'. He claimed, 'The more disturbed men's minds are, the more Utopias multiply'.[1] In Wells's account, utopias have proliferated during historical turning points, including the Renaissance with its discovery of foreign lands. Wells differentiated between 'utopias of freedom and conduct' and 'utopias of organization'. Of the latter type, Campanella's *City of the Sun* was the first utopia to define socialism, and More's *Utopia* was the first to deal with organization.[2]

The period at the end of nineteenth century and the beginning of the twentieth gave rise to another wave of disturbances and utopias. Edward Bellamy's *Looking Backward* (1888) and Wells's *When the Sleeper Awakes* (1899) might be the most well-known examples, but they represent only the tip of the iceberg.[3] At the time, the emergence of monopoly capitalism and the scientific management of labour coupled with urbanization, the invention of new technologies of transportation and communication, shifts in the perception of time, movement and subjectivity, and the rise of the new modes of entertainment, and a culture of consumption produced a multitude of distresses that provoked utopian fiction. In this time of transition, Wells imagined in *When the Sleeper Awakes* an archetypal welfare state.[4] Janet Steiger has argued that this book also featured a 'super-city', simultaneously utopian and dystopian.[5] A precursor to cinematic future cities, it took the form of a glass-roofed climate-controlled environment where people were surrounded by advertisements, and treated to 'babble machines' which provided constant news. In this city, a Sanitary Company burned books, and people were rather forced to watch 'kineto-tele-photographs'. Yet, despite a governmental ordering of social services, hierarchies continued to exist, with labourers (living and working underground) separated physically from nobility.[6] Such architectural motifs and the plot structure of *When the Sleeper Awakes* – which involves the efforts of a couple escaping the tyranny of the city to reach the countryside – recurred in a series of dystopic films throughout the twentieth century.[7] Unlike their cinematic incarnations, however, the protagonists of Wells's book choose to return to the city. In some sense then, Wells's dystopia – of an all-powerful, but failing, welfare state – is also his utopia.

In the 1920s, Fritz Lang's film *Metropolis* (1927) and Yevgeny Zamyatin's novel *My* (1924), also titled *We*, initiated a new tradition of science-fictional dystopia.[8] *My* was soon to be followed by even more famous science-fictional dystopian novels: Aldous Huxley's *Brave New World* (1932) and George Orwell's *1984* (1949). Meanwhile, new dystopian films adopted the visual and architectural language of *Metropolis*: that of a modernism of towering high-rises occupied by the ruling classes, and a medieval underground allocated to labourers and common folk. David Desser has contended that, 'While much science-fiction or fantasy literature of the pre-cinematic age was concerned with the creation of utopias, cinema would carry forward the dystopic tradition inaugurated by *Metropolis*'.[9] Films produced in the second half of the twentieth century also adopted or adapted the political structure of *1984* in their scripts. The tradition of dystopian filmmaking continues to be used today to critique the false utopian visions of corporate and state monopoly capitalism.

In discussing the modernity of urban capitalism and the city of the welfare state and its representations, two issues arise – Fordism and science fiction – both of which will be central to our analysis of the two films in this chapter. In the early twentieth century, artists and thinkers became disillusioned with industrial modernity, often because of the exploitation it produced and the alienation it induced. While workers laboured to produce goods they could not afford, consumers were becoming increasingly detached from the conditions – both ecological and human – of their production. One may argue that alienation from the product underwrote alienation from the activity of production and led to the alienation of human beings from each other and from humanity itself. Such a condition of disconnected production and consumption, coupled with the provision of new infrastructural technologies, however, also created fascination for the prospects of an imaginary dual city – a subterranean world of workers, industrial production, criminals, and the wretched versus an above-ground environment of cafes, urban strolling, parks, department stores, and consumption. Tom Gunning has summarized literature's fascination with the underground world that comprised the first half of this equation:

> This underground technological subcity excited curiosity (such as the tours of Parisian
> sewers) and flights of imagination (such as the underground literary fantasies Rosalind

Williams has chronicled). It also served as a metaphor for the subterranean world of urban underclasses, the city of dreadful delights which likewise excited the voyeurism of urban spectatorship in the form of explorations of the new city's 'other half' by journalists and social reformers.[10]

It is not surprising that one of the greatest utopias of the twentieth century would be a model from within the capitalist system, which would attempt to bridge the distance between these two worlds, as well as between workers and their products. This, of course, was Fordism, which grew from the social idealism of the automobile mogul, Henry Ford.

Fordism promised a better mode of life within the industrial age. Yet, it also relied upon a combination of corporate power and centralized state authority under the economic paradigm of Keynesianism.[11] In this way, Fordism imagined that state power could be used to provide social rights through the welfare state that compensated for the damaging side effects of monopoly capitalism. Indeed, 'postwar Fordism has to be seen less as a mere system of mass production and more as a total way of life'.[12] It aimed to programme not only work but all aspects of life.

In this chapter, we will use two science-fiction films, Lang's *Metropolis*[13] and Terry Gilliam's *Brazil* (1985),[14] to talk about the utopian/dystopian aspects of twentieth-century modernity. Both allow us to see and understand the complex relationship between capital, the state, and the city. While *Metropolis* stands as the ultimate example of how capitalism was imagined to shape the city and its urban forms in the early part of the twentieth century, *Brazil* illustrates how the welfare state of the mid-century – which emerged in response to the excesses of capitalism – was imagined to create its own form of totalizing state control over the economy.

A key aspect of the political systems depicted in the two films, and of twentieth-century dystopian visions in general, is a comprehensive system of surveillance. In order to manage leisure and regulate the consumption that was to drive production, the managers of industry needed to create an apparatus that would keep track of the lives of its citizens. Infrastructure provision, schools, police, secret services, health services, and financial organizations thus spread out as an official system of services, which also functioned as a network of controls and a surveillance apparatus. 'This gaze was organized under the premise that no citizen should have anything to hide'.[15] Indeed, those who hid were assumed to be guilty, and those who surveilled were also to be under surveillance.

In the late 1960s and 1970s, Michel Foucault termed this web of state social services 'disciplinary apparatuses'.[16] In a series of books, he described the enclosed institutions of the prison, the mental hospital, and the school as the identifiers, containers and tamers of the deviant. Using Jeremy

Bentham's panopticon, a mechanism for the control of prisons, as an ideal, he also described the internalization of this system of surveillance. Foucault contrasted two forms of social control. At one extreme was the blockade, the enclosed institution, established on the edges of society, turned inward toward negative functions – arresting evil, breaking communications, suspending time. At the other extreme was panopticism, an internalized mechanism that improved the exercise of power by making it lighter, more rapid, and more effective. The movement from one project to the other, from a schema of exceptional discipline to one of a generalized surveillance, rested on a historical transformation – the gradual extension of the mechanisms of discipline, and the formation of what might be called, in general, the disciplinary society.[17] Foucault conceptualized disciplinary normalization as a general attribute of modernity. But clearly, Fordism, with its totalizing rationality and orientation towards self-regulation, was the realization of the disciplinary society.

Another key aspect of both *Metropolis* and *Brazil* is that they rely on references to architectural modernism. In particular, while the rest of the urbanscape is depicted through an eclectic mix of architectural styles, the high-rise building in the city is prescribed as the archetypal image of monopoly capitalism. Set fifty-eight years apart, in equally defining moments, such symbolism shows how the films share a similar view of technology (as out of control and as a domineering system). Modernism and the drive toward ever more dominant technology are seen as threats to the 'nature' and wholeness of humankind. Beyond such similarities, however, the two films evoke very different versions of utopia from within their respective dystopias. *Metropolis* proposes the union of spirituality/emotion and rationality, while *Brazil* proposes fantasy and the creative potential of the individual.

The City of Capitalist Modernity

It is very hard to talk about a single *Metropolis* since it is a celluloid film, a cinematic city, and a referenced real city.[18] *Metropolis*, the film, borrows its name from 'Metropolis', the city which is the setting, topic, and structuring device of the film. In turn, this city was inspired both by the Manhattan skyline, and by 1920s Berlin as it appeared in debates on architecture, urbanization and society in Weimar Germany.[19]

The story of *Metropolis* takes place in a future, generic city where spatial levels correspond to social hierarchy and function. Above the subterranean workers' city exists an upper-class world of nightclubs, outdoor sports, and heavenly gardens. As the film begins, Freder Fredersen (played by Gustav Frohlich), the son of the Master of the city, is being entertained at the

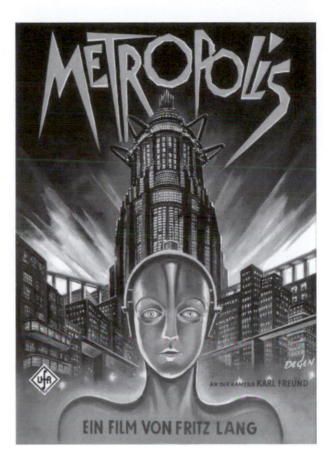

Metropolis (1927).
Film poster.

pleasure garden. However, Maria (played by Brigitte Helm), a beautiful, good-hearted girl from the working sector, makes a sudden and unwelcome appearance there along with a group of working-class children. She instantly, but inadvertently, grabs Freder's attention. Their attraction is shown to be mutual before guards intervene and take Maria and the children away. Afterwards, Freder sneaks into the world of subterranean factories to quench his curiosity about Maria's identity. What he sees there causes him to agonize over the labourers' appalling conditions. He frantically approaches his father, Joh Fredersen (the 'Master' of Metropolis), to discuss the matter, but his father evades him. Highly suspicious of his son, Fredersen recruits a spy to report on Freder. Freder goes to the Machine Room and exchanges identities with a worker so that he can find Maria.

Maria's power is based on her female sexuality. Although, Federson sees her as a challenge because the workers listen to her, she preaches patience to the labourers in the catacombs. It does not matter that Maria is diffusing revolutionary tendencies; her revolutionary potential alarms the ruler of the Metropolis. Federsen next decides to ask the mad scientist Rotwang to make the robot he has been working on look like Maria to sabotage her influence.

Rotwang traps Maria in one of the tunnels with his flashlight, and uses an electrochemical process to transfer her human character into the robot.[20] Once her sexuality is sucked out of her, the real Maria becomes an impotent mother figure.[21] Meanwhile, the robot becomes Maria's double – a powerful combination of human and machine. In particular, Maria's double now has an overt sexuality with which she eludes Rotwang's control and ignites social discontent among the working classes. After an inflaming speech, they rebel, and the city's foundations are shaken. However, when a flood begins to inundate the workers' houses, they realize their uprising will not lead to emancipation but only to their own destruction. Thereafter, the workers turn against Maria's double and burn her at the stake. However, when her outer flesh melts away to expose her machine interior, her subversive potential is undermined.[22] It is at this point that Freder assumes the role of the saviour. He rescues the children from the flood and the real Maria from Rotwang. In the final scene, in front of the cathedral, Freder mediates for the reconciliation of the labourers (people) and Joh (Jehovah) Fredersen.

At the centre of the film is a message that only the heart can mediate between the hand and the mind. In the world of *Metropolis*, the hand is unthinking labour, while capital is the mind. Religion, which is the heart, is the only thing that offers the possibility of reconciliation.[23] Religious symbolism and Biblical references may be found both in the film's plot and the organization of its spaces. However, there is far more nuance in *Metropolis* than a simple dichotomy of heaven and hell, upper ground and underground. Critics have argued a better analogy may be the Tower of

Metropolis. The master of the Metropolis and the scientist Rotwang deliberate over the robot in the making.

Babel, a famous Biblical story, to which Maria actually refers during the film.[24] Babel (or Metropolis) is a utopia. For having challenged the divine by building it, mankind is doomed by God to a life where nobody can speak the same language.

In *Metropolis*, the contrast between worlds is extreme. Above the catacombs are the slums where the workers live. Nondescript tall apartment buildings, with regular grids of windows, are cramped together around a square with a bell in the middle. The general atmosphere here is dark and dingy, and there is no natural light. Tunnels and industrial lifts connect this workers' city to the machines, on the third level. As the workers submissively queue in the tunnels for their shifts, the camera frames them from behind as a 'mass' without faces (individuality). The central machine consists of a multilevel theatrical stage of stepped balconies with workers each facing a separate display device on its walls. The workers run three types of machines and, hence, spaces: Moloch, Paternoster, and the Heart Machine.[25] Their mechanistic movements operate as they the machines serve to critique the inhumane conditions under which they labour.

Meanwhile, above ground, the privileged occupy spaces elevated according to their status within society. The architecture of the high-rise apartment buildings here appears in both Art Deco and Modernist styles, but both utilize glass and iron extensively. Inspired by New York City, this is a city of multiple levels.[26] Biplanes and airships frequent the sky, and

Metropolis. When their shifts are over, workers descend to their underground city.

Metropolis. Workers operate the 'Moloch' machine.

above the streets are skywalks and high-altitude bridges. The ground level features nightlife, particularly Yoshiwara's – named after a neighbourhood in Japan famous for entertainment. It is here that Maria's double does her tempting dance, and where the Gothic cathedral is located that appear in Freder's hallucinations of the Seven Deadly Sins. Here, streets are dark with smog and shadows of buildings above. Rotwang's house is located here, a thatched-roof Germanic house set amid skyscrapers. This house triples as a secret entry to the catacombs, a shrine to Rotwang's beloved, deceased wife (Hel),[27] and a laboratory where scientific experiments take place.[28]

In these utopian upper levels, social reproduction is substituted by physical reproduction, as represented by sports. The stadium is the civic centre for youthful upper-class males. But women are excluded from it. They make an appearance only in the Eternal Gardens and Yoshiwara – where their purpose is to please men. Their outfits and hairstyles emulate those of the Weimar Republic's famous flapper girls. On these upper levels of Metropolis, servants are old, and they serve to regulate and monitor. The highest level belongs to its Master of the Metropolis, Joh Fredersen. His office features high ceilings, oversized furniture, and a huge carpet, all of which enhance the feeling of a modernist monumentality. Federsen's circular desk faces a large glazed wall, which provides views onto the city. But in the back of his office, this master capitalist has an audiovisual device with which he can survey and also communicate with his workers. This device anticipates

Metropolis. Multi-levelled traffic flows in this city of the future.

the use of video surveillance in today's city. But in Metropolis, surveillance serves only the private capitalist, allowing him to maximize output from factories. In this sense, the film portrays an incredibly simple world where politics is driven not by diverse economic factors but solely by the needs of its production. In contrast, surveillance will become the logic and function of the state apparatus in *Brazil*, having attained a far more complex quality similar to the more complicated social structure of the welfare state.[29]

The City of the Welfare State

As in *Metropolis*, 'Brazil' is the name of an imaginary city that is the setting and topic of the film. Brazil, the city, is characterized by bureaucracy, state oppression, blandness, and suspicion, and it is plagued by a system of failed hyper-planning. The protagonist, Sam Lowry (played by Jonathan Pryce), finds refuge in dreams that, as a superman, he saves a beautiful girl from the dark forces of ruin. He works at the Department of Records, 'Information Retrieval', the sanguine name given to a ministry which conducts torture. He prefers being an insignificant clerk at Records rather than being promoted 'up the ladder of Information Retrieval', like his former friend Jack Lint (played by Michael Palin).[30] However, his socialite mother, Ida Lowry, who is well connected to people such as the Deputy Minister of Information Retrieval, Mr. Helpmann, has higher ambitions for her son.

Brazil (1985). Film poster.

The film opens to reveal the cityscape, and then descends to street level and a scene of Christmas shopping. The first failure of the techno-bureaucratic system, which is seemingly unnoticed by the passers-by, is the snow-like fire-fighting foam that is emerging from a shop front. An interview with Mr. Helpmann, broadcast on TVs in shop windows, reveals that the ongoing fight with terrorism is perceived as a game by the authorities, rather than a symptom of dissent. The 'terrorists' – those that the government sees as potential dissidents – are to be charged, he explains, with the expenses of their arrest and litigation. System failures follow one after the other. A typo on an arrest warrant leads security troops to break into the flat of the Buttle family instead of that of the Tuttles, and to the abduction of Mr. Buttle instead of Mr. Tuttle, the supposed terrorist. Meanwhile, in Sam's flat, basic services go out of control, and he has to call for Central Services, which turn out to be slow, inefficient and complicated. Coincidentally, to his aid comes Mr. Tuttle, the real rebellious engineer (played by Robert de Niro). All the first sequences in the film establish the ineptitude and violence of the state apparatus and the climate of paranoia and manipulation in which this operates against ordinary citizens.

With citizens vulnerable to an arbitrary and unaccountable bureaucracy,

Brazil. Sam and Tuttle, the alleged terrorist outside Sam's apartment.

it falls to the film's independent-minded heroine, Jill Layton (played by Kim Greist), to attempt to redress Mr. Buttle's arrest. At the Ministry of Information, however, Sam recognizes Jill as the woman he has been repeatedly saving from monsters in his dreams. But the real Jill defies such objectification, and turns out to be a truck driver in overalls, with short hair. She does not seek, or need Sam's help. The real Jill will transform Sam, and inspire him to exit from his protective cocoon.

It is the Buttle arrest, a typical failure of the system, that ultimately connects Sam and Jill through a series of coincidences. Sam visits the Buttle family to deliver a cheque in compensation for the wrongful arrest. But in the process, his delusions are stripped away and he realizes he is a part of this system that devastates innocents. There, he catches a glimpse of Jill again. But when he attempts to investigate her at work, he realizes that her documents are classified. In order to access them, he accepts the job promotion his mother has arranged. But his new job is infinitely more dehumanizing than his previous one.

Soon, Sam discovers it will not be easy to find information on Jill. Because she witnessed a wrongful event (the Buttle arrest), the ministry now treats her as a terrorist. Sam next 'volunteers' to trace her whereabouts for the ministry. But when Jill shows up in the ministry lobby once more, Sam protects her from the other officers using his new rank. Jill is highly suspicious and tries to evade Sam, who, to her, looks just like any bureaucrat. However, after Sam finally imposes himself on Jill, they learn to trust each other.

Eventually, Sam's associations with Jill and Tuttle turn him into a suspect, too. Jill and Sam share an affectionate moment at Sam's mother's apartment after which Sam decides to save his new-found love by deleting her files

Brazil. The security apparatus at the reception of the Ministry of Information puts Jill on display to herself.

at the ministry. To do this, he sneaks into Mr. Helpmann's office after hours. However, upon his return, a Buttle-style attack disrupts the couple's bliss: Jill is exterminated, and Sam is arrested for interrogation. During his interrogation, Sam escapes from reality by dreaming of being saved by Tuttle and escaping with Jill to the countryside. In Gilliam's version of the film, the end remains ambiguous.[31] It is unclear whether Sam really escapes, or just dreams of doing so. Sam's torturers, Mr. Helpmann and Jack, conclude, 'He's gone,' as Sam hums the movie's theme song, 'Brazil', to himself.

In the making of the film, the spaces of the city and the settings for the ministry scenes were mostly appropriated from unused industrial buildings. Although the genre is science fiction, the film did not necessitate elaborate studio-created 'imaginary' sets and was shot mostly on location in the UK and France. Commenting on its setting, Gilliam has said he favours science fiction as a genre because it allows the abstraction of the real.[32] Thus in Brazil, the landscape of the city is only perceptible as fragments, and no overall view is ever given. The milieu is one of calculated deception. Promotional billboards on either side of the highway block views of adjacent industrial wastelands just as propaganda signs and posters within the city seek to mask social realities. Many such billboards feature Orwellian slogans, similar to those in *1984*: 'Happiness: We're All In It Together', 'Mellowfields', 'Top

Brazil. Clerks hurry about in the Department of Records. When the boss disappears, they tune their TVs to an old western.

Security Holiday Camps', 'Luxury Without Fear', 'Fun Without Suspicion', 'Relax In A Panic Free Atmosphere'. Meanwhile, at the Department of Records and the Ministry of Information, workers are barraged with slogans: 'The Truth Shall Make You Free', 'Information Is The Key To Prosperity', 'A Ministry Of Information', 'Help The Ministry Of Information Help You', 'Be Safe: Be Suspicious', 'Loose Talk Is Noose Talk', 'Suspicion Breeds Confidence'.[33] Often tautological in structure, these messages stand in for the self-defying purpose of the techno-bureaucratic system.

The residential area, where the Buttles (and above them, Jill Layton) live, is called the Shangri La Towers.[34] Far from the suggested utopia, however,

Brazil. Sam and Jill drive on a highway lined with commercial ads that block out the grey, polluted industrial landscape.

its run-down units are reminiscent of those in public housing projects from the 1960s and 1970s in America or social housing projects in France from the same era. Jill and the Buttles, though, belong to a lower social class than Sam and Ida. Shangri La Towers is littered with trash, and crime is widespread, with youthful mobs having taken control of open spaces. On the other hand, Sam's tidy apartment building presents the image of a futuristic scheme – a utopia. In actuality, these scenes were shot in Marne-la-Vallée, at a huge apartment complex, Les Espaces d'Abraxas (The Spaces of Abraxas, 1978–1983). Designed by Ricardo Bofill,[35] these buildings used inexpensive concrete technology with echoes of Classicism in a self-conscious effort to create a 'palace' for low-income residents.[36] In the film, Sam's apartment – and indeed all other upper-class spaces shown, including his mother's, the plastic surgeon's, and the restaurant – are hardly connected to the messy ground at all.

Such an expectation of physical order carries over to Sam's workplace at the ministry. There, Sam is scolded not for poor performance but for having a pile of documents on his desk that are supposed to be filed away. After his promotion, Sam moves to an office on a higher floor, but both environments share the same décor of exposed ducts and piping. John Mathews has suggested that these architectural elements are reflective of the control of the individual by the state – 'as if the ducts are umbilical'.[37] The world of state control starts in the private realm of the home, such that any unsanctioned individual act, even fixing a broken duct, may be interpreted as a terrorist act. In *Brazil*, it is the unchecked access to technology, coupled with the lack of individual agency, that creates a sense that the world is out of control. But in *Metropolis*, it is the technology, itself, that goes out of control.

Brazil. Inside the torture chamber, a microcosm of the whole city and nation.

The Place of *Metropolis*

Metropolis emerged out of the specific economic, political and artistic concerns of Weimar Germany and its relationship to the US as both competitor and model. *Metropolis* triggered immense public debate then, as now. Even its making was a spectacle.[38] Theorist Siegfried Kracauer was one of those who condemned the film because its symbolism was comparable to that which allowed the Nazi Party to rise to power between World Wars I and II. Indeed, Kracauer argued that the film was proto-Nazi:

> The whole composition denotes that the industrialist acknowledges the heart for the purpose of manipulating it; that he does not give up his power, but will expand it over a realm not yet annexed – the realm of the collective soul. Freder's rebellion results in the establishment of totalitarian authority, and he considers this result a victory.[39]

Elsaesser has further argued that the depiction of crowds, as sheepish and easily manipulable, reinforced the acceptability of totalitarian points of view. 'Little did it matter that Nazism detested modernist architecture and that it promoted an anti-urban, "blood-and-soil", back-to-the-land settlement policy'.[40] On the contrary, for parts of *Metropolis*'s set designs, Lang chose the language of architectural modernism, which was at the time associated with socialist politics. Nevertheless, Lang voiced fears of technology and industrialization, and proposed the heart as the mediator. This was a role which the Nazi Party, and Hitler himself, would claim for itself in the next decade.[41] Hence, although the architectural aesthetic might not have been shared by the Nazis, they were able to embrace its narrative and its central mediator/saviour figure.[42] Kracauer's tainted and angry opinion, connecting the film to Nazism, has greatly influenced interpretations of it to this day. But these have distracted from the more important aspects of it that relate to the modernity of capitalism.[43]

Andreas Huyssen's interpretation in 'The Vamp and the Machine' (1981) brought a new approach to the criticism of *Metropolis*. Huyssen argued that Maria's double was a harbinger of destruction that affirmed the Weimar fear of out-of-control technology, and more archaic fears of out-of-control sexuality.[44] In Elsaesser's review:

> Huyssen saw the robot's female gender as a conservative counterstrategy: through the false Maria, *Metropolis* demonizes female sexuality, and her threat justifies the male fantasy of strong leadership, needed to keep the forces of the feminized masses as well as of a potentially destructive technology under firm control.[45]

The figure of the robot, however, allowed *Metropolis* to discard the dangerous side of feminine sexuality and tame what remained. After her sexuality is transferred to her double, Maria is no longer attractive to Freder.[46] Meanwhile, her dangerous attractive qualities are burned at the stake.

Recent literature on the Weimar period has unearthed other literary and artistic works that reflected fears of industrialization and the public visibility of women.[47] Indeed, the 'Whore of Babylon' and the myth of Babylon were part of the popular imagination to which Lang's film contributed.[48] On the other side of the spectrum, the *avant garde* celebrated the film's depiction of a modern city, for which Berlin had come to stand. In 1912, Egon Freidel described Berlin as:

> a wonderful modern engine-room, a giant electric motor, which executes with incredible precision, speed and energy a plethora of complicated, mechanical tasks. True, so far the machine lacks a soul. The life of Berlin is the life of a cinematograph theatre, the life of a brilliantly constructed homunculus-machine.[49]

Elsaesser argued that Freidel's description was equally suited to *Metropolis* and *Berlin* both of the late 1920s. He suggested:

> *Metropolis* is not so much a film about machines as it is itself a machine, made up of parts fitted together, whose intricate clockwork elements are as much the human passions, anxieties and aggressions as they are the pistons, flywheels and dials.[50]

As this description of the film makes clear, this is not only industrial modernity but machine modernity; not about the machine dictating human action and movement, but about humans being, invoking, evoking and emulating the machine in matters of social organization.

Lang was critical of the dehumanization that was brought by industrialization, yet at the same time he was fascinated by machines. Elsaesser maintained that:

> Unresolved in this debate and yet wholly underpinning it, was the relation of Weimar Germany to America. If *Metropolis* did not get to grips with the real effects of mechanization and rationalization, it was not least because Weimar Germany did not finally come to grips with Fordism and Taylorism just as the film industry never resolved its schizophrenic attitude to Hollywood.[51]

Steiger has explained that in 1920s and 1930s film, set and story lines were highly influenced by H.G. Wells's super cities, and maintained a conversation with the unbuilt architectural projects of modernism, such as *La ville contemporaine* (the Contemporary City) by Le Corbusier.[52] For example, Le Corbusier himself advocated a social formation, of hierarchy and paternalism, similar to that portrayed in *Metropolis*.[53] The formal features of architecture were also similar:

(slab-block high rises and peaked skyscrapers, breathtaking vistas from the more significant buildings, diffused lighting); symmetry and balance in the cityscapes; orderly and rational mass transportation systems; and efficient, immediate, and extensive methods of communication.[54]

Yet, *Metropolis* did not only feature modernist architecture; it displayed an array of eclectic architectural styles and was not up-to-date in its depiction of mechanization and rationalization. One of the main criticisms of the film had to do with the representation of contemporary technologies. Why would workers have to carry out tasks requiring intense labour when Ford's assembly line had reorganized the working environment? Why would people walk up the stairs when escalators were now common in many department stores? Why, finally, would the city of the future be vertical when urbanism was spreading horizontally into sprawl?[55] Clearly, today we can see how architecture portrayed in these films was nowhere near as 'futuristic' as the systems of governance and control they depicted. In Metropolis, there is no state as such, no politicians or bureaucrats, but only the capitalists who envision all – who oversee the division of labour and production, and maintain order and infrastructure. In *Brazil*, it is the state that has assumed this paternal role.

'The Location of Brazil'[56]

The question, 'Where is Brazil?' (or 'What is Brazil?'), has caused much speculation. Is it located in the real, geographic Brazil? In an imaginary place? In the song that precedes the film? Or in a time past? Commentators have responded differently to these questions, but all have emphasized the importance of the title. Perhaps, no other film title has been so enigmatic. For example, Salman Rushdie, one of the film's long-term admirers, has observed that 'The location of Brazil is the cinema itself, because in the cinema the dream is the norm'.[57] The prevalence of fantasy sequences in *Brazil* and the particular evocations of the song 'Brazil' avoid any direct reference to the country, Brazil. Indeed, Gilliam recently stated in an interview with Rushdie that he chose the title not because of its references to a modern country but because of a song with the same title.[58] He is quoted as saying the same in a 1985 newspaper article, and subsequently in the book *The Battle of Brazil*.[59] According to these sources, Gilliam also originally wanted to call the film '1984½' as a dual tribute to George Orwell's novel *1984* (1949) and Federico Fellini's film 8½ (1963). But when Michael Radford's cinema adaptation, *Nineteen Eighty-Four*, came out before his film, Gilliam had to search for another title.[60]

Thematically, the most likely location of Brazil is Thatcherite England, where Gilliam lived in the 1980s, a milieu that witnessed the collapse of the welfare state and the emergence of neoliberalism. The welfare state had previously granted many concessions to the working class to pacify and control it. But starting in the late 1970s, governments of many developed countries started to take back these privileges through privatization, declining relative wages, and restrictions on access to health and social services. After her party's election in 1979, Margaret Thatcher advocated severe cutbacks, and the privatization of public housing stock in the UK, hoping to turn the working class into the middle class. A year later, Ronald Reagan, who shared these views, was elected President of the US. Reagan advocated the withdrawal of state services, reduced government size, cutbacks in social spending, and an expansion of the military. Both Thatcher and Reagan also launched invasions of other countries to distract popular attention from the implications of their economic reforms at home. Linda Williams contextualized *Brazil* by arguing that if in the 1960s the question of utopia was reinvented, then:

> the 1970s and 1980s also saw its dystopian Other explored afresh... It may also be that by the time Terry Gilliam and Michael Radford came to make *Brazil* and *Nineteen Eighty-Four* respectively in the mid-1980s, dystopianism was not primarily a means of articulating feared futures of fending off an alternative (socialist) social structure (as was Orwell's original novel), but a shrewd engagement with Britain's present...[61]

Gilliam's film does not embody nostalgia for the welfare state, or even negative views of the neoliberal policies that replaced it. Indeed, he portrays the welfare state in terms of its own failures. But he does point to the similarities between the welfare state and monopoly capitalism. Thus, both are seen to depend on induced hierarchy and bureaucracy; and both dupe citizens with false choices and an almost theological drive and zeal for consumption.[62] In the end, *Brazil* depicts a world of bureaucracy and consumption where 'choice' is actually 'false consciousness'.[63] In the department store, the banner reads, 'Consumers for Christ'. In the luxurious restaurant, the dishes arrive as similar lumps. The failure of the air-conditioning in Sam's flat is a double critique of the utopian aspirations of the welfare state and the weakening of the citizens' trust in it. The state, which posed itself as a paternal provider, is revealed as a surveillance device that denies citizens control over their own lives and offers them nothing in return. Following this, the *mise-en-scène* is a fusion of the architectural aspirations of the different moments of history the film critiques.

In the world of *Brazil*, there is no 'real' choice, either in the welfare state where the lower classes occupy decayed mass housing, or in advanced market-driven neoliberal capitalism of the upper classes. As Steiger has contended:

> In *Brazil*, the impressive and oppressive lobby to the Ministry of Information leads to absolutely uniform corridors and closet offices in which desks are shared through walls. References to *Brave New World* and *Nineteen Eighty Four* abound as Lowry works for an institution that habitually invades private homes because 'suspicion breeds confidence'. Classes and hierarchies abound isomorphically with the architecture: police are stationed in the ministry's subbasement and the CEO's office is on the top floor.[64]

Another architectural motif is that of pristine, modernist interiors. According to Steiger, 'Lowry's home is most reminiscent of the International Style, with the exterior similar to Le Corbusier-influenced 'Silver Towers', home for New York University faculty and staff'.[65] She went on to identify four aspects of *Brazil*'s *mise-en-scène*, according to which the present and the future are brought together in a postmodern way. Thus, modernist high-rises, urban sprawl, and revivalist architecture are used side by side. The city is dark, without a clear sense of orientation, and 'characterized by debris, decay, and abandonment'.[66] Yet, the deliberate use of modern aesthetics is also coupled with the dystopic effects of capitalist commodification: 'Or again, as in *Brazil*, the criticism may be of false appearance of options in a choice-less social order'.[67]

Following these views, it is possible to argue that *Brazil* is a postmodern film about a modernist reality.[68] The modernist aspect is emphasized through the commodification of space and views. 'Lowry cannot look beyond billboards or through glass walls as he travels.'[69] Yet the landscape portrayed is postmodern in the sense that we cannot get an overall sense of it; it is eclectic and fragmented. Finally, the narrative is postmodern in the sense it has multiple endings and is left open to interpretation.[70] Linda Williams has suggested that:

> *Brazil* is set in an enclosed world when even outdoors feels like indoors, when social stratification is keen, but success is particularly marked both by the pleasures of conspicuous consumption and by the power to manipulate bureaucratic processes. But all inhabitants seem to be equal prisoners of their disastrous world; this is not *Metropolis* (1926), the golden palace built on the slavery of workers doomed to pay for others' excesses which benefits an elite strata, here there are no winners.[71]

Because of its ending, *Brazil* remains unique in its depiction of Orwellian modernity. Indeed it may be seen as a post-Orwellian view of a pre-Orwellian world.

Orwellian Modernity and the City

Within this Orwellian modernity, the protagonists of both films are upper-class men in search of themselves. However, both seek refuge in dreams whenever their subjectivities are threatened – by the conditions of monopoly capitalism in *Metropolis*, and by state-capitalism's techno-bureaucracy in *Brazil*.

In *Metropolis*, there are two dream sequences. When Freder ends up in the Machine Room by mistake in search of Maria, he takes over for a fatigued worker. The machine starts heating up, and eventually explodes, killing and injuring many. However, in Freder's hallucination, this machine transforms into a flaming Moloch, the pagan god, a monstrous head that eats workers. This particular transformation has been widely interpreted as representing capitalism's consumption of workers. The second dream sequence happens after Freder sees Maria's double at a nightclub with his father, without realizing it is not the real Maria. While Maria's double does her provocative dance, Freder imagines, under the impact of brain fever, that the statues of the Seven Deadly Sins in the church come alive, and that the figure of Death approaches him. In *Metropolis*, the dream sequences foretell the fears and struggles of the characters.

Brazil features various dream sequences. We are introduced to Sam Lowry well into the film in a dream where he appears as an angel-like figure flying through the clouds looking for his dream girl – a blonde, helpless version of Jill. In a second dream, the landscape is disturbed by an eruption from underground, and Sam awakens to find that his thermostat is out of order. On his way back to his apartment in a transport cage, Jill appears to Sam in a third dream and calls out for him. Sam imagines that he has to fight the 'Forces of Darkness' and the sequences that follow feature combat scenes with a giant samurai warrior while Jill's cage floats upward away from him. Of course, in 'real' life, Sam misses his exit platform. In another dream, when Sam finally has time with Jill, he becomes a mechanical bird with a liberated Jill holding on to him. And in the final dream sequence, in the torture chamber, Sam imagines that Tuttle comes to his rescue and that he eventually joins with Jill to settle in a pastoral valley. If Freder in *Metropolis* is afraid of being consumed by technology, in *Brazil*, Sam is afraid of the state. The state even appears to him as an oversized, samurai warrior – impenetrable and menacing.

Interestingly, the modernity of both *Metropolis* and *Brazil* also results in the creation of doubles with extraordinary powers: a robot in the former, and a technological superman in the latter. Maria's double is forced upon her by the advent of modern technology; Sam's is an imaginary superhero that allows him to escape his sense of oppression by the state. In both cases, however, the characters are powerless in comparison to their doubles.[72] Yet, it is also their doubles that allow them to become agents of social trans-formation and change. The idea of the cyborg, a cybernetic organism, as articulated by Donna Haraway, may also be useful in understanding how doubles appear in these films.[73] In Haraway's view, a cyborg is both a creature of science fiction and social reality.[74] In recent debates about science and politics, she points out that power has shifted from people to machines with unforeseen repercussions, since the machine is seen as modernity gone awry.

Science fiction, in a general sense, may help us understand state-induced modernity, since it allows the depiction of a non-realistic 'future' space, and features 'spectacular environmental changes'.[75] In this sense, it is also important that a clear correlation emerges between the twentieth-century dystopic imagination and the genre of science fiction. In both films examined here, the transformations of institutions and spaces serve to articulate that what is meant and designed as a utopian vision – comprising the division of labour in *Metropolis*; consumer culture in *Brazil*; and panopticism and technology in both films – is actually a dystopia. Utopia is the harbinger of dystopia. In both films, social segregation is mapped through vertical segregation.[76] The upper levels control the lower levels. The upper levels are interpreted as utopia and the lower levels as dystopia.

In the light of these similarities, how can *Metropolis*'s rise to cult status in the 1980s be explained? Why is *Brazil*'s creation of a world fraught with fears of imaginary terrorist attacks – and politicians speaking of civil-rights struggles as sports events – so disconcerting today? The function of science fiction in the twentieth century was to speak to current conditions. In both of these films we may find aspects of our present dystopia. In the new Bush-Blair world, where Homeland Security reigns supreme, *Brazil*'s evocation of a world where 'terrorists' are eliminated before they have terrorist thoughts is prophetic.

The issue of panopticism and control has also received attention among commentators of utopia and dystopia. Orwell's *1984*, one of the inspirations for Gilliam's *Brazil*, has been central to these discussions.[77] The science-fictional world of *1984* is clearly dystopic in character, and its 'nihilistic and reactionary' politics have generally been cited as a powerful critique of authoritarianism.[78] Yet, as part of a wider discussion on science fiction, an enduring debate has developed around whether *1984* was originally intended as a prophecy, and whether it has now been fulfilled. According to Frederic Jameson, 'Orwell's novel, indeed set out explicitly to dramatize the tyrannical omnipotence of a bureaucratic elite, with its perfected and omnipresent technological control'.[79] Yet, in the context of the socialist utopias of its time, Orwell's critique was comparably ideologically burdened.[80] And against discussions of the reliability and success of the foretelling, Jameson has argued that science fiction does not provide the 'image' of the future, so much as it 'defamiliarizes and restructures our experience of our own present'.[81] Since we can no longer imagine the future, he has claimed science fiction is almost always dystopic.[82] While nostalgia can be counter-productive, dystopia (and the dystopian nature of science fiction) has the capacity to incorporate the utopian by provoking and reinventing it.[83]

In parallel to Jameson's views, Rushdie, comparing *Brazil* with Orwell's *1984*, has observed that the latter does not leave any possibility for individual action and agency; it becomes pointless to speak out in an all-powerful oppressive system.[84] But Rushdie has argued that there is always space for resistance.[85] Yet, our analysis here suggests that space can be brought to life only by the double, the technologically enhanced figure of the cyborg who can fight against the all-oppressive power of the state or monopoly capitalism.

Orwellian modernity affirms the dystopian strands within utopian ideas that have dominated the first half of the twentieth century. It is a modernity that was made possible through the increasing role the state started to play in the everyday life of its citizens. Although this intrusion and the services it brought applied to all citizens of the state, it was mainly in the social life of the city that it acquired its most obvious manifestations. Having considerably urbanized by that time, the nation-state first had to establish a bureaucracy to provide social and welfare services. Transformed over time to an oppressive apparatus of surveillance and control, the state not only managed political dissent, but every aspect of urban life. Orwellian modernity was not only utopia gone awry; it was an arena where the possibilities of the future – including the relationship between people and the state, and people and machines – could be charted, explored, and contested.

Notes

1   'Utopias' (January 1939) is a public talk Wells gave. H.G. Wells, 'Utopias', *Science Fiction Studies*, No. 27, Vol. 9 Part 2, 1982, p. 199. Retrieved from http://www.depauw.edu/sfs on 7 July 2005.

2   *Ibid.*

3   Janet Steiger has maintained: 'As a literary genre in the United States, utopian fiction seems to have hit a cycle in the period between 1889 and 1912, when more than a hundred works appeared following the publication of Edward Bellamy's *Looking Backward* in 1888. It is also generally considered that 1880 to 1920 marks a transitional stage in American capitalism and society; the ending of entrepreneurial capitalism and the unveiling of monopoly capitalism... Cultural historians describe this period as including a major shift in individuals' self-conception... A culture of production gives way to one of consumerism.' J. Steiger, 'Future Noir: Contemporary Representations of Visionary Cities', in Annette Kuhn (ed.) *Alien Zone II*. London: Verso, 1999.

4   *Ibid.*, p. 104. Quoted from Mark R. Hillegas in *The Future as Nightmare: H.G. Wells and the Anti-Utopians*. Oxford: Oxford University Press, 1967, p. 3.

5   *Ibid.*

6   *Ibid.*

7   *Ibid.* Steiger cited *Metropolis*, *Fahrenheit 451*, *1984*, *Brazil* and *Blade Runner* as such films. The list can be extended.

8   The word 'dystopia' emerged in opposition to utopia in the middle of the twentieth

century. Dystopia as a literary genre was invented by Yevgeny Zamyatin in his novel *My* (1924; *We*), *OED Online*.

9   D. Desser, 'Race, Space and Class: The Politics of Cityscapes on Science Fiction Film', in A. Kuhn (ed.) *Alien Zone II: The Spaces of Science-Fiction Cinema*. London: Verso, p. 84.

10 T. Gunning, 'From the Kaleidoscope to the X-Ray: Urban Spectatorship, Poe, Benjamin, and *Traffic in Souls* (1913)', *Wide Angle*, no. 19, vol. 4, 1997, p. 39.

11 *Ibid.*, p. 126.

12 *Ibid.*, p. 135.

13 Fritz Lang (1890, Vienna – 1976, Beverly Hills) was the son of a construction company manager and a Jewish mother turned Catholic convert. In the early 1910s, he travelled around Europe and received training in painting in Vienna and Paris. During World War I, he was drafted into the Austrian army and was severely injured in 1916. After the war, following a brief period when he worked in a theatre in Vienna, he started a career in filmmaking as a scriptwriter in Berlin. He subsequently directed enormously successful films based on scripts he wrote in collaboration with his wife, Thea von Harbou. He fled Germany in 1933, leaving his wife, a Nazi-sympathizer, behind, and directed films in Hollywood from 1936 until 1956. He resumed his career in Germany in the mid-1960s. Retrieved on 11 July 2005, http://www.imdb.com/.

14 Terry Gilliam (1940–) was born in Minneapolis and grew up in Los Angeles. He studied Politics at Occidental College in LA. After working in New York, Paris, and travelling throughout Europe, he settled for a job in LA working for an advertising company. He confesses to witnessing police brutality and a general state of terror in LA, which led him to leave the US in favour of the UK where he entered television in 1967. He eventually joined the television show, 'Monty Python's Flying Circus'. The Monty Python group became a popular hit, migrating from TV to feature length films. Gilliam contributed to the Python films as co-director and production designer. In 1980, he left the group to make his own films. Viewed on 11 July 11 2005, http://www.imdb.com.

15 N. K. Denzin, *The Cinematic Society: The Voyeur's Gaze*. London: Sage, 1995, p. 115.

16 M. Foucault, 'Panopticon', in *Discipline & Punish:The Birth of the Prison*, reprinted in N. Leach (ed.) *Rethinking Architecture: A Reader in Cultural Theory*. New York: Routledge, 1997, pp. 366–367.

17 M. Foucault, 'Panopticon'.

18 T. Elsaesser, 'A Ruin-in-Progress: Release Versions and Restorations', *Metropolis*, London: BFI, 2000, pp. 30–42.

An original, or a first print, of *Metropolis* does not exist. It already had three separate releases by August 1927. The version of the film we use in this chapter is the commercially available, 124-minute, 2002 version, commercially distributed by Kino International and Eureka. This was restored using the original score under the supervision of the Murnau Foundation. The German release was two-and-a-half hours in length while the American version was reduced to a little less than two hours to fit American schedules. The new edit concentrated on Maria and Freder's relationship and downplayed that between Rotwang and Fredersen. In the 1980s, restoration efforts culminated in two additional versions: one by Giorgio Moroder (1984) as a commercial venture that turned out to be very successful and gave the film a 'cult' status; and another by the Munich Film Museum (1995) whose goal was archival restoration rather than commercial distribution. According to Elsaesser, Moroder's is not a version, but a re-edit; it is based on editing for continuity in which the narrative was instead generated by *mise-en-scène*.

19 D. Neumann, 'The Urbanistic Vision in Fritz Lang's *Metropolis*', in T.W. Kniesche and S. Brockmann (eds.) *Dancing on the Volcano: Essays on the Culture of the Weimar Republic*. Columbia, SC: Camden House, pp. 143–62.

20 Andreas Huyssen interprets this scene as the male desire to control and as symbolic

rape. A. Huyssen, 'The Vamp and the Machine: Technology and Sexuality in Fritz Lang's *Metropolis*', *New German Critique,* no. 24–25, 1982, p. 230.

21 *Ibid.*

22 *Ibid.,* p. 236.

23 It should be noted that the reductionism of urban life in the film has made it the subject of critique.

24 According to Biblical scripture, the descendants of Noah wanted to build a tower high enough to reach the heavens. God, furious with this act of infidelity, prevented the project from continuing through a confusion of languages making communication impossible. 'Tower of Babel', *Encyclopædia Britannica Online*. Retrieved on 14 June 2004.

25 J.L. Bowen, 'Metropolis (1927)'. Retrieved on 14 June 2004, http://orbitalreviews.com.

26 Lang had travelled to the US (accompanied by the architect Eric Mendelsohn) for the opening of his film *Siegfried's Death* in October 1924. It was a revealing experience in terms of differences between the European and American filmmaking practices and industries.

27 According to the plot of the original novel by Lang's wife and collaborator, Thea von Harbou, and the original German release, Hel ran away with Fredersen and died while giving birth to Freder. H. Bachmann, 'The Production and Contemporary Reception of *Metropolis*', in M. Minden and H. Bachmann (eds.) *Fritz Lang's* Metropolis, *Cinematic Visions of Technology and Fear.* Rochester, NY: Camden House, 2000, p. 12.

28 Hel's departure is Rotwang's symbolic castration, also signified by the hand he lost to his machines. Yet this reference is removed from the English release because of the phonetic proximity of Hel to Hell. T. Elsaesser, *Metropolis.*

29 Where in *Metropolis* was the middle management, and where were the politicians, the police or security forces?' in T. Elsaesser, *Metropolis,* p. 43.

30 Script. Jack explains his position as 'Security Level Five'. J. Mathews, *The Battle of Brazil: Terry Gilliam v. Universal Pictures in the Fight to the Final Cut.* New York: Applause, 1987.

31 In our discussion of the film, we will refer to Gilliam's American theatrical release. The LA-based journalist Jack Mathews has devoted his book, *The Battle of Brazil*, to documenting this dispute. Gilliam and Universal Studios disagreed on the film's final form and content. The studio edited its own version, which is referred to, after the studio's chairman, as Sid Sheinberg's edit. This version was released with the title *Love Conquers All*. Although Universal initially refused to distribute the Gilliam version in the US, when Gilliam's received a number of the 1985 Los Angeles Film Critics Association's Awards, including one for best picture, the studio was compelled to release it according to his wishes. To date, there are five versions of the film. The principal reason for the fallout between the studio and the director had to do with the ending. The studio executives and specialists thought that in order for the film to be commercially viable, it had to have a happy ending and less fantasy overall. In Gilliam's cut, *Brazil*, Sam escapes oppression, but only in his imagination, while in Universal's, he is rescued by his friends.

32 Terry Gilliam, interviewed by Salman Rushdie (March 2003). Viewed on http://www.believermag.com/.

33 J. Mathews, *The Battle of Brazil.*

34 'Shan·gri-la' means: (1) An imaginary remote paradise on earth; utopia; (2) a distant and secluded hideaway, usually of great beauty and peacefulness. (After Shangri-La, the imaginary land in the novel *Lost Horizon* (1933) by James Hilton.) *The American Heritage Dictionary*, 4th ed. Retrieved on 5 July 2005, http://www.bartleby.com/.

35 D. S. Cowen, '*Brazil*, Frequently Asked Questions'. Viewed on http://bau2.uibk.ac.at/sg/python/Scripts/Brazil/Brazil-FAQ.

36 Among locations used are the Croydon Power Station for the Ministry of Information basement; an abandoned grain mill in Docklands, London, as the corridors of the Ministry of Information; Leighton's House, London, for Dr. Jaffe's surgery room;

Mentmore Towers, part of the former Rothschild mansion in Buckinghamshire, for the restaurant; and the Liberal Club, London, for Sam's mother's apartment.

For information on the Bofill's social housing, see http://www.bofill.com.

37 J. Mathews, *The Battle of Brazil*, pp. 99–100.

38 H. Bachmann, 'The Production and Contemporary Reception of *Metropolis*', p. 12. The film was produced by the German film studio Ufa. Trade journals informed their readers of its making. Thea von Harbou's novel was serialized, and appeared in the press with photos from the film set.

39 S. Kracauer, *Caligari to Hitler: A Psychological History of the German Film*. Princeton, NJ: Princeton University Press, 1974 (1947), p. 164.

40 Elsaesser remarked, 'Lang's film now puts forward a right wing utopia, giving the Weimar body-politic the shape of a social-fascist allegory. Furthermore, in its crowd scenes, its spectacles of violence and destruction, it had like no other Weimar film inspired the Nazi aesthetic of the "mass-ornament" …Especially reprehensible for Kracauer was the visual depiction of crowds. Pleasurable to the eye but politically totalitarian, Lang's geometrical forms in *Metropolis* deprive the masses of a will and reduce their public participation to a demagogic reflex'. T. Elsaesser, *Metropolis*, p. 45.

41 R.L. Rutsky, 'The Mediation of Technology and Gender: *Metropolis*, Nazism, Modernism', *New German Critique*, vol. 60, Fall, 1993, pp. 3–32.

42 *Ibid*. It is often quoted that the Nazi Party leaders, including Hitler, were very influenced by the film and wished to see Lang do a film for the Party. Lang declined this proposition and emigrated to the US, but his wife opted to remain and enter the service of the Party.

43 T. Elsaesser, *Metropolis*, p. 48.

44 A. Huyssen, 'The Vamp…', pp. 221–237. Also cited in T. Elsaesser, *Metropolis*, p. 55.

45 A. Huyssen as cited in T. Elsaesser, *Metropolis*, p. 55.

46 A. Huyssen, 'The Vamp…', p. 230.

47 D. Rowe, *Representing Berlin: Sexuality and the City in Imperial and Weimar Germany*. Aldershot: Ashgate, 2003.

48 A. Huyssen, 'The Vamp…', pp. 221–237.

49 E. Freidel quoted in T. Elsaesser, *Metropolis*, p. 64.

50 *Ibid*.

51 *Ibid*., pp. 43–44. *Metropolis*'s making was part of an attempt by the German film industry to compete with Hollywood. At the same time, the film was financed by an agreement between the two industries.

52 J. Steiger, 'Future Noir', pp. 108–109.

53 *Ibid*., p. 110.

54 *Ibid*., p. 111.

55 'Lang's city was organized top-down, when the city of the future would sprawl outwards into suburbs rather than stack its workers vertically.'

'To see workers exert huge physical effort manning a machine incensed every engineer, not only because it did not correspond to the facts of modern factory conditions but because the very purpose of machines was to reduce industry's dependency on manual labor.' Elsaesser, *Metropolis*, p. 43.

56 The subtitle is borrowed from the title of an essay by Salman Rushdie in *Imaginary Homelands: Essays and Criticism*. New York: Viking, 1991, pp. 118–125.

57 *Ibid*.

58 Terry Gilliam, interviewed by Salman Rushdie (March 2003). Retrieved, http://www.believermag.com/. The song, Brazil, was copyrighted in 1939 by Irmaos Vitale in Rio de Janeiro and by Southern Music Publishing, Inc. in New York. The music is by Ary Barroso, and the English lyrics are by S.K. Russell. The version in the soundtrack is performed by Geoff and Maria Muldaur in London. J. Mathews, *The Battle of Brazil*, p. 89.

59 Gilliam explains that Port Talbot of Wales gave him the inspiration: 'Port Talbot is a steel town, where everything is covered with gray iron ore dust. Even the beach is completely littered with dust, its just black. The sun was setting, and it was quite beautiful. The contrast was extraordinary; I had this image of a guy sitting there on this dingy beach with a portable radio, tuning into these strange Latin escapist songs like "Brazil". The music transported him somehow and made his world less gray'. J. Maslin, 'The Screen: "Brazil" from Terry Gilliam', *The New York Times* 18 December, 1985. J. Mathews, *The Battle of Brazil*, p. 47.

60 Terry Gilliam, interviewed by Salman Rushdie (March 2003).

61 L.R. Williams, 'Dream Girls and Mechanic Panic, Dystopia and Its Others in *Brazil* and *Nineteen Eighty-Four*', in I.Q. Hunter (ed.) *British Science Fiction Cinema*. London: New York, Routledge, 1999, p. 158.

62 *Ibid.*, p. 100.

63 *Ibid.*

64 J. Steiger, 'Future Noir', p. 113.

65 *Ibid.*, p. 115.

66 *Ibid.*, p. 100.

67 *Ibid.*, p. 115.

68 'This is possible since the films themselves are not part of a postmodern aesthetic; that is these future noir films may display a postmodern *mise-en-scène*, taking the value of spectacle associated with that style, but since that *mise-en-scène*, is represented as the environment for the characters, the filmic effect is that of criticizing that environment'. *Ibid.*, p. 121.

69 *Ibid.*, p. 118.

70 Steiger has explained, 'Satire returns in *Brazil*, where the trip to the countryside is revealed to be the hallucination of protagonist Sam Lowry. Consequently although the motif of escape to nature circulates between the texts, functionally it serves both utopian and dystopian purposes'. *Ibid.,* pp. 104–105.

71 L.R. Williams, 'Dream Girls and Mechanic Panic', p. 154.

72 Various interpreters of *Metropolis* have followed the lead of Huyssen in 'The Vamp and the Machine', calling Maria's double a cyborg.

73 D. Haraway, 'A Cyborg Manifesto: Science, Technology, and Socialist-Feminism in the Late Twentieth Century', in *Simians, Cyborgs and Women: The Reinvention of Nature*. New York: Routledge, 1991, pp.149–181.

74 *Ibid.*

75 'Science fiction', *OED Online*.

76 J. Steiger, 'Future Noir', p. 113. 'Classes and hierarchies abound isomorphically with the architecture'.

77 R.A. Rogers, '1984 to Brazil: From the Pessimism of Reality to the Hope of Dreams', *Text and Performance Quarterly,* vol.10, no.1, 1990, pp. 34–46.

78 N. Khouri, 'Reaction and Nihilism: The Political Genealogy of Orwell's *1984'*, Science Fiction Studies, no. 36, vol. 12, July 1985.

79 *Ibid.*, p. 249.

80 *Ibid.* 'All of this can be said in another way by showing that, if Soviet images of utopia are ideological, our own characteristically Western images of *dystopia* are no less so, and fraught with equally virulent contradictions.' p. 249.

81 F. Jameson, 'Progress versus Utopia; Or Can We Imagine the Future?', *Art After Modernism: Rethinking Representation*. New York: The New Museum of Contemporary Art, 1984, pp. 239–252.

82 *Ibid.*

83 *Ibid.*

84 S. Rushdie, 'The Location of Brazil', in *Imaginary Homelands*.

85 *Ibid.* Rushdie also suggests that *Brazil* differs from *1984* in proposing a way for transgression through imagination.

Chapter 4

Cynical Modernity, or the Modernity of Cynicism

As we have seen, the modernity of the 1920s and 1930s reflected the rising importance of industry in the city and the Taylorist practices of an urbanizing society. Next, the modernity of the 1940s and early 1950s represented the consolidation of the Fordist city and its correlate of suburbanization. By contrast, the modernity of the late 1950s and 1960s was one of revolt and rejection of physical attributes of these new systems as they came into conflict with older urban values. The contrast between old and new at this time was particularly stark in Europe, and especially France. This chapter uses an examination of several films by Jacques Tati to explore further this cynical modernity, which preceded the eruptions in both American and European cities in the late 1960s and early 1970s.

Urban Renewal and the New Consumer Society

During the mid-1950s, the shortage of adequate housing in Paris attracted immense media publicity. Housing conditions there had been problematic since the economic crises of the 1930s, and the situation had only been exacerbated by the disruptions of World War II. Simply put, there had not been enough housing stock in Paris since the nineteenth century. Following World War II, however, decolonization brought a further influx of residents, and eventually many of these migrants, especially those from North Africa, came to occupy *bidonvilles* (squatter settlements) on the outskirts of the city. Meanwhile the old inner-city neighbourhoods, with their antiquated apartment blocks continued to be populated by the white working classes.

As the economic recovery of the 1950s advanced, some of these conditions began to change. The inner city became popular for businesses, property prices rose, and urban renewal accelerated.[1] Perhaps most importantly, the government underwrote the construction of large-scale apartment projects, *grands ensembles*, on the outskirts of the city. These projects, sometimes containing 8,000–10,000 units each, were influenced by 1920s and 1930s ideas of the 'garden city'. However, their scale was much inflated. As a result, the intellectuals who had admired the garden-city ideal grew critical of the *ensemble*.[2] Nevertheless, they remained uninterested in the postwar American housing model based on a sprawling new landscape of single-family houses. The result was a strange amalgam – high-rise suburbanization. According to Laurent Marie:

> A total reorganization of the French capital and its vicinity was made possible by a new law (2 August 1961) which created the 'district of Paris', an institution which was responsible for the preparation, development, and financing of new urban projects across 1,305 towns. A number of high-rise estates were created in the outskirts of Paris. These Zones à Urbanizer en Priorité (ZUPs; Priority Urbanization Zones) were 'based on the separation of accommodation, industry and offices, and increasing use of the car'.[3]

Relocating the working class, from inner-city slums to modern suburban high-rises, did improve housing conditions, if measured by sanitary standards or amount of space per person. However, the relocation could not replicate the social aspects of life in the old neighbourhoods. In particular, the new modernist developments were criticized for their lack of such crucial features of French life as cafés, markets and street life. Norma Evenson has argued that the 'tragedy of evictions' gave further impetus to the nostalgia for a more traditional mode of urban life.[4] She has explained how in the traditional Parisian neighbourhood of the twentieth century, life often spilled from the tight space of the home to the wider physical and social space of the streets, markets, and cafés.[5] In addition, before older areas were cleared for urban renewal projects, class homogeneity allowed residents to consider their entire neighbourhood to be their 'home'. Ironically, some scholars further observed, those same traits that marked the traditional working-class neighbourhoods of Paris before the arrival of modernism would later be refashioned in the modern, luxury blocks of the 1970s.[6]

Following World War II, massive American aid also led to a burst of economic growth and industrialization. Marie has observed, 'Alongside rapid urbanization, France was beginning to enjoy the benefits of the affluent society, as evidenced by the steep increase in the ownership of cars and television sets'.[7] Indeed, immediately following the war, there were very few TV sets in France. But this changed quickly, and by the early 1960s, TV had started to replace radio as the centrepiece of French households, as it had already in American households in the 1950s.

The end of the war also brought a waning of the economic and political power of the imperial European countries, and formerly colonized people demanded their own sovereignty. Despite the paternalistic government of Charles de Gaulle, by the early 1960s all the French colonies in South-East

Asia and North Africa had achieved various forms of independence. The inflow of residents from these territories exacerbated the housing crisis in Paris. The government's solution was a plan to house one-sixth of the population of the metropolitan region in new *grands ensembles*. But these often poorly built projects[8] never fully diffused revolutionary tendencies, and eventually, disenchantment with the political establishment and with the project of modernity it had adopted led to the May 1968 student and worker uprisings.

One important goal of American aid was to create new markets for American products. Thus, throughout the 1950s France was flooded with American appliances, cars, fashions, music, films, and so on – simultaneously provoking anti-American sentiments. Official promotion of the nuclear family also allowed for the reinvention of the home as a 'privatized' sphere in a way that created new demand for consumer products. Kristin Ross has remarked that in postwar France, 'The commodity form does not merely symbolize the social relations of modernity, it is the central source of their origin'.[9] Thus, as opposed to eating at cafés or restaurants, every household would now eat at home, reinventing traditional French recipes, and buying new modern gadgets.[10] Such privatization was enabled by the abundance of American products and technology.[11]

If this new privatization of home life marked France in the 1950s, it was a new regulation of leisure time that characterized the 1960s. Ellen Furlough, whose research focuses on the history of consumerism in France, has reported that the French first became a society of leisure in the early 1960s.[12] For example, it was then that holidays and travel came to be perceived as the right of every citizen.[13]

Plastic and Glass: The Materials of Modernity

Throughout the 1950s and 1960s, the French government actively engaged in a forced modernization by sponsoring and advocating urban renewal, privatization, and the regulation of leisure. But its practices were also facilitated by the introduction of new materials in both the private and public spheres. The US had led the way in developing new household and construction materials. Although plastics had been known since the nineteenth century, they were not put to commercial use before the 1930s and 1940s. In 1933 British chemists at ICI invented polythene, while in 1935 American chemists from the Du Pont Company discovered nylon, and three years later they discovered Teflon, which the company used to make non-stick cooking utensils. In the following decades, many more plastics resins were made commercially available offering strength and durability. Consumer products employing these materials, such as household appliances, had a profound effect on urban lifestyles. For example, the neighbourhood laundry now became unnecessary, since individual households could acquire their own washing machines. Daily small-scale shopping was also eliminated since refrigerators now allowed each home to store and preserve perishable food. Moreover, the aesthetic sensibility of modernity, already developed in architecture and urban form, was applied to the mass production of household appliances. And through advertising, manufacturers started to promote their products as fashion statements.

During the 1950s, in the heyday of the Cold War, the US government also took a role in propagating the International Style in art and architecture, furniture, and design through hotel chains such as Hilton and trade exhibitions.[14] Initially, this new language of capitalist modernity was welcome in France and in countries aligned with the US, as it provided the look of the future. However, with a change of political climate in the 1960s, new designs in plastic, glass and steel came to be resented as extensions of American hegemony. This change also corresponded with the rise of revolutionary movements in many parts of the world. Meanwhile, architectural modernism was increasingly criticized for creating conditions of social alienation. Postcolonial nationalist perspectives also sought alternative forms to express their particular local and regional identities.

Many of these issues surface in the work of French film director, Jacques Tati.[15] Tati's films of the 1950s and 1960s critiqued modern technology, and American-style consumerism, and attempted to call attention to the degradation of established traditions of life in France.[16] We will discuss two of these films in this chapter, *Mon Oncle* (1958) and *Playtime* (1967), presenting two versions of Paris a decade apart, which yield astute observations about the nature of change in the physical and social fabric of the city. In the process, they reveal a deeply cynical view of American-style modernity.

The Cynic as a Figure of Modernity

In the context of the Americanization of Europe, and later the rest of the world, Tati was ahead of his time. His typical hero was a somewhat confused, apolitical, middle-class male lost in a city, Paris, which was becoming increasingly like other cities in the world. In this context of mundane modernist repetition, Lucy Fisher has suggested, Tati uses the 'dialectic of the old and the new' to invoke a previous mode of life that was calmer and richer in its qualities.[17]

Through a number of films during this period, Tati developed a screen *alter ego* named Monsieur Hulot whom he first introduced and played in *Les Vacances de Monsieur Hulot* (1953). The absentmindedness this character suffers was a perfect foil for the emptiness of the new modernist glass structures that were coming to dominate architecture in the 1950s and 1960s. According to Joan Ockman, Hulot is a distracted spectator, lost in the meaningless materiality of the modern city.[18] Hulot lives in a romanticized Paris in which time passes slowly; people do not work much, and consumerist lifestyles have not yet won out. He is clumsy in his movements and actions, and he does not speak very much. When he does speak the camera does not follow him, but the *mise-en-scène*.

In Hulot, Baudelaire's *flâneur* meets Simmel's *blasé*. Reviewers of Tati's films have also pointed to similarities between the character of Hulot and the figure of the tramp used by Chaplin in many of his films of the 1920s and 1930s.[19] Indeed, they have compared *Mon Oncle* to Chaplin's *Modern Times* because of the many comical scenes created by the confusing array of gadgets Hulot seems so inept at mastering.[20] Both characters inhabit a world of machines they have difficulty comprehending.[21] In an interview with André Bazin and François Truffaut in French cinema journal *Cahiers du Cinéma* (May 1958), Tati argued, however, that he and Chaplin had different 'styles'. For example, while Chaplin's tramp would invent gags for the viewers, the everyman Hulot would not.[22] He also suggested that while Chaplin's tramp may seem naïve, he still manages to adapt brilliantly. Hulot, in contrast, remains passive, and, because of his inability to adapt, he frequently damages the new environments he encounters.[23]

Using the character of Hulot, the two films discussed here present a cynical view of modernist urban life. They also comment directly on the changing form of cities. *Mon Oncle* depicts how Taylorism has reached beyond the modes of production to pervade the ways human beings operate or are expected to operate in their own personal spaces, with all their movements synchronized with their intended desires or objectives. In the film, the entire urban landscape is modern, except for the romantic city block in which Hulot lives, as part of the small population that remains unchanged by modernity. In *Playtime*, a new vision of a Parisian suburb is presented. This is a Paris without monuments except for the ones reflected ephemerally on glass doors or windows of its suburb as they capture a distant reality. It is a Paris that has disappeared to become part of the blurry and anonymous urban edge. In this Paris, citizens live in glass boxes that resemble stacks of television sets piled on top of each other in a store window. This notion of maximum standardization of space percolates not only in the space of work and dwelling, but also in the body space, where the attire is also the same. Tati did not only make films with a strong visual emphasis on architecture but also designed and built architecture. As someone who pursued both film directing and set design, he once declared that he did not see much difference between directing films and designing architecture.[24]

From Tradition to Modernity: Urban Renewal and Change in *Mon Oncle*

In *Mon Oncle*, the young Gerard Arpel lives with his father and mother in an ultra-modern suburban house. Gerard is bored with the disciplinary mechanisms of modern living and uses every opportunity to subvert the rules. His father (played by Jean-Pierre Zola) is an executive in Plastac, a company that produces plastic pipes, and his mother (played by Adrienne Servantie) is a housewife who enthusiastically cleans the house all day. However his uncle Hulot (played by Jacques Tati), who does not fit in this sterile, new milieu, is his greatest source of entertainment. Hulot, Madame Arpel's brother, lives in the 'old' part of the town on the top floor of a makeshift building near a market. The film continuously contrasts the traditional warm sounds and colours of community life in Hulot's neighbourhood with those of the imported, consumption-driven, sterile and alienated modern living elsewhere in the city, but especially in the Arpel household.

Mon Oncle starts and ends at construction sites. In the opening sequence, a crane moves partially secluded behind a construction sign to the sound of drilling. The sign in the foreground is actually the film's titles. In the second sequence, a cut is made to the historical part of the town. The name of the film again appears hand-drawn with chalk on a building wall. The action then begins at the suburban house of the Arpel family. Monsieur

Mon Oncle (1958). Monsieur Hulot lives in a ramshackle apartment building that creates the backdrop for his nostalgia.

Arpel prepares for his workday. He drives Gerard to school, and then heads to Plastac. In another part of town, Monsieur Hulot shops for his groceries on foot from street vendors. Later that day, Hulot picks up Gerard from his school in the new district. When he arrives, he finds the kids are having fun by tricking some drivers into thinking that the following car has hit them. One car, driven by Madame Dubrevil, does actually get hit. But Madame Dubrevil assumes it is part of the kids' joke. Afterwards, she heads to the Arpel home for a short visit. Upon hearing the bell ringing, Madame Arpel quickly removes her housecoat and switches on a fish-shaped fountain in the garden to impress her. Dubrevil does not sit, but rather inspects the house. In return, Madame Arpel exhibits her mechanized domestic domain with pride. In the evening, Monsieur and Madame Arpel resume their daily routine sitting in their uncomfortable wire furniture, consuming mass media.

In an attempt to reclaim their son's attention from uncle Hulot, the Arpels decide to introduce Hulot to a neighbour in the hopes he will become interested in her and ask her to marry him. The garden party organized to set Hulot up, however, is spoiled by a series of technical malfunctions. In the longest sequence of the film, lasting around twenty minutes, water spouting from pipes soaks all the guests.

Monsieur and Madame Arpel both think that Hulot is a loser, but they also continue to believe they can help him. Monsieur Arpel next asks a friend named Lambert, president of the 'SDRC Coal Derivatives', to arrange for

Mon Oncle. In Monsieur Hulot's imagined 'old Paris', neighbours use public spaces actively.

him to have an interview there. But Hulot fails the interview when he tracks mud into the personnel manager's office. Arpel then decides to take him on at Plastac. But Hulot manages to mess things up there when the machines he is running start churning out plastic sausages instead of plastic pipes. Pichard, Arpel's right-hand man, argues Hulot must go, as 'He is not cut out for factory work'.

Monsieur Arpel desperately wants to get Hulot out of his family's life. Finally, he arranges a sales job for him in the provinces. He drives Hulot to the airport, but in the carpark Arpel's whistle to Hulot distracts a passer-by who crashes into a lamp post. Arpel is embarrassed, but Gerard is amused, and comforts his father by holding his hand. As father and son enjoy this Hulot-esque moment, they return to the city, which has become a giant construction site where the old buildings are being torn down one by one.

As this action unfolds, one of the most important sets is the Arpel home, a modernist suburban house with subdued colours, an aesthetic of steel and glass, and lots of electric gadgets. In terms of its layout, however, it is quite conventional: the living room and kitchen are on the ground floor, and Gerard's bedroom is above the Arpel's. The living room features grey wall-to-wall carpet, straight-run stairs, white walls, green-upholstered furniture (to match Madame Arpel's housecoat) and wire chairs like those in Lambert's executive offices. Meanwhile the kitchen is characterized by dentist-like hygiene, and contains much noisy, factory-like equipment. This is Madame Arpel's perfect privatized domain of child rearing and Taylorist household management. She wears a nylon pinafore and rubber gloves and sterilizes all the utensils. She adjusts Gerard's chair and feeds him with scientifically cooked dishes. Gerard protests with hiccups.

Outdoors, the house features a garden secluded behind tall walls and an iron gate. A concrete driveway provides access to a garage, and a twisting concrete garden path leads up a flight of stairs to the entrance porch. On the occasion of Madame Dubrevil's visit, Madame Arpel and Madame Dubrevil approach each other on this twisting path and display superficial greetings while it forces them to walk in opposite directions. Ironically, they talk about the efficiency of the house. This gag is repeated at the garden party to emphasize the convolutedness of the design, which consists of an abstract composition of coloured sands and gravel overlaid with loose stepping stones.

The focal piece of the garden is a small pool with a fish-shaped fountain that is operated from the entrance. When Monsieur Arpel arrives from work and rings the bell, Madame Arpel hurries to turn on the fountain, but her husband shouts from outside to switch it off. The fountain is reserved for important guests and remains off for service people and close family. At the garden party, the sophisticated next-door neighbour arrives with a shawl the

Mon Oncle. Only Monsieur Hulot appears not to recognize the importance of the car as the icon of postwar modernity.

Arpels mistake for a carpet. They switch off the fountain and tell her to leave before they realize who she is. Meanwhile, on the other side of the garden, on a blank wall, the Arpels are cultivating a pair of shrubs in the shape of candleholders. During the garden party, Gerard accidentally breaks a branch of one of them, which has been trained to grow symmetrically on an espalier. However, when he asks his uncle to fix it, Hulot ends up trimming the whole plant.

Gerard, being a lonely child, loves to go to the old town with his uncle. In the urban wasteland that lies between the new district and the old, he also finds friends and has fun. Characterized by overgrown vegetation, derelict railway tracks, and crumbling walls, this 'no-man's land' doubles as a playground for children and a hideout for lovers. The most famous sequence from the film happens here when Hulot replaces a brick in a crumbling wall there and passes through a broken iron fence onto an asphalt road leading to modernist apartment slabs. Although it is located in the middle of the old district, the riverside also has a similar quality of play. It is reserved for the lovers and the mock suicide of the sausage-formed pipes.

While Gerard is able to have fun with the people he meets in such places, his parents must go to a specialized entertainment space to celebrate their wedding anniversary. This is a posh restaurant, Rington's, with a concierge, neon lights, and expensive cars outside. Its stodgy formal arrangement and rigid patrons provide a stark contrast to the public spaces of the old district.

Tati chose a recently-built Parisian suburb, Creteil, as a location to shoot the scenes depicting the Arpels' neighbourhood.[25] James Harding reported that since no sense of community had formed in Creteil's highly regulated setting at the time, Tati and his crew had great difficulty working there. By contrast, they were welcomed in Saint-Maur-des-Fosses, the setting where the scenes of Hulot's neighbourhood were shot.[26] The exterior shots in Saint-Maur-des-Fosses were filmed at Place d'Armes. Tati erected a false four-storey building in front of the existing café, to serve as the supposed location of Hulot's apartment. But he was not satisfied with the look of the place as it was, so he also put up false fronts on a series of shops and sealed off two of the six streets leading into the square. In his view, this neighbourhood would always be full of people and street vendors. In this fictional world, the local café, Chez Margot, would also be the centre of the social life. People would spend their days, hold their meetings, and receive their telephone calls there. But the café would not just be a contained interior. It would spill outside. Indeed, Tati refrains from showing interiors in the old district even those of the café. Life in the old district is shown to take place outdoors in public on squares and streets, which are crooked and cobbled, inhabited by people of all ages, and filled with music and conviviality.

This nostalgic vision of the old district contrasts starkly with views of the new modern world. In the Arpels' neighbourhood, wide asphalt streets are populated only by American cars, stuck in orderly rows. The parking

Mon Oncle. The Arpels organize a garden party.

areas at factories are marked by white signs that speak of hierarchy and social status. The president of SDRC Coal Derivatives works in a minimalist, oversized office with see-through wire chairs, a desk with embedded phone, and a world map on the wall. Monsier Arpel works in a similar enclosure at Plastac bounded by glass walls and filled with functionalist furniture. Meanwhile, Plastac's typists share space with identical desks and typewriters, and wear identical outfits and hairdos. And the company's production plant is mechanized according to Fordist principles; here, machines do the work while the workers, now spatially separated, see to quality control while inhaling fumes that make them drowsy.

The characters in *Mon Oncle* reinforce this contrast in physical environments. Monsieur Arpel, a representative of the emerging executive class, prefers plastic flowers to real ones because plastic, a modern product, does not decay. Yet even if he is the boss at work, Madame Arpel reigns over the domestic world. Everything in the Arpel house is coordinated according to her wishes, while her obsession with cleaning and household management reflects trends in contemporary French society.[27] Hulot, however, represents traditional France. He rides a bicycle and has no interest in cars or other consumer products. Although he lives alone, he is not by any means lonely. He communicates with few words – and as effectively with his neighbours as with animals. Opening a window, Hulot is taken by how its reflection makes a nearby canary sing, so he adjusts it to let the canary sing and participate more fully in the neighbourhood conversation.

Mon Oncle. Monsieur Arpel's home is a cubist villa, a stage for modern life; one that is not comfortable.

Subsidiary characters also embody aspects of class relations in the new modern France. There are the upper-class neighbour and her jockey friend; SDRC's president and manager; Plastac's manager who brings the artificial flowers to the Arpels' garden party and fixes the fountain; Plastac's secretarial and blue-collar workforce; Madame Dubrevil who wears designer clothes that look like carpets; the superstitious maid who declines to activate the garage door; the fruit delivery man who is shocked at the sight of the Arpels' remote-controlled door and fish fountain; and others. As Monsieur Arpel is inspecting a new car, an anniversary present for his wife, the salesman refuses to talk about its engine but instead argues that its superficial qualities are most important, 'Let's not talk about the number of cylinders, since they will never open the hood… Let's just talk about the comfort and the paint job…'.

Among the cinematic devices Tati uses to enhance the contrast between old and new are the complexity, level, and pitch of sounds. In the Arpels' house, Monsieur Arpel is hardly ever heard, whereas his wife's voice is exaggerated and acute. Footfalls are heightened to emphasize the coldness of modern spaces, while they are muted in the historical district. When Arpel calls Hulot at the café from Lambert's office, Hulot does not hang up, letting the sounds of the café intrude into the modernist office space, disrupting its silence. At Rington's, the exaggerated sound of the crushed tip emphasizes how the musicians are performing here for money, not personal satisfaction. This is contrasted in parallel editing to the fun Hulot and Gerard have with gypsy music in the old district.

Tati also 'humanizes' the suburban villa by visual associations and mental transformations.[28] When the Arpels come back from their evening out on their wedding anniversary, they find Hulot sleeping in the living room on an uncomfortable couch he has turned upright to make into a comfy chaise longue. At night, as the Arpels look out of their circular bedroom windows, the windows resemble cartoon eyes, the pupils their heads.

François Penz, in his book *Cinema and Architecture*, notes how Tati uses housing space as a focus for his critique of modern architecture. From the very way he conceived the setting of *Mon Oncle* (designed as a montage of images from magazines) to the sounds and colours he applied to emphasize the absurdity of a life full of gadgets and useless spaces, we are presented with a cynical view of modernity.[29]

The Uniformity of Modernity: *Playtime* and the 1960s

Playtime starts where *Mon Oncle* leaves off. The old world has been banished to the provinces with Hulot, and, only the new world of glass, plastic and electro-mechanical living remains. Hulot (again played by Tati) returns temporarily for an appointment. The plot, simply put, consists of a series of vignettes describing his chance encounters with an American tourist named Barbara (played by Barbara Dennek) during the twenty-four hours she spends in a Parisian suburb. In the first part of the movie, during daytime, Hulot, unsuccessfully tries to keep an appointment in a high-rise office building. In the second part, in the evening, he starts establishing human contact. In the third part, which takes place in a restaurant, he acts as a catalyst for social cohesion.

As the film begins, Barbara's group, comprised mainly of middle-aged, middle-class, American women, arrives at the Paris airport, chattering and gossiping loudly. The hostess hands them over to the tour operator who herds them onto buses. There does not seem to be much to distinguish this city from any other destination they have been. As they arrive in the city centre, Hulot exits from a public bus. He has an appointment with a Monsieur Giffard, but ends up getting lost in this world of transparency and reflection, and misses every opportunity to talk to him. As soon as he manages to step out to the street, he is again hoarded into another disorienting interior. An announcement declares that it is a trade exhibit: 'While our international expo is going on, don't forget to visit Spaceland!'. Arriving at the top floor, to which the elevator takes him by mistake, Hulot steps out on a terrace with views of the Parisian roofscape. Eventually, Barbara's group arrives at the same exhibit. Barbara is reluctant to go in, but she complies with the group. Inside the exhibit are peculiar items such as a floor mop with headlights and a trash can in the form of a Greek column. All the women are enchanted.

As the sun sets, Hulot meets an old friend from the army, who insists he has a drink at his home. He introduces Hulot to his family and shows off his flat. They then gather around the TV without conversation. Hulot excuses himself and starts wandering around in the city. Eventually, he comes across a construction site where the installation of huge sheets of glass has turned into evening entertainment, some sort of a street festival for the local crowd. Teenagers blow circus music on kazoos to accompany the construction workers, turning them into a children's puppet theatre. It is here, at this instant spectacle and public gathering that Hulot finally gets the chance to meet Giffard.

Barbara and her entourage return to their hotel from a trip to the Eiffel Tower. The interior of the hotel room possesses a confused aesthetic, an extension of the building exterior. Next Barbara joins the rest of her group in a series of escalator rides and lobby meanderings, before they reach a restaurant, The Royal Garden. The place is just being completed and as the first couple arrives in a Rolls Royce, the architect is still on site. But soon things start failing. Hulot, who has been dragged to the scene from 'Le Drugstore' by the doorman, again an old friend from the army, first accidentally runs into the glass entrance door, breaking it, and then tears down the central hanging panel inadvertently. These acts of destruction of the décor create the opportunity for the patrons to mingle and have fun until early morning. To conclude the evening, Barbara and Hulot have breakfast at 'Le Drugstore', which is part pharmacy part eatery, and whose design and artificially coloured foods are well-suited to this glass and steel Paris. Hulot fetches presents for Barbara from a tourist store as she departs to the airport.

Playtime (1966). Modernist apartments become television screens stacked on top of one another for Tati's camera.

An entire film set had to be built for the filming of *Playtime* designed by Eugène Roman, a miniature town on wasteland in Vincennes.[30] Completed in five months, it had real streets with tarmac and zebra crossings, habitable multi-storey buildings with air-conditioning, electricity, and movable walls to accommodate camera positioning. James Harding reported, 'As news of Tativille spread, many people came to see and wonder at the miniature township. Visitors from England, America, Sweden and Russia saw streets alive with traffic and shops filled with merchandise. A fashionable couturier presented his spring collection there'.[31] Tati's Paris in *Playtime*, often called Tativille, resembled other global tourist destinations more than anything else. Highways connect airports to glass and steel corporate office blocks and spaces for mass consumption. Intended to be experienced as a framed image or from a moving vehicle, it presents a street-level pedestrian experience that is highly disorienting.

To emphasize these qualities, the film starts with a title sequence that is simply a still image of clouds, the framed view from an airplane. This is followed by a static and overwhelming image of the Esso building, the first office building at La Défense, and then a shot of an interior lobby.[32] Barbara's tour bus has wide glass windows on the sides and the top to maximize viewing. On the way from the airport to the city, it passes through a landscape of traffic, asphalt roads, painted road signs, and lamp posts to arrive in the middle of grey, regularly placed modernist slabs. In their conversation, the tourists confuse some of these structures with major historical landmarks. By contrast, Hulot appears in a more 'traditional' green, public bus. Unlike the white tour bus, it does not blend with the cool grey and white of its environs.

As he arrives for his appointment with Giffard, Hulot first waits in the glazed, sterile entrance of an austere office block. With apparent trouble, the concierge reports Hulot's arrival using a convoluted door phone. In a deep-focus longtake, Giffard approaches from the other end of the hallway, but he only takes Hulot to a glass chamber with identical chairs where he asks him to wait some more. The chamber's glass walls allow its occupants maximum viewing from inside but it also exposes them to view by those outside. This all glass, transparent space appears like a cage. Frustrated, Hulot leaves to track Giffard, enters an executive meeting to the annoyed glances of those inside, accidentally steps into an elevator and ends up travelling up and down in the building. Finally, he enters an 'open' office where employees are working in identical cubicles and where a secretary sits in the middle at a rotating table. Presumably this is Giffard's office floor, but whichever way Hulot goes, he ends up facing the secretary. The modernist office layout becomes Hulot's labyrinth.

Although Hulot occupies the same space as Giffard, because of the illusions glass creates, Hulot thinks Giffard is elsewhere, and he steps

Playtime. Monsieur Hulot is disoriented when he finds himself in a modern office space with identical cubicles.

outside. On the pavement, Barbara is trying to take photos, but the only suitable subject she can find is a lady selling fresh flowers in a ragged outfit. The flower lady resists being photographed because of her attire, but at last gives in. However, Barbara does not want to contaminate the picture with 'modern' items or characters like Americanized youth and she takes such a long time to shoot her authentic Paris photograph that she ends up being crowded into another similar picture being taken by a passing US soldier. Colourful and old, the flower lady is reminiscent of the old Paris. However, other signs of old Paris – the Arc de Triomphe, Eiffel Tower, Sacré Coeur, Hôtel de Ville, Champs Elysées – merely exist as advertisements or reflections on moving glass.

With the exception of Houlot, the characters of *Playtime* are more abstract in both their presence and actions than those in *Mon Oncle*. Brent Maddock and Penelope Gilliatt have commented on the de-emphasis of Hulot in *Playtime*.[33] In many instances, Hulot appears almost incidental. He hardly talks, and when he does, such as when he bumps into Giffard, the camera may drop him out of the frame. When he visits his friend in his flat, the camera keeps its distance regardless of the barrier of glass. The alienation of Hulot from the camera serves to emphasize how Hulot still belongs to the 'old' world and represents the traditional French everyman struggling with the changes in his city.

Barbara is distinguished from the rest of her fellow travellers by her youth, elegance, relative quietness, disinterest in consumption, and – particularly – by her observation of and receptiveness to her surroundings. While entering the trade exhibit, she notices the reflection of the Eiffel Tower on the glass door and is taken by surprise. In fact, she is delighted to catch any glimpses of the old Paris, and is the only one among her fellow travellers who is disturbed by the architectural streamlining and homogeneity. Looking out from the window in her hotel room, Barbara is tantalized. On the window edge is a radio that bears a resemblance to the lit-up high-rises. Lucy Fisher has analysed this scene as follows:

> It (the radio) is not there, however, simply as a realistic detail, nor is it there merely to allow Tati an opportunity to burlesque the commercials that it is spewing. Rather it is there to look like the skyscrapers outside the window and thereby formulate the message of absurd design uniformity, where even radios look like high-rise buildings.[34]

In the tourism agency, it is only Barbara who notices the absurd similarity of the posters for Hawaii, Mexico, London, and Paris, which all feature identical buildings that dwarf their landmarks. In the trade exhibition, the only image decorating the exhibition space of the firm specializing in silent doors is a poster similar to the one used to advertise world cities in the tourism agency. These silent doors are made for such modernist slabs. Finally, Barbara acts, in the restaurant scene, as a catalyst. When the orchestra members, who are black, leave, she plays the piano along with other patrons.

Although Tati is clearly critical of mass consumption and mass tourism, he is not critical of the tourists, *per se*. Before the end, the tourists are able to establish contact with the locals and are endowed with a transformed vision despite the regulated nature of their visit. Penelope Gilliatt has observed that,

> The tourists are never mocked. Tati finds few people foolish because he sees few people as being finally incapable of unbending. One of his American visitors asks softly, 'How do you say "drugstore" in French?', a little ashamed of her ignorance and sweetly ignoring the signs reading 'drugstore' everywhere.[35]

The tourists were played by the wives of the American service officers in Paris at the time. They wore their own clothes and behaved as they would have under normal circumstances. Tati had a penchant for using non-professional or unknown actors. Barbara, too, was Tati's discovery. She was a German au pair working in his neighbourhood when he cast her for the role.

As in *Mon Oncle*, the transformations of spaces in *Playtime* are achieved by sound effects, visual associations, and use of colour. In the opening sequence, actors move with considerable silence in what appears to be a waiting room: a couple whispers quietly; a cleaner in a uniform mops the floor; a nurse passes by carrying a crying baby; a soldier walks up and down; a man hurries away with a large bouquet of flowers. All these actions create the illusion that this room is in a hospital. But an announcement soon reveals that this is an airport, and the sounds of planes and arriving passengers suddenly transform the sterile room into an airport lobby. Tati's comedy often derives from the surprise that such spatial transformations generate, rather than dialogue or action.

In the city, as the sun sets, executives leave the towers in their private cars while office clerks crowd into buses. Lights go on and without curtains, glass surfaces, which acted like mirrors during the day become transparent. In the flat of his old army friend Hulot and his friend share a drink and watch television, a very fashionable household product at the time. Although Hulot excuses himself and leaves, the camera remains outside on the street. The television is embedded in a wall that separates the flat from the one next-door. As the camera pulls back it reveals that the next-door neighbour and the residents of flats on the floors above, are all facing each other, but instead of socializing with each other, they all watch televisions placed in the walls that separate them. Tati is suggesting here that the residents are peeking into others' private lives via television, and hence metaphorically looking at each other without knowing, interacting, or participating. The camera also suggests that, as spectators, we are in the same position. The flats become different TV monitors, and we as spectators of the film are watching them.

Another important and lengthy sequence in the film is that which takes place towards the end in the Royal Garden. Dietrich Neumann, a distinguished scholar of cinematic architecture, has observed that, 'The restaurant, itself, serves as a metaphor for the city'.[36] No clear story emerges in this one-hour sequence. Rather a series of gags take place first by visual associations, then through the transformations of the space itself by the patrons. A series of failures first creates confusion, but then as the patrons relax and take things into their own hands, the resultant chaos allows them to socialize.[37] Significantly, the patrons rip the space apart with their bare hands, creating a club within a club. As the physical world is deconstructed, social hierarchies also come apart and people who otherwise would not talk mingle and have fun. A Texas millionaire buys drinks for everyone. Since the entrance door is wide open, anyone can enter. Eventually, the patrons play songs about Paris, and boundaries between the spectators and spectacle dissolve.

Playtime. Monsieur Hulot's inadvertent destruction of the restaurant set encourages spontaneity.

As the film ends, the tourists' perception of the city is transformed through their interaction with French people. In the tour bus, Barbara opens Hulot's presents – a scarf with historic Parisian monuments printed on the them and a bunch of lilies of the valley, which now resemble the lamp posts on the highway. The highway traffic is shot to remind the spectators of a

Playtime. A round-about in the modernist city: congestion leading to nowhere.

carousel; the new city turned into an amusement park.[38] Tati aims to show that it is possible to reconcile the brutality of the new by highlighting the absurd and recasting it as comical.

Marie has argued that it is not modern architecture or technological products that Tati is critical of but rather their fashion-driven use and fetishization. 'Tati explains that he is "against a certain way of life, a sterile, homogenization which affects the way we think as much as the place where we live".'[39] Through all these aural and visual and physical transformations, spaces are interpreted in a new light, and in the narrative they serve to connect the tourists to Hulot. Hilliker has called this a 'humanizing possibility', which was, in the context of the 1960s, also a reconciliation between the global and the local:

> As he did in *Mon Oncle*, Tati in *Playtime* brings a sense of humanizing possibility into contemporary architectural space from which it had been absent, and the reconciliation which takes place between father and son in the 1958 film is here effected between the tourists and their desire for an authentic Paris, and between city dwellers and the alienating, confusing work, living, and leisure spaces of their everyday lives.[40]

In what could be considered a filmographic critique of modern architecture, Tati's real attack was not targeted at the architecture but at the homogeneous, sterile and banal ways of life.[41] Architecture becomes here the *vedette*, the central attraction of the film, and the character of the *flâneur* becomes almost minuscule in the middle of the overwhelming uniformity of places and glass reflections.[42]

Cynical Paris or Parisian Cynicism

Mon Oncle and *Playtime* are markers of a particular kind of European, mid-twentieth-century modernity. According to Ockman:

> the decade between the making of *Mon Oncle*, and *Playtime* was decisive in transforming France from an insular, agrarian, and empire-oriented society into an urban, industrial, and decolonized nation. The face of Paris, 'capital of the nineteenth century,' was permanently reshaped during these years by a sweeping new wave of Hausmannization.[43]

Consequently, this is a modernity still concerned with equality in distributing the benefits of progress. In the 1920s and 1930s the Bauhaus had framed modernity as an ideology in the service of society. These ideas were now accepted and often implemented – but in ways, Tati suggests, that have enslaved the people they were supposed to serve. In other words, this is a physical environment of efficiency that is no longer efficient; one that conceals its hegemonic workings; one that divides society; and finally, one that causes some to fear change and others to welcome it. It is an environment where Taylorist calculations no longer just organize the activities of human beings, but create their own logic. It is Lang's *Metropolis* in the garb of the architecture of the Bauhaus, wearing the socio-economic hat of the 1960s. The expectation is no longer just efficiency of production as this expectation has by now been achieved. It is now a normative operation within the mandated space of the modern house or the office cubicle. Thus, Hulot's cinematic portrayal of the cubicles adopts a bird's-eye perspective, but there is no panopticon or observing authority. The workers are no longer prisoners who behave or perform because of the expectation of surveillance, rather, they perform to attain the expected benefits of the welfare society in which they now believe. Ironically, having the physical manifestations of efficiency have made achieving efficiency very difficult, if not problematic. In *Mon Oncle*, the factory and the home have similar kinds of machines. Similar processes of production and sterilization take place. The home is no longer a refuge from work, but an extension of it.[44]

Just as leisure has been enabled by the assembly line, Tati shows that it has also become mechanized.[45] Thus, tourists move passively according to a predetermined route that can be likened to an assembly line. In homes, excessive numbers of labour-saving devices not only do not save labour, but also tend to break down and create havoc. Similar to high-tech architecture in Tati's view, they engender passivity in their users.[46] In this milieu, humans have little agency left. Their perceptual apparatuses are numbed by mechanical gadgets, mass media, advertising and consumerism.

By addressing and challenging this condition, Tati seeks to endow the spectator with agency. He uses high-resolution film, deep focus and long shot camera techniques, sound editing, and colour to subvert viewers' reception of the films. Tati was very vocal about his aims. He said:

> The trouble with today's audiences is that they're not used to participation, they're used to television, which makes no demands on the part of the viewer. I do not make close-ups of people so the audience must see what they see with their own eyes, not what the camera tells them.[47]

Perceptually, *Playtime* is difficult for an audience accustomed to passive viewing.[48] Tati demands their engagement and participation. He eschews the usual techniques such as shot reverse-shot, which have become transparent through mainstream cinema, in favour of the long-duration deep-focus shot. In *Playtime*, nothing is centred or foregrounded, and the narrative is less important to the film than the *mise-en-scène*. Therefore, Hulot enters the film as late as in the seventh scene, and disappears from the frame intermittently throughout. Each frame shot comprises a multitude of gags which render successive viewings different. At the end of the film, as the tourist group heads back to the airport, the highway on which they travel is transformed into a circus environment.[49] In this sense, Kristin Thompson has identified a 'perceptual playtime' in the films. The tourists are not working, so they are at 'play' (vacation). The destruction of the restaurant décor enables another kind of 'playtime'. On top of these more literal references, playtime has a metaphorical application and perceptual implication. Fisher calls this 'metaphoric vision': 'the ability to see things in a figurative fashion, to "transform" one thing into another'.[50]

The linkage between the city's 'superficial rationality and its underlying rationality' has also been important in Tati's work.[51] In *Playtime*, Paris is displaced to the suburbs, confounding our understanding of its location and creating a fundamental absence.[52] The underlying and pervasive concept is 'the absence of a "real" Paris, the lack of substance at the heart of a consumerist society founded on nothing but exchange value, the emptiness of glass architecture'.[53] In this regard, *Playtime*, 'conflates and confounds the nothingness of cinema with the immateriality of the new modern construction with its excessive use of glass'.[54]

Tati's work emerges out of and is part of the transformation French society underwent as a result of rapid urbanization and the establishment of a new sense of class relations as a result of consumerism.[55] Marie has claimed that this political dimension of Tati's work has not been adequately addressed in previous reviews.[56] He claimed Tati's work at the time paralleled views presented in *Situationist International*, a French-language magazine established in 1957 by a group of *avant-garde* artists and intellectuals. The Situationists wanted a revolution that would be facilitated through art and imagination. Marie has also pointed to the timing of another important text, Guy Debord's *Society of the Spectacle*, which was published a month before the release of *Playtime*.[57] In it, Debord theorized the 'spectacle', and he discussed the 'colonization of everyday life' by capitalism. While he may not have shared Tati's cynicism, Debord maintained that 'What is now missing in life can only be found in spectacle in the form of separated independent representations'.[58] The Situationists had developed concepts and techniques to deal with these conditions that included what they termed psychogeography, unitary urbanism, and constructed situations. Hence *Playtime*'s characters may be seen as 'determined by the geography or the architecture of the place in which they find themselves.[59]

The sequence in which strange household products are displayed at the trade exhibition is a critique of consumer society along the lines of the Situationists. Remarkably, Marie has pointed out that the restaurant scene is a model that would fit well with ideals of Unitary Urbanism.[60] In it the patrons gain their agency and take control of the space, following a series of 'anarchic' disruptions in which they establish direct contact with each other without regard to class and gender boundaries. Ockman also pointed to the similarity between *Situationist International* and Tati's work. But she has argued, that Playtime is not Situationist because it does not end triumphantly in anarchy – for example, in the restaurant sequence.[61] Instead, *Playtime* ends on the highway, where it cannot express either 'avant-gardism' or 'utopianism'. Rather, it seeks to reconcile old and new ways of living.

Following earlier work by Simmel about the character of the *blasé*, Walter Benjamin identified distraction as an important mode of urban experience. Benjamin was not concerned with the tourist's gaze before a famous building or the intellectual Baudelairian *flâneur* enjoying its cafés; rather he wanted to examine the everyday perceptions of working masses.[62] According to Ockman, 'Hulot is Benjamin's distracted spectator par excellence'.[63] He is the 'Collective non-utopian embodiment of the Benjaminian viewer', a distracted middle-class individual who looks 'without seeing'.[64] The distracted cynic is both a product and a representative of this modernity and all its disappointments.

This is a modernity then that calls for more than physical reform. It calls for a change in our very perceptions, or 'the way we live'. Here is a society that is both obsessed with material products and ideologies of efficiency yet nostalgic for a disappearing 'real' world of social relations and personal interactions. This cynical modernity was produced by the ultimate Parisian cynic at a time in the middle of the twentieth century before the great transformation of French society brought by the student/worker riots of 1968. In the decades that would follow modernity, its products, and its tropes, would undergo fundamental changes.

However, in both Europe and America, there was a certain calmness to the early 1960s that preceded this turmoil. The cynicism that appears in much of the artwork of that period, including cinema, appears now as the calm before the storm.

Notes

1   N. Evenson, *Paris: A Century of Change (1878–1978)*. New Haven, CT: Yale University Press, 1979, p. 236.
2   *Ibid.*, p. 249.
3   L. Marie, 'Jacques Tati's *Playtime* as New Babylon', in M. Shiel and T. Fitzmaurice (eds.) *Cinema and the City*. Oxford: Blackwell, 2001, p. 258.
4   N. Evenson, *Paris*, p. 237.
5   *Ibid.*, p. 255.
6   *Ibid.*, p. 264.
7   L. Marie, 'Jacques Tati's *Playtime*', p. 258.
8   J. Ockman, 'Architecture in a Mode of Distraction: Eight Takes of Jacques Tati's *Playtime*', in M. Lamster (ed.) *Architecture and Film*. New York: Princeton Architectural Press, 2000, pp. 171–195. The reference is from pp. 182–183.
9   K. Ross, 'Starting Afresh: Hygiene and Modernization in Post-War France', *October*, vol. 67, no. 23, 1994, p. 34.
10 *Ibid.*, p. 33.
11 *Ibid.*, p. 34.
12 E. Furlough, 'Making Mass Vacations: Tourism and Consumer Culture in France, 1930s to 1970s', *Comparative Studies in Society and History*, vol. 40, no. 2, 1998, pp. 247–286.
13 *Ibid.*
14 A.J. Wharton, *Building the Cold War: Hilton International Hotels and Modern Architecture*. Chicago: University of Chicago Press, 2001.
15 J. Tati (1908–1982) was born into an upper class family of Russian descent. His real surname was Tatischeff. His artistic career started in music halls. In 1945, he started making comedy shorts, such as *L'Ecole des Facteurs* (1947) in which he determined his targets as postwar Americanism and the drive for efficiency and consumerism. The success of *Mon Oncle*, his third feature, allowed him to establish his own production company. But his subsequent film, *Playtime,* brought bankruptcy because of the length of the operation and the size and detail of the set. Unlike many set designers and directors similarly meticulous about their work, and despite his take on architectural modernism, Tati did not have a close relation to the architectural profession. D. Bellos, *Jacques Tati: His Life and Art*. London: Harvill, 1999.
16 L. Fisher, 'Critical Survey', *Jacques Tati, A Guide to References and Resource*. Boston, MA: G.K. Hall, 1983, p. 5.
17 *Ibid.*, p. 25.
18 J. Ockman, 'Architecture in a Mode of Distraction', p. 185.
19 B. Cardullo, 'An Interview with Jacques Tati by Andre Bazin, with the participation of François Truffaut', *Quarterly Review of Film and Video*, no. 19, 2002, pp. 285–298.
    In 1959, Tati visited Yale Drama School and discussed his dissimilarity from Chaplin in a talk he gave. J.K. Simon, 'Hulot, or, The Common Man as Observer and Critic', *Yale French Studies*, no. 23, 1959, pp. 18–25.
20 F. Penz, 'Architecture in the Films of Jacques Tati', in F. Penz and M. Thomas (eds.)

Cinema and Architecture: Melies, Mallet-Stevens, Multimedia. London: British Film Institute, 1997, p. 51.

21   B. Schwabach, 'A Silent Comedy Surrounded by Sound', *New York Times*, Dec 10, 2000, p. 2.26.

22   B. Cardullo, 'An Interview with Jacques Tati'.

23   *Ibid.*, pp. 289–290.

24   Marie writes, 'In an interview for *Les Lettres Françaises* in May 1958, after the release of *Mon Oncle*, Jacques Tati explained that he had not made up his mind as to what his next film would be about, adding that, instead of shooting a film, he would not mind constructing a building'. L. Marie, 'Jacques Tati's *Playtime*'.

25   J. Harding, *Jacques Tati, Frame by Frame*. London: Secker and Warburg, 1984, p. 90–91.

26   *Ibid.*

27   K. Ross, *October*, pp. 23–57.

28   L. Hilliker, 'In the Modernist Mirror: Jacques Tati and the Parisian Landscape', *French Review*, vol.76, no.2, 2002, pp. 318–329.

29   F. Penz, 'Architecture in the Films of Jacques Tati'.

30   J. Harding, *Jacques Tati, Frame by Frame*, p. 22.
     Production took place from October 1964 to October 1967. Filming began in April 1965.

31   *Ibid.*, p. 122. Previously mentioned in B. Maddock, *The Films of Jacques Tati*. Metuchen, NJ: Scarecrow Press, 1977.

32   *Ibid.*

33   B. Maddock, *The Films of Jacques Tati*, p. 79. 'Tati had been steadily de-emphasizing his main character, which became apparent in this film. He had reached a level of comic observation in this film where the masses of people in the street were playing as important a role as Hulot himself. Entire scenes were played with only the incidental appearance of Hulot'.
     P. Gilliatt, *Jacques Tati*. London: Woburn Press, 1976, p. 59. Gilliatt reports, 'Hulot begins to disappear in *Playtime* because everyone is the hero', said Tati. In fact, every now and then in the film, there are glimpses of a back view, hoisted trousers, a furled umbrella, angles of posture that look like Hulot's and turn out to be someone else's'.

34   L. Fisher, 'Critical Survey', p. 39.

35   P. Gilliatt, *Jacques Tati*, pp. 53–54.

36   D. Neuman, 'Playtime', in D. Neumann (ed.) *Film Architecture: Set Designs from Metropolis to Blade Runner*. Munich: Prestel, 1996, p. 142.

37   *Ibid.*

38   L. Fisher, 'Critical Survey', p. 71.

39   L. Marie, 'Jacques Tati's *Playtime*', p. 259.

40   L. Hilliker, 'In the Modernist Mirror', p. 326.

41   *Ibid.*

42   J. Ockman, 'Architecture in a Mode of Distraction', p. 179.

43   *Ibid.*, 182.

44   L. Fisher, 'Critical Survey', pp. 19–21.

45   *Ibid.*, p. 19.

46   *Ibid.*, p. 21.

47   Tati interviewed by K. Thomas in 'Jacques Tati: Silent Comedy's Heir', *Los Angeles Times*, 24 November, 1972, and quoted in L. Fisher, 'Critical Survey', p. 34.

48   K. Thompson, 'Playtime: Comedy on the Edge of Perception', *Wide Angle*, vol. 3, no. 2, 1979, p. 20.

49   *Ibid.*

50   L. Fisher, 'Critical Survey', p. 26.

51   J. Ockman, 'Architecture in a Mode of Distraction', p. 178.

52 *Ibid*, p. 183.
53 *Ibid*, p. 185.
54 *Ibid*, p. 188.
55 L. Marie, 'Jacques Tati's *Playtime*', p. 258.
56 *Ibid.*, pp. 258–260.
57 *Ibid.*
58 G. Debord quoted in *Ibid.*, p. 261. For full text of *Society of the Spectacle* (1967) see, www.marxists.org.
59 L. Marie, 'Jacques Tati's *Playtime*', p. 260.
60 *Ibid.*, p. 263
61 J. Ookman, 'Architecture In a Mode of Distraction', p. 192.
62 W. Benjamin, 'Work of Art in the Age of Mechanical Reproduction', in H. Zohn (Trans.) *Illuminations: Essays and Reflection*. New York: Schocken, p. 237.
63 J. Ockman, 'Architecture in a Mode of Distraction', p. 185.
64 *Ibid.*, p. 192.

Chapter 5

From Postmodern Condition to Cinematic City

The postmodern condition has often been defined as one of fragmentation. If modernity is about a unified narrative, a single, all-pervasive truth, post-modernity is a condition of several narratives, and many simultaneously valid truths. If the modernist city was one with a single centre that held more or less the same meaning for all its inhabitants, the postmodern city offers varied cultural and spatial experiences and no single unified vision.

To discuss the postmodern city necessitates an engagement with postmodern ideas of utopia and dystopia. The idea of a postmodern dystopia may seem self-contradictory. A utopian vision is necessarily singular and ideal, while a postmodern condition accepts that the ideal cannot be the same for everyone. Thus, while a postmodern utopia would appear to be impossible, there is every possibility for a modernist utopia. Indeed, modern-ism – and especially the modernist urban experience as depicted in film – frequently regresses into utopianism.[1] The postmodern condition then only appears dystopic when contrasted with the idealized modern experience.

Attributes of Postmodernity

Time, fragmentation, decentralization, militarization and surveillance are among the most important attributes of the postmodern city. In such a city, utopian aspirations frequently turn into dystopic hell. This chapter will attempt to illustrate these ideas by focusing on cinematic representations of Los Angeles, a city known for having dismantled public space and turned itself into a series of military camps. Every fragmented compartment of this city is ready to defend itself; paranoia pervades, and law enforcement exists to make sure that everybody is accounted for and in his or her place.[2] Mike Davis has argued that this process of militarization is achieved through practices of architectural and spatial separation, and the use of technologically driven surveillance systems. The city is thus divided into spaces that are individually defensible, and all undesirable bodies are forced to huddle together out of sight.

In Los Angeles, fragmentation occurs along class and ethnic lines and is manifested both economically and spatially. The new mode of global economy renders fixity of capital, labour, and resources irrelevant. Harvey has called this 'flexible accumulation', and has explained how it involves circumvention of the vertically organized Fordist economy by employing subcontracting and outsourcing strategies.[3] Steven Flusty and Michael Dear have further used the term 'flexism', as a variant of flexible accumulation to describe the experience of Los Angeles. They have defined this newer term as 'a pattern of economic and cultural production and consumption characterized by near instantaneous delivery and rapid redirectability of resource flows'.[4]

Coupled with the use of new technologies and increased financial centralization, these new flexible processes are controlled by large corporations – especially those that no longer engage in the actual manufacturing. Instead, these corporations exercise control over production processes through a system of subcontracting. The Fordist contract no longer holds for this postmodern condition. One can no longer assume that a worker will automatically become a consumer of the goods that s/he produces within an inclusive economic system. Processes of flexible accumulation also intersect with processes of globalization. The classic relationship between the city, as a centre of production, and the periphery, often the suburbs or the countryside, that owes is existence to Fordist processes, no longer holds. Rather it is the market that is then the 'rational' arena where new forms of social and economic organization take shape. Being rational, the market is also considered naturally 'just', and it is assumed it will mete out justice in the natural course of business. In the postmodern city then, the idea of an unfettered market as an ideal natural system replaces older capitalist ideas and state oversight.[5]

Although it may be a global process, flexible accumulation has an immense effect on the local urban economy and environment.[6] In particular, as capital becomes increasingly mobile, cities must adopt an entrepreneurial approach to governance if they want to prosper. This frequently requires that scarce resources be allocated to creating spectacular events and spaces of consumption, at the expense of services for the poor.[7] Of course, the return on investments in such facilities as stadia, convention centres, and theme parks bound to be short-lived, because the intense competition between cities soon decreases their novelty.[8] As a result, a 'noncontiguous collage of parcellized, consumption-oriented landscapes devoid of conventional centers' has come to replace the Chicago School's model of concentric city form.[9]

What do these new systems of organization mean for the urban landscape? In describing the geography of Los Angeles, Edward Soja has traced the evolution of a series of fragmented communities, cultures and economies that reflect varied divisions of space and power.[10] Key to this process is what Soja has characterized as 'decentralization'.[11] Here, the old core of production – and hence older patterns of employment and urbanism – is challenged; yet, rather than being abandoned, as with late modernity, it is simply restructured.

As an example of these processes, Frederic Jameson has used the Bonaventure Hotel in downtown Los Angeles. He likened the hotel to an enclosed miniature city, in which simulations play against and with each other. In the case of a modernist building, such a disjunction from the surroundings would be deliberate and visibly symbolic. But the Bonaventure's glass skin simply repels the outside by reflecting its surroundings.[12] Thus the Bonaventure fails to engage its surrounds through bold intervention. Rather, it repels them by disengaging from them.

As urban governments turn cities into centres of consumption, their particular innovations – downtown stadia, festival marketplaces, shopping and restaurant complexes – soon circulate and are imitated by other cities. Such centres of differentiated consumption for the wealthy are then sustained through so-called public-private partnerships, often at the expense of the urban poor.[13] The postmodern façade thus often masks spaces of urban decline.[14]

Moreover, the underlying ordering and exploitative mechanisms of patriarchy, race relations, and labour divisions are still present in this new urban landscape, however fragmented and incoherent it may appear. But the politics of these exploitative mechanisms has disappeared from public discourse and come to inhabit more secretive and unaccountable private processes.[15] As Soja believes, 'everything seems to come together in Los Angeles, the totalizing Aleph. Its representations of spatiality and historicity are archetypes of vividness, simultaneity, and interconnection'.[16] Davis has echoed these sentiments in describing the 'militarization' of Los Angeles, where 'armed response' is used to defend luxury lifestyles, repress unwanted movement, and contain undesirable spaces. Davis has also looked to the pop-apocalyptic cinematic narrative for an expression of this kind of urbanism: 'images of carceral inner cities, high-tech police death squads, sentient buildings, urban Bantustans, Vietnam-like street wars…'.[17] In his view, privatization of social control also leads to the disappearance of the 'rhetoric of social welfare' that underpinned the controlling mechanisms of the modern state. In spatial and architectural terms, this has allowed a merger of security and aesthetic concerns in a world of labyrinthine, contained, and closely monitored edifices.[18] Davis has further drawn attention to the fact that it is not only the built environment that has attained a policing function, but the police have armed themselves to control spaces better.[19]

Through the later decades of the twentieth century, conservative social critics called increasingly for the state's withdrawal from all manner of social control, including public welfare and criminal corrections. In the new fragmented landscape of individually policed territories, it was seen as easier to practice mass urban segregation than to pay attention to the needs of the individual.[20] The result has been an urban landscape of racially segregated populations.

Finally, the postmodern city is characterized by the development of highly standardized modes of consumption. Among other things, Clarke has written of how the postmodern city allows the 'reconfiguration of capitalist society as consumer society'.[21] One implication of this transformation is that, while corporations may no longer be manufacturing goods within urban communities, they must still market and ensure the consumption of these goods there. As a result, they invest tremendous energies in producing and maintaining brand identities and constructing sign systems and imagery.

Advertising, rather than fulfilling its original function of promoting products, is now largely concerned with simply creating and manipulating desires and tastes.[22] In such an environment of hyper-commercialism, the ability to consume, in turn, informs the experience of space. As humans, goods, images and signs can all travel faster, flexible accumulation results in space and time compression.[23] But, while the privileged can traverse and consume this world at their ease, others are forced to move in prescribed low-speed, low-prestige routes due to their position in the hierarchy of flexible production processes. While some become increasingly connected via transport and telecommunications networks, others become increasingly disconnected and isolated. Most importantly, however, capital can freely move across this world, setting up new production facilities with the same ease as it abandons old ones, frequently depriving people of their livelihoods in one place while forcing them to migrate to others.

The Cyborg as Postmodern Subject

How can a cinematic subject be created in this landscape of fragmentation and decentralization? Neither the *flâneur* nor the *blasé* can operate in such a space of insidious control and surveillance. Rather it is the cyborg, a hybrid machine and biological organism, first introduced by the feminist scholar Donna Haraway, that emerges as the main actor in this postmodern space. This, however, is not the robot that we saw in the Taylorist spaces of *Metropolis*. It is in fact a new creation that challenges the humanity of urbanites. If postmodern urbanism represents a crisis of cohesion, its subject, the cyborg, represents a crisis in the definition of the living being. Being alive is no longer a result of biological/technological definitions, but a matter of subjectivity.[24] Indeed, the cyborg overcomes the modernist dichotomy of man versus machine.[25]

In her seminal essay, 'A Cyborg Manifesto' (1985, 1991), Haraway argued,

> By the late twentieth century, our time, a mythic time, we are all chimeras, theorized and fabricated hybrids of machine and organism; in short, we are cyborgs. The cyborg is our ontology… The cyborg is a condensed image of both imagination and material reality.[26]

For Haraway, the cyborg is any fusion of the organic and the technological. But these categories are themselves never truly distinct from one another. Cyborgs do not have to be part human, nor evolve from a purely human beginning. Rather, the cyborg comes into being through an exercise of agency that uses technology to enhance human/organic/natural potential.[27] The cyborg exceeds its origins and defies its founding identities, thus blurring the definition of what constitutes self-determination for humans and machines.[28] After Christopher Reeve, the actor famous for portraying Superman, fell from his horse and became paralyzed, he lived some time on life-support machines.[29] As his body was closely integrated with machines, Reeve became an active advocate for greater 'cyborg-ization'.[30] As Chris Hables Gray has suggested, following Haraway, contemporary society is a 'cyborg society'. From pacemakers to vaccinations that re-programme the human immune system, cyborg technology is all pervasive.[31] As Haraway has argued, we are all cyborgs, and Haraway's optimism about the cyborg condition is based on the liberatory potential of technology. The cyborg is the quintessential trope that we need to employ to understand fully the postmodern city. In the two films we will explore in this chapter, *Blade Runner* (1982) and *Falling Down* (1993), the cyborgs are replicants or androids.

Inside the Cinematic Los Angeles

This is where *Blade Runner* comes in. Directed by Ridley Scott,[32] the film is based on the Philip K. Dick (1928–1982) science fiction novel, *Do Androids Dream of Electric Sheep?* (1968).[33] Its main character, Rick Deckard (played by Harrison Ford), is a weary bounty hunter dispatched by a corporation to search for a group of murderous replicants (Leon, Roy, Zhora, Pris) who have escaped from the off-world colonies. Driven by fear of death, the replicants have arrived on Earth to locate and compel their creator to prolong their short life spans.

The film is set in the year 2019 in a Los Angeles that is in physical and psychological decay. [34] In the opening shot, pollution spews out of

Blade Runner (1982). 'Off world' colonies are advertised with the slogan: 'Live Clean'.

smokestacks in an industrial wasteland, and city lights flicker in the misty night air. Futuristic vehicles cruise through a dark sky. At the heart of the city is the pyramidal headquarters of the Tyrell Corporation, a genetic-engineering firm that has become a powerful monopoly by manufacturing replicants who serve as slaves for off-world exploration and colonization. Inside the corporation, Leon, a low-level employee suspected of being an escaped replicant is being interrogated with a Voigt-Kampff test device. The device is used to measure emotional responses by focusing on the iris and evaluating its involuntary fluctuations. Failing the test, Leon kills his tester and runs away.

LA's dark, neon-lit streets are populated by a heterogeneous mix of lower-class people: Asians, Latinos, street gangs, and punks. Amid this crowd, Deckard is approached by a corporation security official who asks him to return to duty to track down escapee replicants. At the Tyrell headquarters, Deckard performs the test on Mr. Tyrell's assistant, Rachael, a test subject. Surprisingly, he determines that she is a replicant – albeit with great difficulty. Upon returning home, Deckard finds Rachael, who aims to persuade him of her authenticity.

Back on the streets, Chew, a specialist in making artificial eyes, offers to take Leon and Roy to meet J.F. Sebastian, a genetic engineer who works for Tyrell. Elsewhere, Sebastian is befriending a hungry and homeless replicant

Blade Runner. The Tyrell Corporation.

Blade Runner. Inside the Tyrell Corporation.

named Pris. Meanwhile, evidence from Leon's flat leads Deckard to search for him in a section of the city called Animoid Row, where synthetic animals are manufactured. Deckard is directed through the crowd to a man named Abdul Ben-Hassan, a replicant-snake manufacturer. Ben-Hassan directs Deckard to a smokey, crowded nightclub called the Snake Pit where Deckard spots Zhora, one of the escapee replicants, and he follows her backstage. But sensing that Deckard is a threat, Zhora unexpectedly attacks him and runs away from him. Deckard chases her through the crowded streets and shoots her in the back. Leon witnesses Zhora's execution. Deckard is informed that Rachael has been added to the list of wanted replicants when he spots her moving through the crowds and traffic. But Leon attacks Deckard before he can reach her. By surprise, Rachael comes to Deckard's defence, and kills Leon. Deckard then corners Rachael and breaks her down with a kiss, instructing her that if she is to appear human she must reciprocate his overtures of physical intimacy.

Back at Sebastian's flat, Roy appears to tell Pris that they are now the only two replicants left alive. During a chess game, Roy and Pris convince Sebastian to smuggle them into Tyrell's headquarters to help them live longer. During a meeting with his creator, Tyrell, Roy confesses that he wants his life extended beyond its built-in four-year span. But Tyrell tells Roy he should be grateful for whatever life span he has. This enrages Roy. He kisses Tyrell passionately on the lips, and then, crushes his skull and gouges his eyes out.

Deckard is informed by car radio of the death of Tyrell and Sebastian. But when he approaches Sebastian's apartment for evidence, Pris attacks him. After a struggle, Deckard kills Pris. Roy, the last remaining replicant, then pursues Deckard. But during the course of the chase, his own life begins to wane. As Deckard is about to slip over the edge of a roof, he mutters 'Kinship?' – perhaps implying that he is also a replicant. Indeed, Deckard shares significant traits with his replicant prey. Both blade runner and replicants have the same feelings: the fear of being hunted.[35] In the voiceover narration that follows, Deckard muses about the replicants' love of life. The corporation officials let Rachael live, thinking that in any case, she had a short life span. Deckard and Rachael leave the city, and in the final scene are seen driving with a light sky in the background.

If *Blade Runner* shows us a Los Angeles of 2019 that suffers the effects of economic fragmentation, outsourcing, decentralization and surveillance, *Falling Down* (1992) – made to appear contemporary and realistic, not futuristic – shows us the effects of ethnic fragmentation, militarization, and the rise of an increasingly privatized world. Directed by Joel Schumacher,[36] the film depicts the rage of a previously privileged white male against the increasingly multi-racial and fragmented society that has made him redundant. The film opens to a typical LA morning commute on a highway. Unable to bear the traffic, the heat, and the stress, the protagonist Foster (played by Michael Douglas) abandons his car and sets off on foot. Yet Foster has no home or work to go to. He's separated from his wife and daughter, and under a court restraining order to stay away. He was recently laid off from his job at a defence plant due to downsizing. Dressed in a white short-sleeved shirt, slacks and tie, and carrying a briefcase, he appears to be a generic white male professional. His car plate reads 'D-FENS', an apt descriptor for his character as it evolves during the movie through a series of encounters with other residents of the city that become increasingly violent.

Foster's first destination is a corner grocery owned by a Korean immigrant. There he finds himself in a confrontation over the cost of an overpriced can of soda. When the Korean proprietor comes after him with a baseball bat, Foster disarms him and proceeds to wreck the shop to give its owner a lesson on price-fixing, inflation and dishonesty. He then

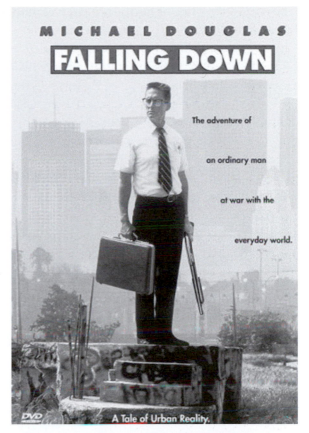

Falling Down (1993).
Film poster.

Falling Down. Los Angeles as a dysfunctional city: traffic jam on the highway.

renegotiates the price of his soda, and leaves with his first weapon, the bat. Foster next crosses into a Latino neighbourhood and is accosted by two Chicano youths. The youths demand his briefcase as a 'toll', and when he refuses to give it to them, they threaten him with a switchblade knife. Using the briefcase and the bat, however, Foster sends them running – and acquires the switchblade, his second weapon. Foster next acquires a sports bag full of pistols and automatics weapons. As he calls his wife on a pay phone, the gang to which the two youths from the last encounter belong roars past in a torpedo-back Chevy, strafing the phone kiosk. But they manage to hit only innocent pedestrians and shop windows. After Foster hangs up, he picks his way through the bodies, and finds that the Chevy has been wrecked against a parked car around the corner. The youths lie sprawled and bloody, their weapons strewn all around. Foster now turns into a true vigilante. He shoots one of the punks in the leg, collects their bag of guns, and walks away.

Falling Down. Foster on the 'turf' of Chicano youths.

After the Korean storeowner files a complaint and news of the shooting gets out, the police become involved. But Detective Pendergast, who is put in charge of the case, has his own problems – a dipsomaniac wife, a demanding mistress who also happens to be a colleague, a boss who despises him, and colleagues who mock him. Yet, he's the one who figures out who Foster is and begins to plot his increasingly violent trajectory across the city.

In a surplus store, Foster next confronts an extreme version of the person he might one day become – a weapons-wielding Nazi. The store owner has been listening to radio reports of Foster's rampage, and welcomes Foster as a kindred spirit in the fight against gays, blacks, Jews, immigrants, and the police. The store owner then offers Foster more lethal weaponry. But Foster is horrified by the store operator's racist attitude. Despite his own earlier racist slurs at the Korean store owner, he does not consider himself a bigot. When he says so, he and the store owner get into a fight. Eventually, the store owner smashes the birthday gift Foster bought for his daughter (a glass snowball). Infuriated, Foster stabs the store owner with the switchblade, and then shoots him.[37]

Falling Down. Foster smashes the grocery store owned by the Korean.

By the time Foster reaches a golf course, he is clearly over the edge and will become more violent at the slightest provocation. At the store he had traded his white shirt and shoes for a black shirt and boots. He has now also armed himself with a missile launcher, which an African-American kid he meets shows him how to use.

In the final scene, the two white men, Foster and Pendergast, face off. Symbolically, they represent two versions of the same past. 'I'm the bad guy – how did that happen?' exclaims Foster, as he stands with his back to the railing of a pier, the ocean behind him. He reaches for his gun, but all

Falling Down. Foster walking through Los Angeles. By courtesy of the UCB Architecture Slide Library

he now has is his daughter's water pistol. With regret, Pendergast shoots at him, and Foster topples backwards into the water. However, falling down into the water does not resolve Foster's personal conflict, leaving the film open-ended.

Like the Los Angeles of *Blade Runner*, the urban landscape Foster traverses is one of fragmentation and social decay. There is no sense of order or any real public space. Neighbourhoods have been taken over by ethnic gangs. The only valid escape comes in privatized spaces such as the golf course, which are possessed by the elite. In other words, there is no space left for a white 'everyman' like Foster.

Cinematic Postmodernity

These two films depict postmodernity according to quite different teleologies. *Blade Runner* depicts a postmodern condition, but it should not be viewed as a postmodern film. Although purportedly set forty years in the future, *Blade Runner* simultaneously depicts a world forty years in the past, owing largely to its *film noir*-inspired sets. As Dietrich Neumann has pointed out, the city it depicts has a history, with buildings from an earlier age that survive amid contemporary mega-structures.[38] In characterizing the Los Angeles of *Blade Runner* as a modernist interpretation of a postmodern condition, David Harvey has also taken issue with its representation of culture.[39] He pointed out that in the film spaces and bodies remain divisible into categories by ethnicity, gender and class, and it is only the blade runner who can traverse these categories. In Harvey's view, the conflicts in *Blade Runner* are between people living in different time scales and spatial resolutions.[40] Although *Blade Runner* provides an evocative portrayal of the condition of postmodernity – and the conflicting experience of space and time on varied scales – the film continues to view this fragmented condition in conventionally unified ways.[41] Similarly, according to Clarke and Doel, this 'account of the postmodern supposedly reflected in *Blade Runner* does nothing less than domesticate it, in line with a thoroughly modernist logic'.[42] A strictly postmodern reading of the film is also flawed because the film presents Tyrell and his corporation as villains, thus critiquing the overpowering apparatus of social and economic power that is a characteristic of the postmodern condition.[43]

In *Blade Runner*, the fragmented landscape of Los Angeles is unified only by the flying pathways for hover cars. This fragmentation is further exacerbated by the fact that people live on different time scales. The replicant's short life spans, in particular, cause them to see and experience the world very differently. As a blade runner, Deckard is in the business of law enforcement, and has the advantage of a top-down view, and he is able to traverse a variety of spaces, from the soaring offices of the Tyrell Corporation, to the streets of Chinatown.

As Scott Bukatman has pointed out, this sense of fragmentation in *Blade Runner* is simultaneously set within an overall sense of order.[44] Although at one level, especially on its streets, this city is complex and constantly changing, at another level or scale, it is dominated by a controlling agency that ensures a balance of order and disorder and, in the end, maintains the status quo of power relations. Here postmodernism is characterized by the insidiousness of power networks that affect all aspects of social and economic life.[45] In *Blade Runner*, the controlling agency is a confluence of the Tyrell Corporation and law enforcement, and Deckard works for both of them.

When Roy, Batty and Leon seek Chew, the 'eye engineer' who runs an outsourcing outlet, Chew indicates that it is the big boss Tyrell who has all the information, and that he is responsible only for providing components to the Tyrell Corporation's genetic programme. Chew is thus part of the apparatus of flexible accumulation; he only produces eyes according to the specifications of the Tyrell Corporation, without any interest or involvement in the final product. Information at higher levels is only controlled by entities such as the Tyrell Corporation. Sebastian is also an independent contractor, designing and producing realistic, genetically designed toys that are sold by the Tyrell Corporation under its own brand name.

In *Falling Down*, which depicts the 'real' Los Angeles, urban fragmentation as a condition of postmodernity is pervasive. The landscape that Foster traverses – ethnic neighbourhoods, abandoned parks, gated communities, and private golf courses – has no sense of unity. The freeway is all that connects the parts of this sprawling non-city. As Carol Clover has pointed out, Foster represents a category of man, the white, male, worker who used to have a place in this city.[46] But this category is no longer the standard against which all other differences are measured.[47] Hence, to Foster, the city seems both unreadable and fragmented.[48]

The Los Angeles of *Blade Runner* is a city of postindustrial decay. The interiors of empty warehouses and abandoned industrial plants drip with leaking rain. Its services are poor, its infrastructure is disintegrating, and vagrants scavenge in its streets. Sebastian, the Tyrell Corporation's genetic designer, lives in an abandoned downtown building, outside which the street seethes with small-scale production, and where a mongrel language (a hybrid of Japanese, German, Spanish, English, etc.) prevails. The streets are populated with various formerly third world people who provide the informal labour that produces the various components that go into the Tyrell Corporation's products.[49]

Above the chaos and decay of street level, there exists a world of zooming transporters and advertising screens selling the products of such large corporations as Coca-Cola and Budweiser.[50] None of these products or advertisements is ever directed to the level of the street. The billboards are meant to be viewed from the hover car. Repeatedly, a Japanese woman advertises products, and a voice urges the inhabitants of this fragmented city to emigrate to off-world colonies.[51] Thus, consumption in this postmodern dystopic city is targeted at the few who can afford it. The rich have all manner of toys, and J.F. Sebastian produces many of them. Sebastian is one of the few who have choice, who have elected to stay on Earth rather than explore the new frontier of the off-world colonies. But he has had to manufacture his own toys for companionship. The only places of entertainment in the central part of the city are sleazy nightclubs of the kind where Deckard finds Pris. The old core of production, the Earth, is thus represented as a place where only the debris of humanity is left to operate. This debris is essential to processes of flexible accumulation. But it is not permitted to enjoy the benefits of the 'off-world colonies', an analogy for the decentralized bliss of postmodern suburbia. The massive pyramidal building of the Tyrell Corporation, however, remains in the city since it must police the system of flexible accumulation that fuels its 'assembly lines'.

Similarly, the landscape of *Falling Down* is amply stocked with standardized consumer products and services: soda, fast food, and guns. They are sold through franchises and small businesses, some run by immigrants. The Whammy Burger represents the retail end of a large organization, and in a sense Foster is expressing his anger at such entities when he complains about the quality of service and the food.

In this world, public space also does not exist; the public park, a site of vagrancy and vandalism, is a travesty of such an institution. Indeed, both *Blade Runner* and *Falling Down* depict cities that no longer coalesce around shared public spaces. Rather, a series of shared images and texts proliferate through various media – television, Internet, electronic billboards, etc. According to Clarke, the postmodern city and society as a whole practices *flânerie*.[52] Bauman has termed the postmodern city a 'managed playground'.[53] Rather than subjects of action, individuals become spectators of increasingly homogenized images. To paraphrase Paul Virilio, the space of multiple screens that projects simultaneously dispersed images, gives this society a sense of 'false cohesion'.[54]

Falling Down has been viewed as portraying the marginalization of the white male in a city where the majority population will soon be Latino. As John Gabriel has stated:

> … it is whites, allegedly, who have lost their rights to employment (through the use of minority quotas), free speech (for example, through the introduction of nonracist guidelines on college campuses and corporations), and their rightful claims to territory and space.[55]

In a sense, Foster is left without a frame of reference. The freeway that once connected the private sphere of the suburban family to the public sphere of the Fordist workplace has been overloaded to the point where it no longer works. Meanwhile, Foster's work has disappeared overseas through outsourcing practices, and his family has disintegrated as a result of the emotional strain this has caused him.[56]

Nevertheless, Elana Zilberg has critiqued *Falling Down* for its inability to provide a complete picture of the displacement of its subjects through space and time. While focusing on Foster's travails, the film ignores the displacement stories of the Latinos and blacks it depicts. For instance, the 'fifteen-second shot in the film of a Latino immigrant selling oranges in a hot dusty crowded inner-city neighborhood' opens a possibility of a different story of postmodernity.[57] Zilberg has argued that both Foster and the Latino immigrants in Los Angeles live within the same global process, though they occupy different places within it. The film fails to bring the (re)Latinization of Los Angeles and the displacement of its Anglo subject into an empathetic relationship because of the 'defensive cognitive map which undergirds its narrative'.[58]

By contrast, in *Blade Runner*, the chaos in the street is tolerated because it is easily controlled. Elements of law enforcement can rapidly descend from their positions of surveillance to ensure that everything is in its place.[59] One is left with a sense that the streets depicted are only a small part of the space controlled by powerful entities such as the Tyrell Corporation. Meanwhile, frequent references to off-world colonies imply that those who are more fortunate may retreat from this chaos. Although the streets are chaotic, they represent a small, easily controlled ghetto, much like those of contemporary Los Angeles.

Davis has suggested that a dominant characteristic of the contemporary postmodern American city is the destruction of any semblance of democratic public space. What we now build are simulacra of public spaces – the nostalgia-driven aesthetic which created the streets and 'town-squares' advocated by the neo-traditionalist/neo-urbanist movement. These spaces, along with 'megastructures and super malls', have replaced the truly public space of the street. Such inward-looking spaces are subject to private surveillance mechanisms and information systems, and access to these networks is what defines and structures the various fragments of the city. This is evident in the Los Angeles of *Blade Runner*.

As Davis has also pointed out, in the Los Angeles of today, 'the ghetto is defined not only by its paucity of parks and public amenities, but also by the fact that it is not wired into any of the key information circuits. In contrast, the affluent Westside is plugged – often at public expense – into dense networks of educational and cultural media'.[60] Davis sees this as an end of the earlier Olmstedian, modernist vision of public space. Although not inclusive either, this vision helped create New York's Central Park as a nineteenth-century 'social safety-valve' where the classes could mix. In the bygone age of industrial modernity, the park was also envisioned as a piece of nature in the city, whose function was to be recreational as well as morally uplifting.[61] The abandoned spaces of *Falling Down* are evidence of the end of this modernist imaginary.

Finally, we must take note that many Los Angeles suburbs have withdrawn their streets from the public domain by turning themselves into 'gated communities'. Access to these communities is restricted by electronic codes, and the largest mansions and their grounds are further wired for 'absolute security'. The desirability of such devices is indicated by the fact they invariably raise property values.[62] In such a city, surveillance takes on a new definition. Law enforcement officers armed with information technology ensure that everything is in its designated place. According to Davis, 'airborne police terror', has replaced the individual police officer on patrol, as law enforcement agencies have become more concerned with categories of people and space than with intimate knowledge of real communities. In the Los Angeles of today, Davis has noted that the police department has an air force equipped with helicopters fitted with night vision cameras that can also register heat images such as from a burning cigarette. In an ironic simulation of Hollywood images of police terror, they practice by swooping down on high-rises in downtown Los Angeles.[63] In *Blade Runner* the hover car exemplifies this quality of technology-driven surveillance. It 'hovers' over the city, ready to swoop down and enforce control at any time.

In 'Time and Space in the Postmodern Cinema', Harvey has argued that conflict in the postmodern era is 'between people living on different time scales, and seeing and experiencing the world very differently as a result'.[64] In his analysis of *Blade Runner*, he noted how the main conflict, that between the Tyrell Corporation (the privileged) and the replicants (the underclasses), has to do with time.[65] Tyrell and his creation and killer, Roy, have different understandings of life precisely because they have different lifespans.[66] The replicants might have a short lifespan but the intensity with which they live it, according to Tyrell, is 'compensation'. A similar conflict underlies *Falling Down*. Like Roy, Foster has been discarded now that his job is done. But Roy's desire is to extend his life beyond what can be expected. Foster, on the other hand, wants to continue his life according to his, and society's former, expectations. Both reveal time in the postmodern city is not simply an objective measure but, rather, a subjective experience, that cannot be dissociated from an individual's role in the urban economy.

The Replicant as the Displaced Subject of Postmodernity

In *Blade Runner*, the Tyrell Corporation is engaged in the business of producing simulacra; genetically produced owls, snakes, and, of course, human replicants. Creative destruction is actively present in the figure of the replicants. They have been created to possess extraordinary powers, but are to be destroyed after a limited lifespan. If they develop feelings or desires, they need to be prematurely retired.[67]

The replicants in *Blade Runner* are all perfect specimens of simulated humanity, and they are all white. By contrast, the 'real' people in the city are all either handicapped or members of ethnic groups. Sebastian is a case in point. Although a mere twenty-five years old, he suffers from a disease called 'Methuselah syndrome' that causes him to age prematurely. However, in *Blade Runner*, human beings are distinguished from replicants on the basis of their authenticity of memory. The replicants have only manufactured histories.[68] Thus, Rachael tries to claim a personal history by producing a picture of herself with her mother.[69] Although they are products of genetic engineering, they carry photographs in an attempt to validate their human selves, since 'to have a past, whether your own or one you have created, is also to have a future'.[70] Photographs are perceived as proof of a real history in the case of the replicant Leon. Likewise, Rachael transcends her category of replicant by her willingness to search for a history and an identity.[71] Thus, the terms 'human', or 'android', are moral, rather than biological definitions:

humans can become human androids by technological enhancement, while androids can acquire humanity by developing empathetic traits.[72] In the film, Deckard questions whether he is not simply an advanced replicant himself. He wonders whether his dreams express a real past or simply planted memories.

Although individualized, the replicants produced by the Tyrell Corporation are mass products. However, as an industrial product, the replicant induces a nostalgia for the authentic, the unique and 'context-bound' product.[73] In their Marxist reading, Doel and Clarke suggested that the replicant is a commodity, and like capital itself, 'dead labor simulating life'.[74] However, by demanding to become human, the replicants refuse to remain as mere objects, and therefore transgress the capitalist contract between humans and their products.[75] Unlike the romantic theology dividing the human and the divine that underlies Mary Shelly's *Frankenstein, Blade Runner*'s narrative accepts the postmodern inevitability of humans creating life from machines. The film, however, treats humans as having 'violated morality and decency by treating their creations as nonhuman'.[76]

The replicants are authentic reproductions, indistinguishable in almost all respects from human beings; they are simulacra, not robots. Walter Benjamin's early nineteenth-century notion of 'aura' addresses some of these same questions. Benjamin emphasized that a quality of 'uniqueness' underlies an object's 'material specificity and history'.[77] But *Blade Runner* imagines a world in which new technologies of human reproduction have substituted plurality for uniqueness. Thus, just as the mechanical reproduction of artwork may destroy the sense of authenticity and uniqueness upon which aura depends, the mechanical reproduction of replicants threatens the sense of individuality that undergirds notions of the human.[78]

Designed as efficient, short-term labour power, replicants are perfectly equipped to adapt to the conditions of flexible accumulation. A Marxist reading of this situation would emphasize that in the manner of all workers, the replicants object to a shortening of their working life, and hence to their four-year lifespan.[79] In *Blade Runner*, the replicant emerges as a product of this dystopic postmodernity. A cold Deckard, with his non-human character, and Roy, with his idealized human traits of striving, vitality, and emotional yearning, ultimately evolve into human beings.[80] In his last moments, Roy meditates on the loss of memories that death will bring; he thus mourns the loss of memory more than life.[81] The act emphasizes how memory, whether real or implanted, may be pivotal for the definition of humanity. So unlike the robot in *Metropolis* whose programme merely goes awry, the replicants of *Blade Runner* desire and ultimately require humanity through experience. They are what the postmodern city needs to function.

As repeatedly mentioned in the film, the Tyrell Corporation has created replicants that are more human than humans. But perhaps the most significant aspect of the production and use of replicants, as far as the postmodern city is concerned, are its implications for labour. The labourer here is not a man or woman, despite appearances, but a machine which acts also as a medium, one that squashes the meaning of labour power itself.[82] Baudrillard reminds us that Benjamin and McLuhan saw that the real message lay in reproduction itself, and that production, as such, has no meaning as 'its social finality gets lost in seriality'.[83]

Falling Down's Foster is part of the same postmodern machinery. He was trained to work in the defence industry according to a pact between the state and the corporation. Even his license plate 'D-FENS' identifies him as an extension of this machinery. However, in his societal function, he is no more than a replicant. And now he's being discarded because there are cheaper and more efficient ways to do his job. Like a cyborg, Foster's technical knowledge also plays a very important role in his capacity to survive this moment. Foster's job as a defence engineer may be considered similar to Chew, the Chinese subcontractor of artificial eyes who works for the Tyrell Corporation. However, Foster's is also different because he loses his job to the overseas subcontractor who, in science fiction, is portrayed as either the Asian body or the replicant. As the city's economy is transforming, Foster is discarded; his job is moved as a result of outsourcing. Foster's story reflects the 'erosion of traditional survival mechanisms in urban communities' due to increased competition and 'urban stress' under flexible accumulation.[84] The allocation of resources to the rich creates economic impoverishment, but also increased class polarization and social stress that are manifested spatially.

While all of these constitute profound changes, 'this postmodern urban process remains resolutely capitalist'.[85] Urban scholars based in Los Angeles[86] forefront the city as the paradigmatic postmodern space and use metaphors such as the 'gaming board' to conceptualize how the city operates. However, it becomes paramount to understand what Los Angeles has become among the hierarchy of cities in a post-industrial era. In 1976, Jean Baudrillard had argued that we live in a system with no fixed determinants, in a world where anything can be anything else, and in a society where everything is either equivalent or indifferent to everything else. These two films produced a few decades later affirm Baudrillard's pessimistic conclusion that in this era dominated by the digital code, the only escape is death, which emerges as the only act without the possibility of return, an act that defies the world of simulacra, models and codes.[87] But this symbolic death of the figures of the postmodern city is not a death of the city itself. On the contrary, the city is alive and well. But it is important to conclude that neither can the arbitrariness of the city, Los Angeles in this case, be generalized as a postmodern condition, nor could its urbanism be naturalized as a postmodern space. Both the cyborg and the discarded human worker are reduced to direct agents of production and consumption in this economy of outsourcing and flexibility and, as a result, they become the significant figures of this new postmodernity. Like Chaplin's tramp, they are small parts within a machinery which they do not control or comprehend. And, if these figures develop the requisite consciousness of their roles within it, and their subsequent enslavement to it, they are left with no choice but to rebel against it. A radical rebellion that allows them to inhabit postmodern space, while totally rejecting the postmodern condition that created the cyborg in the first place, becomes the new radical position that forces us to reconsider the meanings and achievements of earlier forms of modernity.

Notes

1   Y. Chevier, 'Blade Runner or, The Sociology of Anticipation', *Science Fiction Studies*, vol. 2, part 1, March 1984, pp. 51–60, p. 57.
2   M. Davis, 'Fortress Los Angeles: The Militarization of Urban Space', in M. Sorkin (ed.) *Variations on a Theme Park: The New American City and the End of Public Space*. New York: Hill and Wang, 1992, pp. 154–180.
3   D. Harvey, 'Time-space Compression and the Postmodern Condition', in *The Condition of Postmodernity*. Oxford: Blackwell, 1990, p. 284.
4   S. Flusty and M. Dear, 'Invitation to a Postmodern Urbanism', in R.A. Beauregard and S. Body-Gendrot, (eds.) *The Urban Moment, Cosmopolitan Essays on the Late 20th Century City*. Thousand Oaks, CA: Sage, 1999, pp. 24–49. The reference is from page 39.
5   D. Harvey, 'Social Justice, Postmodernism, and the City', *International Journal of Urban and Regional Research*, vol.16, no. 4, 1992, pp. 588–601.
6   D. Harvey, 'Flexible Accumulation through Urbanization: Reflections on "Postmodernism" in the American City', in Ash Amin (ed.), *Post-Fordism: A Reader*. Oxford: Blackwell, 1994, pp. 361–386. The references are to pages 377–379.
7   *Ibid.*
8   *Ibid.*
9   Flusty and Dear, 'Invitation to a Postmodern Urbanism', p. 39.
10 E. W. Soja, 'Taking Los Angeles Apart', in *Postmodern Geographies: The Reassertion of Space in Critical Social Theory*. London: Verso, 1989, p. 244.
11 *Ibid.*, p. 233.
12 F. Jameson, *Postmodernism, or, the Cultural Logic of Late Capitalism*. Durham, Duke University Press, 1991, pp. 40–42.
13 D. Harvey, 'Flexible Accumulation through Urbanization', p. 366.
14 M. Featherstone, 'City Cultures and Postmodern Lifestyles', in Ash Amin (ed.) *Post-Fordism*, p. 401.
15 *Ibid.*, p. 246.
16 *Ibid.*, p. 248.
17 M. Davis, *City of Quartz: Excavating the Future in Los Angeles*. London: Verso, 1990, p. 223.
18 *Ibid.*, p. 224.
19 M. Davis, 'Fortress Los Angeles', *Variations on a Theme Park*, p. 174.
20 *Ibid.*, p. 178.

21   D.B. Clarke, *The Consumer Society and the Postmodern City*. London: Routledge, 2003, p. 4.

22   D. Harvey, 'Time-space Compression', p. 287.

23   D. Harvey, *The Condition of Postmodernity*.

24   V. Casimir, 'Data and Dick's Deckard: Cyborg as Problematic Signifier', *Extrapolations*, vol. 38, no.4, 1997, pp. 279–291.

25   *Ibid.*, p. 290.

26   D.J. Haraway, *Simians, Cyborgs, and Women*. London: Routledge, 1991, p. 150.

27   D.J. Haraway, *Modest_witness@Second_Millenium.FemaleMan_Meets_Oncomous: Feminism and Technoscience*. London: Routledge, 1997, p. 51.

28   *Ibid.*, p. 281.

29   C.H. Gray, *Cyborg Citizen: Politics in the Posthuman Age*. London: Routledge, 2001, p. 1.

30   *Ibid.*

31   *Ibid.*, p. 2.

32   Sir Ridley Scott (1937–) studied photography at London's Royal College of Art in the 1960s. On graduation he started working for the BBC as a set designer. In the 1970s, he worked for his own advertising firm. He then moved to Hollywood where he gained international fame with *Alien* (1977). *Blade Runner* received mixed reviews from film critics in North America when it was released in 1982. However, academics loved it, and it soon gained cult status. Viewed on http://www.imdb.com.

There are five different versions of the film. We are using the US Theatrical Release (1982).

33   P.K. Dick, *Do Androids Dream of Electric Sheep?* New York: Doubleday, 1968.

Dick was born in Chicago and raised in Berkeley, California. In the 1950s, he started his first science fiction pulps. He was prolific between 1959 and 1964, publishing sixteen novels. In the science fiction community, he received an early recognition for his 1963 'The Man in the High Castle', which tells of a world in which Japan and Germany are the victors of the Second World War. However, international fame arrived shortly after his death after the 1983 release of *Blade Runner* which is loosely based on the plot of his 1968 novel, *Do Androids Dream of Electric Sheep?*. The film takes key concepts of the book such as human identity, a recurring theme in Dick's work. Viewed on http://www.philipkdick.com.

The title, 'Blade Runner' comes from a story by Alan E. Nourse. Ridley Scott purchased the rights to the title. Viewed on http://www.brmovie.com.

34   *Do Androids Dream of Electric Sheep?* is set in a future San Francisco of 1992 while the film takes place in LA, in the year 2019. According to the script, the film was to be set in 2020. However it was changed to 2019 to prevent any confusion with the State of California's 2020 vision. Viewed on http://www.brmovie.com.

35   The idea that blade runners were supposed to be without feelings suggests that Deckard may himself be a heartless replicant with implanted memories – a hypothetical theme that keeps reappearing in the film.

36   Joel Schumacher (1939–, US) studied at the Parsons School of Design in New York. He first worked in the fashion industry designing window displays. Then he became a costume designer and moved to TV and cinema. He directed his first film in 1981 (*The Incredible Shrinking Women*). He made *Falling Down*, his eighth film, during an economic recession, when many engineers, who had actually worked exclusively on defence applications in Los Angeles, found themselves unable to deal with unemployment. In his later career, Schumacher went on to direct the Batman series.

37   Viewed on 10 August 2005, http://www.imdb.com.

38   D. Neumann, 'Blade Runner', in D. Neumann (ed.) *Film Architecture: Set Designs from Metropolis to Blade Runner*. Munich: Prestel, 1996, p. 150.

39   D. Harvey, 'Time and Space in the Postmodern Cinema', in *The Condition of Postmodernity*, chapter 18.

40 *Ibid.*

41 S. Aitken and L. Zonn, 'Representing the Place Pastiche', in S. Aitken and L. Zonn (eds.) *Place, Power and Spectacle*. Lanham, MD: Rowman and Littlefield, 1994, p. 10.

42 M.A. Doel and D.B. Clarke, 'Blade Runner, Death and Symbolic Exchange', in D. Clarke (ed.) *The Cinematic City*. London: Routledge, 1997, p. 151.

43 J. Abbott, 'The 'Monster' Reconsidered: *Blade Runner's* Replicant as Romantic Hero', *Extrapolations*, vol. 34, no.4, 1993, pp. 340-350, p. 347.

44 S. Bukatman, 'Blade Runner and Fractal Geography', *Terminal Identity: The Virtual Subject in Postmodern Science Fiction*. Durham: Duke University Press, 1993, p. 134.

45 F. Jameson, *Postmodernism, or, the Cultural Logic of Late Capitalism*.

46 C. Clover, 'White Noise', *Sight and Sound*, no. 5, May 1993, pp. 6–9.

47 *Ibid.*

48 E. Mahoney, '"The People in Parentheses": Space Under Pressure in the Postmodern City', *The Cinematic City*, p. 174.

49 D. Harvey, 'Time and Space in the Postmodern Cinema', pp. 312–313.

50 *Ibid.*

51 S. Bukatman, 'Blade Runner and Fractal Geography', p. 134.

52 D. B. Clarke, *The Consumer Society*, p. 95.

53 Bauman 1993 in *Ibid.*, p. 95.

54 P. Virilio, *The Aesthetics of Disappearance*, Philip Beitchman (trans.). New York: Semiotext(e), 1991, 1980.

55 J. Gabriel, 'What Do You Do When Minority Means You? *Falling Down* and the Construction of "Whiteness"', *Screen*, vol. 37, no.2, 1996, pp. 129–151.

56 E. Zilberg, 'Falling Down in El Norte: A Cultural Politics and Spatial Poetics of the ReLatinization of Los Angeles', *Wide Angle*, vol. 20, no. 3, 1998, pp. 183–209.

57 *Ibid.*

58 *Ibid.*

59 D. Harvey, 'Time and Space in the Postmodern Cinema', pp. 312–313.

60 M. Davis, 'Fortress Los Angeles', p. 155.

61 R. A. Mohl, *The New City: Urban America in the Industrial Age, 1860–1920*. Arlington Heights: Harlan Davidson, 1985, p.75. It was hoped that the parks would be a distraction from grog shops and other activities that were viewed by the institutional apparatus as immoral and undesirable. In the Los Angeles that Foster traverses, there is no institutional apparatus to mediate between him and his rampage.

62 M. Davis, 'Fortress Los Angeles', *Variations on a Theme Park*, p.175.

63 *Ibid.*

64 D. Harvey, 'Time and Space in the Postmodern Cinema', p. 313.

65 *Ibid.*, p. 309.

66 *Ibid.*, p. 313.

67 D. Harvey, 'Time and Space in the Postmodern Cinema', pp. 312–313.

68 *Ibid.*, p. 313.

69 *Ibid.*, p. 312.

70 D. Dresser, 'Science Fiction and Transcendence', *Literature/Film Quarterly*, vol.13, no.3, 1985, pp. 172–179, p. 175.

71 D. Harvey, 'Time and Space in the Postmodern Cinema', p. 312.

72 J. Abbott, 'The "Monster" Reconsidered', pp. 340–350, p. 349.

73 M.A. Doel and D.B. Clarke, 'Blade Runner, Death and Symbolic Exchange', p. 153.

74 *Ibid.*

75 *Ibid.*

76 J. Abbott, 'The "Monster" Reconsidered', pp. 342–343.

77 W. Benjamin, *Illuminations*, Hannah Arendt (ed.), Harry Zohn (trans.). New York: Schocken Books, 1969.

78   V. Shetley and A. Ferguson, 'Reflections in a Silver Eye: Lens and Mirror in Blade Runner', *Science Fiction Studies*, vol. 28, 2001, pp. 66–76, p. 69.
79   D. Harvey, 'Time and Space in the Postmodern Cinema', p. 309.
80   R. Morrison, 'Casablanca Meets Star Wars: The Blakean Dialectics of Blade Runner', *Literature Film Quarterly*, vol.18, 1990, pp. 2–9, p. 4.
81   M. M. Deutelbaum, 'Visual Memory/Visual Design', *Literature/Film Quarterly*, vol.17, 1989, pp. 66–72, p. 68.
82   J. Baudrillard, *Selected Writings*, Mark Poster (ed.). Stanford, CA: Standford University Press, 2001, p. 141.
83   *Ibid.*
84   D. Harvey, 'Flexible Accumulation through Urbanization', p. 377.
85   S. Flusty and M. Dear, 'Invitation to a Postmodern Urbanism', p. 46.
86   S. Flusty and M. Dear are part of this school for example.
87   J. Baudrillard, *Selected Writings*, p. 5.

Chapter 6

Voyeuristic Modernity: The Lens, the Screen, and the City

In an era when cameras and other systems of surveillance are ubiquitous in both public and private spaces, the boundaries of the city are no longer defined by monumental entrances, but by electronic devices. The constricting walls of medieval towns have been replaced by the recording of images. The French philosopher Paul Virilio has argued that with the proliferation of images, the 'opacity of building materials is reduced to zero', creating a city where everyone and everything can be seen inside out.[1] The screen and the lens become new modes through which the city is experienced and policed, leading to a 'revision of point of view and a radical mutation of our perception of the world'.[2] This new point of view is mediated through the virtual media, which appear as an alternative to the physical experience of the city. In this virtual city, the physical spaces are overlaid with, or replaced by, the virtual image. According to Virilio, 'the screen abruptly became the city square, the crossroads of all mass media'.[3]

The transparency of the virtual city has been created primarily through a grid of surveillance systems that aim to exclude the dangers of urban life from the lives and spaces of the wealthy. Mike Davis has argued that in Los Angeles, 'the defense of luxury lifestyles is translated into a proliferation of … physical security systems, and collaterally, with architectural policing of social boundaries'.[4] In this environment, the camera – operated by the media, the state, and the private security company – also becomes a tool for recording the violence of the city. According to Davis, the media 'carelessly throw up specters of criminal underclasses' as a means to 'bury and obscure the daily economic violence of the city'.[5] Meanwhile, the police have adopted 'technologized surveillance and response' as a strategic means of social control. New technologies, particularly aerial surveillance, have eclipsed the importance of 'the traditional patrolman's intimate "folk knowledge" of the city'.[6]

Such a 'new epistemology' exemplifies the panopticon as a tool for knowing and controlling behaviour. Jeremy Bentham first proposed the panopticon in the late eighteenth century as a model for a prison that would maximize the state's ability to modify the behaviour of prisoners. Its defining architectural feature was an arrangement of individual cells that would all be visible from a single command tower. In this model, surveillance would be constantly present, exposing the object of discipline to constant view. According to Foucault, it is this 'conscious and permanent visibility that assures the automatic functioning of power'.[7] In this scheme, 'visibility is a trap' which allows a single observer to control the behaviour of others remotely, extinguishing the need to apply physical punishment.[8]

In dystopian visions such as George Orwell's *1984* (1949) and the films discussed in Chapter 3, this panoptic apparatus is applied generally upon an entire society through two-way screens placed in both public and private spaces. Using this mechanism, a remote authority can monitor large masses of people, and modify behaviours through occasional reprimands from the screen or interventions by security forces on the ground. In the same way, Foucault has argued that the principle of the panopticon may act not as a 'schema for exceptional discipline', but as a 'generalized surveillance' by which the 'basic functioning of society is penetrated through and through with disciplinary mechanisms'.[9]

The surveillance state within the city of Los Angeles, as described by Davis, exemplifies this power of the image to control. However, in the 'overexposed city', a label coined by Virilio, this power to view is not limited to the state, but is extended both to private corporations to protect property and to individuals for their own personal pleasure. Thus, in an age in which direct views have been replaced by screen views, the figure of the *flâneur* is reborn and magnified as the voyeur. The voyeur behind the screen or camera lens, like the *flâneur*, adopts the gaze as a means of knowing. However, the voyeur differs from the *flâneur* in his invisibility. He no longer occupies the spaces he observes, but remains physically remote, a 'Peeping Tom' behind the cloak of his technological devices. Although the city is exposed to him, he gains power by retreating into the panopticon's opaque centre.

The perspective of the *flâneur* is normally thought to be exclusively male. Indeed, Elizabeth Wilson has questioned whether the *flâneuse*, a woman of the city streets, could ever enjoy the same position.[10] In particular, she has argued that despite the public presence of women in the city as journalists, prostitutes and shoppers and the new openness of urban spaces, women still do not share the same experience of the city. Instead, their activities remain commodified by their roles both as consumers and consumed, and they are limited by ideals that continue to restrain them within the domestic sphere. Thus, she believes, the 'male gaze' still defines the *flâneur* and the voyeur, articulating a new 'modern sexual economy'. Wilson has argued, however, that the modern technology of voyeurism, as exercised through the Internet and reality shows on television, has partially democratized this arena, at least in terms of access.

This chapter will examine the voyeur as an emblematic character of the 'exposed city', who takes 'visual possession of the city' using new technologies, and observes new social phenomena. The films discussed here will chart the way in which the lens and the screen have been utilized in response to the changing conditions of urban life. In Alfred Hitchcock's *Rear Window* (1954), a housebound journalist gazes from his window into the courtyard to watch beautiful women and spy upon his neighbours.[11] The lens is thus depicted as a tool for both pleasure and security. This dual purpose of the gaze is also depicted in Phillip Noyce's *Sliver* (1993), in which the internal surveillance system of a New York apartment complex is co-opted as a personal pleasure theatre by the building's owner.[12] Last, in Wim Wenders's *The End of Violence* (1997) surveillance systems are examined within a larger social context involving the social production and control of violence and fear.[13] All three of these films address power inequalities that arise when one person or group has access to views of another, and is able to project their own meanings and interpretations upon the images they collect. Although there are many films that deal with the phenomenon of voyeurism in urban society, these three films provide insight on two distinct urban periods. *Rear Window* presents New York at the height of modernity, while both *Sliver* and *The End of Violence* capture New York and Los Angeles in the mid-1990s, an era of postmodern urban discourse.

A Courtyard in Greenwich Village

In *Rear Window*, Hitchcock tells the story of a mysterious murder in New York of the 1950s through the eyes of a voyeur who uncovers clues by spying on his neighbours. The main character, L.B. Jefferies, also called Jeff (played by James Stewart), is an injured photojournalist, who is confined to a wheelchair for seven weeks with a broken leg. During the final week of his internment, Jefferies has nothing to do but look out of his window, often using binoculars, watching his neighbours in the courtyard behind his Greenwich Village apartment building. Each window in the surrounding buildings provides a view into the lives of its inhabitants.

Jeff's only social interaction during his confinement is an occasional call from his boss and visits from his nurse Stella and his girlfriend Lisa Freemont (played by Grace Kelly). During his interaction with his visitors, Jeff reveals that he is uninterested in marriage, fearing that he will be unable to live his desired life of travel and adventure if tied down in a relationship. Lisa, on the other hand, is hoping to convince Jeff to settle down with her in New York. As the couple struggles to define their relationship, the neighbours displayed in the windows around the courtyard reflect their hopes and fears for the future. In particular, one of Jeff's neighbours, Thorwald, is an unhappily

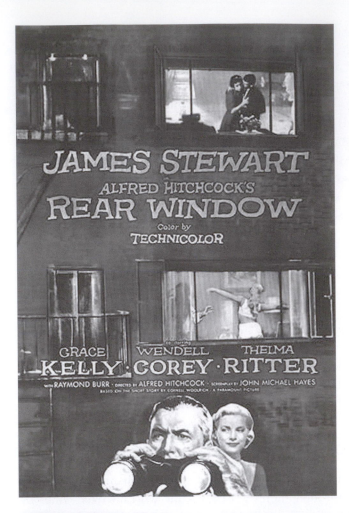

Rear Window (1954). Film poster.

Rear Window. Jeff is able to see what others cannot.

married salesman with an invalid wife. Jeff argues that if he began 'rushing home to … a nagging wife' (like Mrs. Thorwald), he would 'never be able to go anywhere'.[14]

One night Jeff sees Thorwald acting suspiciously, leaving the apartment several times in the middle of the night with his large briefcase. The next morning there is no sign of his wife, and Jeff begins to suspect that Thorwald has murdered her. He watches Thorwald as he cleans his knives, and as he has a large wooden box removed from the apartment. With the help of Stella and Lisa, Jeff continues to observe Thorwald, weaving evidence of wrongdoing into possible explanations of the murder. As their suspicions increase, Jeff calls upon Thomas J. Coyne, an ex-army buddy, now employed as a police detective, to investigate the murder. Coyne is unable to corroborate any of Jeff's observations, and instead reports reasonable explanations for each of the suspicious behaviours. He explains that Mrs. Thorwald has travelled to see her parents, and that the trunk, on route to their home, has been examined and contains no suspicious materials. Jeff and his companions are prepared to forget the mystery and return to their own lives, when they hear a shriek from the courtyard. A woman has found her dog lying motionless in the courtyard. All the neighbours come to the windows to see what has happened, except Thorwald who sits suspiciously in his dark apartment smoking a cigarette.

Jeff and Lisa resume their 'investigation' with renewed zeal. No longer satisfied to merely watch and wonder, they seek to analyse his actions. Lisa even enters his apartment to search for evidence. But when she is caught in the act and screams for help, Thorwald notices that she gestures toward Jeff's window. As Lisa is arrested, Thorwald leaves his apartment unnoticed, in order to confront Jeff. He enters Jeff's dark apartment and asks menacingly, 'What do you want?' Jeff uses his camera flash to blind Thorwald, stalling him until the police arrive. As Jeff calls out to the detective, Thorwald tries to strangle him, and the men struggle. Jeff is pushed out the window, and falls, breaking another leg. Thorwald is taken into custody after confessing to murdering his wife. In the end, Jeff is shown back in his apartment, sleeping with two broken legs, while Lisa sits nearby, pretending to read.

In *Rear Window*, the entire story takes place in Jeff's Greenwich Village apartment building, making the set a star in itself.[15] The courtyard was designed from photographs taken of real buildings that fit *Hitchcock*'s specifications for a setting with views of the sky and the city.[16] The courtyard is shown to consist of many buildings built intermittently, creating a 'labyrinth' of fire escapes, balconies, alleys and gardens. These features fragment the courtyard into many semi-private spaces, rather than one unified public space.[17] The stage set included thirty-one apartments; however, the story centred around eight apartments inhabited primarily by artists. These residents depict a slice of life, exhibiting the many professions of the art world, and different relationships. The single residents include an alcoholic musician, a friendly sculptress, an exhibitionist dancer, and a lonely middle-aged woman – the last two of whom Jeff respectively calls 'Miss Torso' and 'Miss Lonelyhearts'. The building houses several couples, including newlyweds, an old married couple with a dog, and Thorwald and his invalid wife.

Rear Window. The courtyard view from Jeff's apartment.

Rear Window. The courtyard reflected in Jeff's lens.

The residents of these apartments are generally depicted as living lonely or unhappy lives, estranged from their neighbours, and at times even from their lovers. Miss Torso is surrounded by men, but she is not interested in any of them; instead, she waits for her lover to return from the army. Miss Lonelyhearts dines with an imaginary boyfriend, too timid to interact with real men. Later, when she does invite a man back to her apartment, she throws him out after he makes a sexual advance. Even married couples are shown to be alone. In a manner that would recur in Tati's *Playtime* a decade later, Thorwald and his wife are to be emotionally disconnected, inhabiting separate rooms. The only residents who appear to be happy are the older couple; however, their relationship is depicted as sterile, as they have replaced their absent children with a dog.[18]

Rear Window. Viewing the neighbours' private lives.

The courtyard is a vigorous environment open to the conduct of everyday life. In the background, we hear a woman singing, the piano playing, children laughing. All this contributes to a sense of the courtyard as an active modern social space. However, beneath the 'superficial bustle' of the neighbourhood, John Fawell has argued that, there remains an 'underlying despair'.[19] In the courtyard, the neighbours go about their business without interacting socially. When the sculptress tries to give Thorwald advice on his rose garden, he rebukes her angrily. After the scene where the older woman finds her dog dead, she calls out to the neighbours: 'Which one of you killed my dog? You don't know the meaning of the word neighbor! Neighbors like each other, speak to each other, care if anybody lives or dies. But none of you do'.[20]

Fawell has further argued that *Rear Window* serves as a 'commentary on the alienation of urban life'.[21] In overview shots that show all the neighbours in their apartments, windows divide them from one another, and their simultaneous proximity and isolation accentuates the feeling of loneliness.[22] Thus, in *Rear Window*, Hitchcock depicts the alienation of modern urban life and the *blasé* attitude associated with it. In a community in which privacy is inhibited by proximity, and by the heat which necessitates open windows, neighbours withdraw from social engagement. However, a series of visual and auditory interruptions are shown to create inevitable conflict.

Behind the Surveillance Camera

In *Sliver*, New York of the 1990s is again depicted as a city where murders remain unsolved, and where amateur sleuths spy upon their neighbours with both pleasure and suspicion. A recently divorced book editor, Carly Norris (played by Sharon Stone), moves into an apartment in Manhattan, in which the former tenant died under mysterious circumstances. Several of the building tenants befriend Carly, including Zeke Hawkins (played by William Baldwin), Vida Jordan, and Jack Lansford, a successful author of crime novels.

One morning, as Carly is jogging, Jack sneaks up behind her. Although irritated, Carly talks to him because she wants to hear about Naomi, the tenant she replaced. Another neighbour, Vida, informs her later that day, shortly before being murdered himself, that Carly bears a startling resemblance to the deceased former tenant. A series of strange occurrences follows. First, Carly receives a telescope from a secret admirer. Reluctantly, she comes to derive pleasure from using it to peek into others' private lives. Then, both Zeke and Jack show up to her flat-warming party without having been invited, and they both ask her out on a date. Only Zeke gets a positive response; Carly has to cajole Jack to leave.

Carly agrees to accompany Zeke to the building's gym on the condition that there are not too many mirrors there. When she arrives, she discovers that, despite Zeke's claims, the room is indeed filled with mirrors, and she must become accustomed to watching herself. After working out, Carly and Zeke return to his apartment to make love. He reveals his secret, that he is the owner of the building, and that he was the one who sneaked into her apartment to give her the telescope. At work, Zeke then uses his skills as a videogame programmer to hack into Carly's computer to send her love messages. Carly seems to enjoy being the focus of Zeke's attention.

Carly next witnesses a dispute between Jack and Vida. Later, she discovers Jack leaning over the body of a brutally murdered Vida. Jack sneaks into Carly's apartment to persuade her of his innocence, blaming Zeke instead.

Mysteriously, however, Zeke arrives at Carly's to break up the increasingly tense *tête-à-tête*. As it turns out, Zeke has witnessed the confrontation through the video-surveillance system he installed in all the apartments. Zeke invites Carly into the surveillance control room attached to his apartment, where dozens of monitors display what is occurring in each of the building's apartments. Carly is initially shocked and angry about the intrusion upon the residents' privacy. However, as she watches the drama of people's everyday lives, she becomes transfixed by the views on the screens. She watches as her neighbours fight, make love, and as a young girl tells her mother that she is being sexually abused by her stepfather. As she becomes engrossed, as if by a soap opera, Carly becomes uncomfortable with the ethics of their position. She questions their responsibility for reporting events that put people in danger. Zeke later calls Carly at work to tell her he has anonymously threatened the stepfather. She comes home and watches as the man asks the girl nervously who she has told about her abuse. He apologizes and promises to stop abusing her. Carly feels empowered by her ability to watch and then control the events around her.

Zeke and Carly do not just watch others as spectacle, but also create spectacles for others to witness. At a restaurant, Zeke initiates a sex game, encouraging Carly to give him peeks at the new underwear that he has bought for her. She experiences a rush of adrenalin as she exposes herself in public. However, she is also uncomfortable with her exhibitionist role, seeming to act less for her own pleasure than to prove to herself and Zeke that she can take risks.

Sliver (1993). Carly is seduced by the equipment of voyeurism.

Later, Carly becomes suspicious of Zeke when she realizes he has videotaped their own sexual adventures. While Zeke is out getting them dinner, she finds tapes of his past lovers including Naomi, the deceased former tenant, and Vida Jordan. She searches frantically to try and find tapes of the murders occurring, but is interrupted when Zeke returns early. Terrified that he is the killer, Carly tries to lock Zeke out of the control room, and defends herself with a pistol. Meanwhile, the tape of Naomi's murder plays, revealing that it is Jack who was the killer. Carly turns the gun away from Zeke, and instead shoots up the television screens, destroying his control room. She ends her romance with Zeke and her brief flirtation with the joy and the power of voyeurism by advising Zeke to 'Get a life!'

Sliver takes place in New York City, in a high-tech, high-rent apartment complex with luxury amenities to ensure the residents' comfort and security. As in *Rear Window*, this building is a popular residence for artists. However, unlike the traditional New York urbanism represented by the Greenwich Village courtyard in *Rear Window*, this building represents late-modern residential architecture. The social centre of the community is not a court-yard but the elevator. Like the courtyard, the elevator/stairwell is a space of encounter, where anonymous neighbours are forced to confront one another. However, unlike *Rear Window*, this film depicts the residents as relatively extroverted, striking up conversations in the building's common spaces – even if this surface friendliness is only a mechanism for coping with the burden of urban living. Meanwhile, the residents have a greater expectation of privacy from their neighbours than in *Rear Window*. The outward-facing windows, climate-controlled interior, and soundproof walls eliminate many of the accidental intrusions upon privacy that occur in Hitchcock's film. However, behind these private walls, the neighbours continue to live complex, secret lives, and the surface friendliness often hides uncomfortable and dangerous interactions between.

Both *Rear Window* and *Sliver*, are concerned with 'windows' into people's secret lives and behaviours. However, in the latter film the real window has been replaced by video surveillance, the 'sliver' that opens up the view. Zeke's control room acts as a panopticon from which he can peek into the everyday dramas of ordinary people's lives. Like Jeff, Zeke spends the majority of his time at home. However, unlike Jeff, he is not incapacitated, but at home by choice. And, as a computer programmer, he often works from his apartment. Zeke is a product of a new system of work management, in which employees no longer have regular face-to-face contact with their offices. Zeke also does not socialize with anyone outside the apartment building; his primary relationships are with the women tenants there. Thus, for Zeke, the act of voyeurism has replaced reciprocal interaction with the world around him.

This late-modern phenomenon reflects many aspects of the urban space

Zeke inhabits. In the city outside, a mixing of traditional public and private spaces has created new forms of hybrid experience. Zeke is thus able to experience the space of the city virtually from his own private sphere, and only secondarily as real social or physical space. It is this alienation from reality that differentiates Zeke's position as a voyeur from Jeff's. Zeke does not watch to judge and apprehend the criminal; instead, he is detached from the consequences of the violence and sexuality he witnesses. He is a prime example of Wilson's urban resident whose 'committed emotion cedes to irony and detachment'.[23]

Screening the Fears of the City

In the third film examined here, *The End of Violence*, Wim Wenders depicts Los Angeles as a city where alienation has led to violence, class division, and fear of the other. The main character, Mike Max (played by Bill Pullman) is a producer of bloody action films who is so involved in his career that he has become estranged from his personal life. He ignores his wife Page (played by Andie MacDowell), who has become so depressed that she is unable to follow through on her threats to leave him. One day, Mike is kidnapped after receiving a mysterious email from the FBI containing information about a secret surveillance system. Two hit-men take him under a freeway exchange, where they plan to shoot him. However, the men disagree over whether to go through with the hit or spare Mike's life. In the end, they appear to shoot each other.

This mysterious sequence is left unresolved, and the film cuts to another character, Ray Barring (played by Gabriel Byrne), who has seen the kidnapping. Ray's job is to monitor the video screens at an FBI crime prevention facility. He witnesses the preceding events from an aerial surveillance camera; however, he is unable to see their final outcome when

The End of Violence (1997). Ray in the control room.

his feed is cut by interference. The next morning the men are found dead, and since Mike fled the scene, he is pursued as a suspect.

Later, Max is found by his Latino gardeners in an injured and semi-conscious state. After he declines their offers to take him to a hospital or to his house, they take him to the home of one of the gardeners, Ramon, where he eventually hides out for many months. Both his hosts and the film audience remain uncertain, however, if he fears being killed or arrested if he is discovered. At Ramon's, Mike seems now to transform into a simple man who prefers hard work and family meals to his past life as a busy, self-centred businessman. Although Mike does return to his house several times, he makes no effort to reunite with his wife.

On one trip to the house Mike retrieves his Palm Pilot in an attempt to discover what the secret FBI message contained. He discovers that the message has been erased, but that the sender, Ray, had also contacted Mike's secretary to warn him of danger. Ray, a computer communications expert, had developed a surveillance project as part of a secret government plan to end all violence. Although Ray was already testing the equipment, its use had not been approved by Congress or the public. Disturbed by the implications of the technology for civil liberties, Ray had begun to search for someone to whom he could reveal his secret work. Ray chose to confess the details of the project in the mysterious email to Mike, who had expressed curiosity about the technology earlier that year. Ray's superior discovered that Ray had leaked information about the project, and had tried to have Mike killed to keep it secret.

While Mike has been in hiding, Ray has discovered, when he is able to recover the surveillance film of the shooting, that Mike was a target . On the film, he also discovered how after the two hit-men abandon their duty, an unseen weapon aims at and misses Mike, but kills the other men. However, when the police officer investigating the shooting tries to meet Ray, Ray

The End of Violence. Surveillance cameras watch over the city.

is shot before he can reveal this information. At the end of the film, the surveillance project is presumed to continue and expand unimpeded. But the audience is left to wonder about its implications and whether it can truly 'end violence'. Mike, however, is depicted as having been 'saved'. He is reborn to actual experience and interaction with people, disconnecting from his former addictions to virtual experience and the power to shape reality.

The End of Violence's Los Angeles is an anti-social city, a hostile environment where people are alienated from one another. Seen primarily from a distance, through the surveillance cameras, it features hard surfaces and an inhumane scale. However, close up, it is a place where people are lonely and afraid. Even when people gather, they do so to share their pain and fears. Thus the members of a poetry group narrate their personal experiences with the hard edges and violent relationships of the city. The film also depicts a number of characters who are so busy they have lost touch with their families, and have replaced emotional relationships with legalistic interactions. Mike is typical of these people. He claims not to trust anyone, saying that he is 'always ready for a sudden attack'. As a hermit, his relationships appear contractual, a series of compromises made without emotional content. Thus, while Page must call him on the phone from downstairs in his own house to get his attention, he dedicates time to visit one of his actresses at the hospital for the purpose of mitigating a possible lawsuit. Mike's interactions are exemplary of what Paul Virilio has called the 'production of distance in discussions', in which people at great distance can be virtually materialized, while those in close physical proximity recede into the background.[24] Other characters, such as Ray, are also shown to be lonely and socially disconnected. Ray lives alone with his aged father. The only social interaction he has beyond this is with the maid at the observatory who, unbeknownst to him, is hired to spy on him.

This Los Angeles is a city of great class division, where the rich and the poor live both geographically and culturally distinct lives, often requiring police protection and surveillance. The rich, such as Mike, live in luxurious

The End of Violence. Looking over the city from the observatory.

homes in the hills, with views of the city or the ocean. Nevertheless, these people are spatially and emotionally distant from one another. On the other hand, poorer families, such as the Ramons, live in small homes and come together each evening over dinner. In this way, the richness of Latino culture, which values tradition, religion, and family, is romanticized to contrast the sterility of upper-class Anglo culture.

In Wenders's Los Angeles, people are afraid of the unknown – of strangers or unseen enemies who may inflict violence upon them. At one point, Mike states that he has 'turned a fear of strangers into a multimillion-dollar enterprise', arguing that in the movie business, 'paranoia is our number one export – everyone needs an enemy'. Thus, Wenders depicts a city that uses cameras both to create and overcome its own fear of violence. The virtual city created by Hollywood is one that exaggerates violence, that capitalizes on people's fears in order to sell them a happy ending. On the other hand, the government surveillance system, aims to 'end violence' and control it by observing the city's inhabitants in their everyday lives. Ostensibly, the FBI is developing the project to 'cut down response time' to crime, by identifying and suppressing violent activity more quickly, but its motivation reveals the desire to create a utopian space free of violence. In the process, however, an oppressive landscape of surveillance and control is created, where men must die to protect the source of the government's knowledge and power. The film thus opens a discussion on a number of contemporary issues that have emerged in the real city in recent years, such as the role of surveillance

The End of Violence. Security men look over the highways.

cameras in identifying the terrorist bombers of the London Underground in July 2005, and their later installation in the New York subway system. It thus indicates how life now imitates art, and how the virtual has become the frame of reference for the real.

In *The End of Violence*, the media and the government use similar technologies to achieve contradictory ends. For its part, the film industry fans the flames of fear and hatred through the invention of violent enemies. Davis has argued in this regard that security mobilization itself leads to fear, and he has suggested that it is the security-mania provoked by violent films, rather than crime itself, that perpetuates the 'social perception of threat'.[25] Meanwhile, the police seek to acquire ever more accurate knowledge in order quickly to apprehend and eliminate these largely fictitious enemies. Indeed, at the beginning of the film Mike questions whether these enemies really exist: 'I came to realize there were no extras or strangers, just a strange world'.[26] In this comment, Mike also uses the virtual world as a referent by which to judge the real world. Thus, he hints at the way Los Angelinos experience their city as if they are the heroes in a film and as if the crowds of people around them are all extras – or possible villains. Virilio has called Los Angeles 'the city of the living cinema where stage sets and reality, tax plans and scripts, the living and the living dead, mix and merge deliriously'.[27]

The Virtual Spectacle as the Enticement for the Real

In these three films, the virtual evocation of the spectacle in the window frame, the camera lens, or the screen serves as an allusion that calls forth the real world. Viewing and fantasizing does not directly replace actual experience or interaction, but instead serves as a referent to and enticement for the physical. In these films, the sexuality and violence in the virtual world, serves as a means of both inciting desire for action or dispelling it.

In *Rear Window*, Jeff projects both his fantasies and fears onto the world outside rather than acting upon these feelings with Lisa in his own apartment. Staring at the figures of the women across the courtyard, he 'would rather look than love', opting for 'a one-way relationship based on voyeurism'. [28] He thus displaces his sexual desire into the virtual realm, to avoid the danger of emotional entanglement in a complicated relationship with Lisa. He is better able to sympathize with the sorrows of these anonymous women than communicate with his girlfriend directly.[29] Thus, fantasy and reality are shown to be at odds, as Lisa must objectify herself to attract Jeff's attention from the 'show' outside. Laura Mulvey has argued that voyeurs become fixated on the erotic pleasure of looking, and thus their 'only sexual satisfaction can come from watching, in an active and controlling sense, an objectified other'.[30] In *Rear Window*, it is only after Jeff watches Lisa from afar, and becomes an audience to her being attacked, that his attention becomes focused upon her. Similarly, in *Sliver*, Zeke uses his surveillance system as a virtual dating service, first consuming the images of women from a distance before deciding to pursue them sexually. His temporary relationships with these women are also recorded on film, and immortalized. Thus, for Zeke the sexual act must be enticed and recorded through the virtual realm in order to be satisfying. In these films the view both replaces and incites the sexual desire.

Similarly, the virtual realm is a place in which violence is both assuaged and provoked. In *Rear Window*, the act of imagining and apprehending a murderer serves as a release for Jeff. Even Lisa, constrained by her attachment to Jeff, shares his 'desire for violence' and expresses guilt over such feelings. In *Sliver*, although Zeke does not seem to welcome the violence he observes through his monitors, his silence reveals his desire for violence above all else.

Such questions of 'rear window ethics' are expanded when the voyeurist activity is no longer limited to individuals, but involves the greater public. In *The End of Violence*, Mike makes violent films that feed upon the fears of the public, and that fulfil their audiences' need to act out aggressions in the virtual realm. Thus, the films reflect and provide an outlet for the violence of the culture. Meanwhile, the government surveillance project does not merely record violent events, but requires that the state try to arrest criminals before their crimes can occur. In both cases the virtual realm does not merely reflect society, but is mutually constitutive of it. The images are forms of action, that require responses that may or may not perpetuate further violence.

The Gaze of Pleasure and Control

These three films depict the way in which the gaze, with the aid of technology, may serve as a method of control. The gaze is a source of knowledge and power over others that may be employed by different agents for different means. In the modern dystopian visions discussed in Chapter 3, the idea of the panopticon, as imagined by Bentham and Foucault, has been appropriated by the state to control society at large. In these visions, government officials occupy the place of power at the centre, and control how knowledge is employed. In the films examined here, however, this power is privatized.

In *Rear Window*, the power of the gaze is personalized, as Jeff surveys his neighbours with the supposed intent to identify and punish a murderer. The state in this film is represented by Jeff's police buddy Thomas J. Coyne, who is more hesitant to snoop into people's private lives. As Coyne admonishes Jeff: 'That's a secret private world you're looking into there. People do a lot of things in private they couldn't explain in public'.[31] He then recites the amendments and laws which prevent the state from engaging in unsanctioned surveillance. Robert J. Corber, in a book on national security, has in fact argued that Jeff's personal surveillance is a 'political act'. It paralleled the power of individuals during the Cold War to criminalize their neighbours through accusations to the House Committee on Unamerican Activities.[32] According to Corber, in the 1950s voyeurism was no longer considered 'a private form of erotic pleasure but a mode of political behavior intended to expose potential enemies of the state'.[33] Thus in *Rear Window*, Jeff's desire for visual pleasure is excused as a public service: to solve a crime.

In *Sliver*, the state is depicted as unable to protect citizens and apprehend criminals. As a result, security has had to be privatized using high-tech surveillance systems to protect the wealthy residents from the outside world. Davis has called this design strategy the 'fortress effect', in which entire residential neighbourhoods are 'partitioning themselves from the rest of the metropolis'.[34] However in the film, Zeke commandeers the privatized surveillance system for his own personal entertainment. Thus, in the neoliberal state of 1990s, the supposed need for public surveillance has been co-opted as a private instrument of pleasure.

Mulvey has termed Jeff's motivation – the pleasure derived from the voyeuristic gaze – 'scopophilia'. As a professional photographer and a Peeping Tom, he has turned the act of looking into both a hobby and a livelihood.[35] Similarly, *Sliver*'s Zeke employs the gaze for pleasure as he spies upon his neighbours. But he controls his view from a privileged position and so does not have to justify it. The difference between Jeff and Zeke's modes of surveillance is informed by a forty-year gap between the making of the two films. The design of the courtyard in Rear Window enables and promotes the reciprocal sociability of residents across the yard (though they might choose not to), but Zeke's building is designed with one-way visibility in mind. This difference represents a real change in the form of the city based on increased demand for privacy.

It is important to note that we cannot talk about surveillance as having a truly panoptic effect in either of these two films, as the observed do not know that they are being observed. Both Zeke and Jeff also tread a fine line between being voyeurs and becoming participants in the dramas they watch and consume. In the beginning of *Rear Window*, Jeff is content merely to enjoy the view of his 'bathing beauties'. However, as he begins to interpret and act upon what he sees, his position changes to that of a 'provocateur'.[36] Thus, Jeff incites Thorwald into action and has Lisa investigate his apartment, moving from merely observing to intervening in the lives of those around him. In *Sliver*, Zeke has access to tapes that reveal who the killer is, and at first does not take action to expose him. However, when Zeke and Carly discover that a girl in the building is being sexually harassed, they act upon this knowledge to try to stop further incidents. Here, the scopophilic pleasure of the gaze is subverted as its recipient is catapulted to act in the world.

In *The End of Violence*, the three forms of surveillance – state-controlled, personalized, and privatized – are interwoven to show how perceptions of violence are employed by the film industry and the state to perpetuate and eliminate fear respectively. The state collects and then acts upon the aerial surveillance images it collects. However, unlike the all-powerful state agencies in the panoptic dystopias discussed in Chapter 3, it is also shown to recognize the dangers of its own power. Ray's boss admits, 'Watching the Earth from the heavens is messier. In a system like this, there is a chance for abuse'.[37]

In this regard, Virilio has argued that the aerial view has the power to diminish the city to the 'theoretical altitudes of scale models'.[38] In fact, *The End of Violence*'s depiction of aerial surveillance and data collection exemplifies Mike Davis's argument that 'public law enforcement has retrenched behind the supervision of security macrosystems'.[39] This distancing of the view has the possibility of alienating the panopticon operator from the humanity that he views. Nonetheless, Ray, as the uneasy representative of the state, is not merely an obedient technician, but an individual who acts upon the images he views according to his own interpretations and values. Despite the all-encompassing apparatus of surveillance in Los Angeles of the 1990s, state control is not shown to be absolute, but rather at odds with individual will.

Power and the Gendered Gaze

In *Rear Window*, Jeff becomes a surrogate for the audience, as Hitchcock's subjective camera techniques enable the audience to identify with him. Through Jeff, the audience projects its fears and fantasies upon the female characters in the film. In *Sliver*, Zeke wields a similar power over women through his camera system. He is shown first to visually consume women he is interested in before pursing them sexually. Even when he shares his power to view with Carly, he ultimately tries to control the images to which she has access. Although Noyce does not use Hithcock's subjective camera techniques, he hints at Zeke's omnipotent view by aligning his angles with possible hidden surveillance locations. This omnipotent view is also present in *The End of Violence*.

In all three films, however, the control of the gaze is clearly in the domain of the male protagonists. Women are mainly its objects, and they are often further portrayed as longing to be objectified by it. *Rear Window*'s Lisa desires this gaze and actively performs in order to sustain Jeff's attention. Her fashionable appearance exemplifies what Mulvey has called 'to-be-looked-at-ness'. According to this idea, women aim to display themselves as a 'passive image of visual perfection' to achieve a 'strong visual and erotic impact'.[40] In *Sliver*, Carly similarly acts to perpetuate her position as an object of Zeke's view. In *The End of Violence*, when Mike's wife Page is shown changing her clothes, she is attempting to vie for his attention. And while she may be unsuccessful with Mike, she manages to capture the audience's attention effectively.

In the 1970s Mulvey argued that female audience members, when viewing such objectified women themselves, occupy the position of the male gaze. However, in response to criticism, she revised this position in the 1980s, formulating a 'more mobile concept of female spectatorship' according to which woman move between masculine and feminine positions.[41] Further scholarship on screen theory has recognized the diversity of spectators, and the ability of commercial films to cater to multiple groups simultaneously.[42] For example, the three films examined here feature female characters who gain control as the film progresses, allowing female spectators to sympathize with them.

This role reversal, the loss of control of the gaze, is depicted as an emasculating experience. In these films, the view is connected to both sexual perversion and power. Jeff's sexuality is questioned covertly in several scenes in *Rear Window*, as the script depicts the tensions between the single life of the playboy in search of exotic sexual frontiers and scopic pleasures, and the normalized male identity of the suburban family life.[43] His masculinity is jeopardized by his injury, which has relegated him to the feminized domestic realm. Lisa, on the other hand, holds a more masculine position, working during the day and choosing when and if she will visit Jeff in the evening. She is thus able to control their relationship, and Jeff is shown to fear her power to alter his lifestyle. His sexuality is questioned because he does not want to marry, and does not show sexual desire for Lisa. Sexuality is also a theme in *Sliver* as Zeke, with his power to view, is depicted as a sexual predator. By contrast, Jack is inferred to be impotent, and thus, must replace sex with violence. Jeff too is shown to seek violence as an escape from his emasculation. As he projects his fears of marriage onto the Thorwalds, the murder investigation dispels his own aggressions and sexual frustrations. Thus, in these films, the control of the gaze is directly tied to gender roles and sexual power.

The Constitution of the Real and the Reel

In these films, the window or the lens of the camera, becomes the screen through which events are seen and recorded. These mechanisms for obtaining the view form new means of knowing, in which reality is understood through reflection. It does not matter if something is real, but rather if it is seen. In this same sense, Virilio has argued that the 'reality effect replaces immediate reality'.[44] The voyeur thus defines the subject through viewing, independent of its physical existence. In essence, the virtual and the real become mutually constitutive, as these dual experiences redefine and recreate one another.

However, the lens can also play an important role in mediating the interaction among people in a community; in other words, it can both replace face-to-face interaction and incite it. The interaction between the characters of the films thus occurs across the medium of the cinema and the screen, an indication that in the modern and postmodern city, 'lives [are] lived next to each other without touching'.[45] However, each character's isolation is not tantamount to privacy; instead, in *Rear Window* and *Sliver*, 'private sorrow spills out for public viewing'.[46] The voyeuristic society, by encouraging visual contact across distance, instead facilitates interaction between people who might not otherwise come into contact. Not only is the quantity of social interaction thus depleted by the growth of the virtual realm, but its quality is also fundamentally altered. The virtual realm accompanies and perpetuates the increase in levels of social interaction that occur. Thus, it may be the excess rather than the dearth of societal information that ultimately leads to alienation. The characters in these films, particularly those who depict a postmodern condition, have thus become desensitized to images of violence and sex through sensory overload. The lens then is a tool for mediating and managing social interactions, and for empowering those individuals who control it. These films thus show how in the contemporary age, the voyeur gaze's, aided by camera lenses and screens, has replaced the wandering eye of the *flâneur*, taking 'visual possession' of an altered cityscape.[47] In other words, the camera itself now acts as the *flâneur*. Serving as the ultimate 'detached observer' that records the scope of human experiences in a range of public and private places.[48] However, behind the lens, a human subject will always have to interpret and direct who is watched, when, where and why. The powerful authority lies behind the lens, whether it is the individual, a private corporation, or the state.

The relationship between voyeurism and surveillance is not a new one. While this relationship is not a product of modernity itself, as its existence has preceded modernity, its form has been aided and conditioned by both modernity and postmodernity. The change that has occurred between the middle of the twentieth century and its end is mainly reflective of the changing nature of surveillance and of those who exercise control over the movements between the individual, the media, and the state. This is a modernity that arises from the mutually constitutive relationship between the real and the reel. Voyeuristic modernity is based on the production, manufacture and consumption of images where power inequalities arise when one person or corporation has access to view another, and to reproject this interpretation as the reality of the public sphere.

Notes

1   P. Virilio, 'The Overexposed City', in N. Leach (ed.) *Rethinking Architecture: A Reader in Cultural Theory*. London: Routledge, 1997, p. 382.
2   *Ibid.*, p. 390.
3   *Ibid.*, p. 389.
4   M. Davis, *City of Quartz: Excavating the Future of Los Angeles*. London: Verso, 1990, pp. 223–224.
5   *Ibid.*
6   *Ibid.*, p. 251.
7   M. Foucault, *Discipline and Punish: The Birth of the Prison*. New York: Vintage, 1977, pp. 200–201.
8   *Ibid.*
9   *Ibid.*, p. 209
10 E. Wilson, 'The Invisible *Flâneur*', in S. Watson and K. Gibson (eds.) *Postmodern Cities and Spaces*. Oxford: Blackwell, 1995, pp. 59–79. The reference is from page 68.
11 Alfred Hitchcock (1899–1980) was born in London, the son of an East End greengrocer. He began his career in film at Gainsborough Pictures as a writer, title designer, and art director. He had his first major success in 1926 with *The Lodger*, a thriller loosely based on 'Jack the Ripper'. Later films, including *The Man Who Knew Too Much* (1934), *The 39 Steps* (1935), and *The Lady Vanishes* (1938), brought him international success and opened the way for him to move to Hollywood. He became one of the most well-known directors in the world in the 1950s and 1960s. Viewed on 24 August 2005 on http://movies2.nytimes.com.
12 Phillip Noyce (1950–) grew up in New South Wales, Australia. He studied law, then fine arts, at the University of Sydney. As a student, he produced short documentaries. In 1972, he started studying at Australia's Film and Television School. Soon, he won recognition for his documentary work, and became a professional. With *Dead Calm* (1989), he gained access to Hollywood where he has since produced films such as *Patriot Games* (1992) and *Sliver* (1993). Viewed on 24 August 2005 on http://movies2.nytimes.com.
13 Wim Wenders (1945–) was born in Düsseldorf, Germany just after the end of World War II. After studying medicine and philosophy in his native country, he aspired to become a painter, but in Paris he discovered cinema instead. He returned to his homeland to attend Munich's Academy of Film and Television from 1967 to 1970, and then started to direct and produce his own films. He is known for his 'road movies' and philosophical explorations. Viewed on 25 August 2005 on http://movies2.nytimes.com.
14 J. M. Hayes, 'Rear Window Screenplay, based on a short story by Cornell Woolrich'. Viewed on 23 August 2005, on http://www.geocities.com/classicmoviescripts.
15 J. Belton (ed.), *Alfred Hitchcock's* Rear Window. Cambridge: Cambridge University Press, 2000, p. 3.
16 S. Curtis, 'The Making of *Rear Window*', in J. Belton (ed.) *Alfred Hitchcock's* Rear Window, p. 29.
17 *Ibid.*, p. 28.
18 J. Fawell, *Hitchcock's* Rear Window: *The Well Made Film*. Carbondale and Edwardsville: Southern Illinois University Press, 2001, p. 112.
19 *Ibid.*, p. 111
20 J. M. Hayes, 'Rear Window Screenplay'.
21 J. Fawell, *Hitchcock's* Rear Window, p. 111.
22 *Ibid.*, p. 116.
23 E. Wilson, 'The Invisible *Flâneur*', p. 73.

24 P. Virilio, 'The Overexposed City', p. 386.
25 M. Davis, *City of Quartz*, p. 224.
26 N. Klein, '*The End of Violence* Screenplay'.
27 P. Virilio, 'The Overexposed City', p. 390.
28 J. Belton (ed.), *Alfred Hitchcock's* Rear Window, p. 7.
29 J. Fawell, *Hitchcock's* Rear Window, pp. 118, 120.
30 L. Mulvey, 'Visual Pleasure and Narrative Cinema', *Screen*, vol. 16, no. 3, 1975, p. 9.
31 J.M. Hayes, 'Rear Window Screenplay'.
32 J. Fawell, *Hitchcock's* Rear Window, p. 113.
33 R.J. Corber, *In the Name of National Security: Hitchcock, Homophobia, and the Political Construction of Gender in Post War America*. Durham: Duke University Press, 1993, p. 98.
34 M. Davis, *City of Quartz,* pp. 229, 246.
35 J. Belton (ed.), *Alfred Hitchcock's* Rear Window, p. 12.
36 *Ibid.*
37 N. Klein*, 'The End of Violence* Screenplay'.
38 P. Virilio, 'The Overexposed City', p. 390.
39 M. Davis, *City of Quartz*, p. 251.
40 L. Mulvey, 'Visual Pleasure and Narrative Cinema', p. 11.
41 W. Broker and D. Jermyn, 'The Spectator and the Audience: Shifts in Screen Theory', in W. Broker and D. Jermyn (eds.) *The Audience Studies Reader*. London: Routledge, 2003, p. 128.
42 For instance, Tania Modleski has argued that women do not objectify other women, but instead empathize with them. T. Modleski, *The Women Who Knew Too Much: Hitchcock and Feminist Theory.* London: Methuen, 1988, p. 80.
43 E. Lemire, 'Voyeurism and the Postwar Crisis of Masculinity', *Alfred Hitchcock's* Rear Window, pp. 67–68.
44 P. Virilio, 'The Overexposed City', p. 389.
45 J. Fawell, *Hitchcock's* Rear Window, pp. 116, 118.
46 *Ibid.*
47 E. Wilson, 'The Invisible *Flâneur*', pp. 64–65.
48 *Ibid.*

Chapter 7

The City through Different Eyes: The Modernity of the Sophisticate and the Misfit

As an industry, filmmaking is heavily based on capital and bound up with power relations. Any discussion of capital necessitates an engagement of class. Class cannot be understood outside of prevailing modes of production and the social structures in which it exists. Class itself is far from static, as class categories are constituted through continuing historical processes and regenerated on daily basis. Moreover, class assumes intrinsic traits and is based in dominant ideologies of power. Susan Hayward has written that 'Different classes are characterized by divergent ideologies', which are rendered most visible through 'cultural artefacts' such as films.[1] Class preferences may often also reveal themselves in the choice of media (cinema, theatre, literature, etc.), or genres (melodrama, science fiction, mystery, etc.). For instance, while melodramas often use class difference as a narrative element, they do not always question class relations – and, in fact, might even be seen to serve the interests of particular classes who control their production. Hayward has cited the example of the 1950s Hollywood melodrama. Subservient to Fordism, it 'naturalized' patriarchy and capitalism simultaneously by promoting the suburban family as an ideal and the notion of men as wage earners and women as housewives.[2] It is important to contextualize individual films to understand why they are produced and what audiences they are produced for. Focusing only on a formal analysis of a film often disguises the actual class relations inherent in its content and in its making.

Like other modernities, the experience of twentieth-century modernity is not only based on class but also vitally linked to two separate domains; the production and consumption of space. The French sociologist Henri Lefebvre was one of the first to apply and extend the Marxist concept of 'alienation' to postindustrial urban society.[3] In explaining the production of space, he shifted the focus of urban studies from a historical to a spatial footing.[4] Lefebvre argued that space is 'vital'. He argued that the production of space is the product of social encounters determined by the individual reacting to other individual urban dwellers. This, he suggested, determines the landscape and geographies of the city. Lefebvre was also concerned with the 'multiplicity' of this production, represented in part by the major division between intellectual and manual labour. This kind of fragmentation creates a phenomenally diverse urban landscape, in which the eyes of one spectator can see the city as a jungle of decay and disease, while another may view it as a playground of creativity and intellectual contribution. Such class-based urban vision is nowhere more evident than in the representation of New York City, the quintessentially modern American metropolis.

Before discussing New York in detail and the city as a meta-space, however, it is important to reflect on recent scholarship related to the concept of performance. Although Lefebvre was not concerned with the individual's existence in urban space, the writings of both Judith Butler and Elizabeth Wilson allow us to understand the nature and motivations of the individual. In the 1990s, the feminist scholar Judith Butler reconceptualized the 'performance' of gender not only as a set of practices but a system of meanings.[5] She wrote that 'performance destabilizes the very distinctions between natural and artificial, depth and surface, inner and outer, through which discourse about genders almost always operates'.[6] She used the analogy of clothing to explain this construction. She argued that 'putting on' a garment is akin to wearing a costume to support a cultural or gender identity. However, the 'self' that this act expressed is very much inspired by the surrounding environment and culture. The social spaces it creates come into play in terms of the kind of performativity towards which a person aspires. Indeed, the cultural or gender performance of a person is very closely allied with their class. What s/he sees, but inversely, what s/he constructs, are reflected in her or his outward portrayal. If Butler's discussion helps us understand how an individual exists in Lefebvrian space, Elizabeth Wilson's work of the early 1990s, which discusses the role of gender and *flânerie*, allows us to examine an individual's movement through space. In her work on the role of the *flâneur*, Wilson has drawn particularly on the nineteenth century as a period when the original 'modern industrial' space was produced.[7] While her seminal work on gender is not the concern of this chapter, it is impossible to separate it here from a concern with class. Wilson has argued *flânerie* is a masculine privilege, because women at the time were not free to move about 'un-molested' outside the home and the market. Thus, the hierarchy of space in the city is one that is forever constructed with regard to a hidden imbalance of power relations between the genders. The protagonists in *Manhattan*, *Annie Hall*, and *Taxi Driver* will illustrate a modernity of class in the American city in the second half of the twentieth century.

Production, Performance, and the Urban Stage

New York City is unique in its density and the intensity of its activities. Hence, as a space it becomes equally important to understand the city not only through class categories but also through exercises of performativity, which are often class and gender-based. A fascination with New York's complexity has sparked the imagination of many film directors. Often they have explored the idea about the city through an intense focus on a single character. For the purposes of this chapter, the protagonist takes two forms: the upper-class urban sophisticate and the tortured urban outcast. The former type is captured by the protagonists in Woody Allen's films, particularly *Annie Hall* (1977) and *Manhattan* (1979). The second can be seen in Martin Scorsese's *Taxi Driver* (1976). Both Allen[8] and Scorsese[9] were born, raised and educated in New York, and have produced many films about the city.

As Donald Albrecht has suggested, in the twentieth century, New York came to be seen as a place where the American dream of social and financial transformation could be achieved.[10] Film was the perfect medium to spread the word, and develop New York's image for a mass audience. During the 1920s and 1930s, cinematic New York was projected as a city of optimism and escapism, a city of endless romance and capitalist triumph.[11] Especially during the Great Depression in the 1930s, America needed hopeful images to help it rebound from financial collapse. Films told stories of perseverance through hard labour and determination, and showed how the American dream could still be achieved against all odds. Ironically however, many of these views were artificially created as film sets in Los Angeles. This was the beginning of the separation between the 'real' and the 'reel' New York. It was only during the 1940s and 1950s, that a unique aesthetic for the city came to be developed. Following World War II and the development of postwar Italian neo-realist films, the actual city of New York came to serve as a 'celluloid stage'.[12] Films were shot on location, and the real, grimy qualities of the city were juxtaposed with its former image of sophistication. During this period, both qualities were glorified, and all that mattered was that the city was not made up from plastic skyscrapers. But by the 1960s and 1970s, the city's poverty was beginning to overcome its more urbane aspects. Albrecht has suggested that as pessimism triumphed over hope, the city came to be seen as a celluloid 'cesspool', ridden with crime, prostitution, pornography, and moral decay. However, the mid-1970s also witnessed the emergence of nostalgia for an older, more refined city, as America yearned for a return to moral clarity after the humiliation of Vietnam, Watergate, and the oil embargoes.[13] A yearning for an earlier New York, not of 'real' history but of a 'reel' history, became a special source of inspiration for many directors at this time. They turned to film techniques such as the close-up, pan, and collage to achieve their personal nostalgic representations.

Woody Allen and Martin Scorsese stand out as the most important re-interpreters of New York. Because the city they filmed was also the city in which they lived and worked, their lives and that of the city are closely linked. In a sense, they are 'New Yorkaholics' as Patricia Kruth has called them.[14] Yet, although the films of these two directors take place in the same city, they occupy different streets and neighbourhoods, portray different types of characters, and mobilize different film techniques. In this sense, the films also draw extensively from their own lives as embodied in their respective protagonists. In *Manhattan* and *Annie Hall*, the protagonists (Isaac Davis and Alvy Singer) are both played by Allen himself, and their stories display strong links to Allen's own experience growing up and coming into his own as an actor and a director in New York City. Although very different, the story and protagonist in *Taxi Driver*, Travis Bickle (played by Robert de Niro), also has traces that connect to Scorsese's urban experience. Here, person and place are tightly linked in these films, and need to be analysed together.

A Tale of Two Cities

The *flâneur* of New York, in this urban framework, sees the city in a manner that often reflects his own performativity within his immediate spatial environment. In both *Manhattan* and *Annie Hall*, Allen tells us the story of such a man whose experience and vision are determined by nostalgia and fantasy for the old bourgeois city of the turn of the twentieth century. Yet the *flâneur* of these two films also has a limited experience, and in his city, there are no beggars or outcasts, only scholars, actors, writers, models, and artists, who attend upscale shows and discuss their content in local ethnic restaurants. The city is glorified as the centre of this ideal cultured American urban life, and we experience it not only through the stories of the characters, but through a spatial collage of the city itself.

The story in *Annie Hall* is related by its male protagonist, Alvy Singer, for whom romance is characterized by the fact that he would 'never want to belong to any club that would have someone like me for a member'. Alvy is insecure, morbid ('the world is divided into the horrible and the miserable'), paranoid, and constantly makes fun of himself in his job as a stand-up comic. Flashbacks of his childhood reveal Alvy refusing to do his homework, because 'the universe is expanding and some day it'll break apart…'. Further flashbacks reveal how in his two previous marriages he chose intellectual 'New York girls'. Eventually, in both cases Alvy lost interest in them sexually. However, his new girlfriend, Annie Hall, provides a refreshing contrast. She is an aspiring nightclub singer; she is fun to be around but extremely unintellectual; and she comes from a small town in the Midwest. The fact that she drives erratically around New York in an old Volkswagen Beetle, likes to smoke grass every time they have sex, and that she is not cerebral makes Alvy uncomfortable. But she represents for him a privileged and normal Christian world that is unavailable to him as a self-conscious New York Jew. He begins to give her books to read and encourages her to take college courses on literary and philosophical subjects.

Scenes of Alvy and Annie walking down New York streets, sitting on benches, feeding pigeons, and watching people provide a backdrop for their romance. Alvy's paranoia resurfaces, after a trip together to the Midwest, and he becomes jealous of Annie's relationship with her college professor. He persuades Annie to undergo psychoanalysis and pays for her sessions. Annie gets angry with Alvy for being jealous of her relationship with the professor, and the two break up.

Alvy walks down the street in New York accosting strangers and asking people about their own relationships. An older woman declares, '… love fades'. He accosts a good-looking couple and asks them about the secret of their evident happiness. The woman says, 'I'm really shallow and empty, and I have no ideas and nothing interesting to say'. The man adds, 'I'm exactly the same way'. Alvy tries to date other women, but Annie intrudes – she calls him with the excuse that there are spiders in her apartment.

The two get together again, and Alvy takes Annie and his friend Rob to see his old Brooklyn neighbourhood. While Annie is singing at the club,

Annie Hall (1977). Alvy and Annie on the rooftop.

Tony Lacey, a music agent from California, hears her and invites them to a party with the tentative offer of a music contract. A split screen shows both Alvy and Annie with their respective psychoanalysts. Alvy complains that sex three times a week is 'hardly ever', and that he feels cheated because Annie is becoming more assertive about her own feelings as a result of the analysis. Annie complains that they have sex constantly – 'three times a week'. She feels guilty for having a right to her own feelings as a result of psychoanalysis since Alvy is paying for her sessions.

Alvy and Annie go to Los Angeles for Alvy's TV appearance to give an award. Rob, who has moved there, drives them around Beverly Hills, revealing he has never felt so relaxed. It is clean – 'they don't throw away their garbage, they make it into TV shows', Alvy proclaims. There is no crime, no mugging – 'no economic crime, but there's ritual, religious, cult murders'. Alvy also complains about the banality of architecture – 'French, Spanish, Tudor, Japanese' – and declares that in Los Angeles, Santa Claus would get sunstroke.

Annie Hall. Christmas in Los Angeles.

Alvy accompanies Rob to the recording studio, where Rob monitors the addition of prerecorded laughter to his hit show. Alvy becomes nauseous and is unable to make his TV appearance. At a Christmas party, Annie is offered a recording contract and the chance to live in Los Angeles. On the plane ride back to New York both Annie and Alvy have doubts about their relationship, and Annie breaks it up.

Alvy is alone in New York and declares he misses Annie. Again, he talks to people in the street – and symbolically to the city. He flies out to Los Angeles, to convince her to come back and get married. They meet at an alfresco restaurant on Sunset Boulevard, where he orders 'alfalfa sprouts and a plate of mashed yeast'. But Annie refuses to return to New York, declaring that she enjoys people more in Los Angeles. She adds, 'Alvy you're incapable of enjoying life. You're like New York City … you're like an island unto yourself'.

A disappointed Alvy gets into his car, tries to drive, and causes a pile-up. He is arrested for not cooperating with the police, and Rob has to bail him out. Alvy pleads with Rob, 'you're an actor – you should be doing Shakespeare in the park'. 'I did do Shakespeare in the park', Rob replies. 'I got mugged'. Back in New York Alvy writes a play about the relationship. In the play, however, the character of Annie returns to New York with the Alvy character. As Alvy confesses to the camera, 'you try to get things to come out perfect in art because it's real difficult in life'. Eventually, Annie moves back to New York, and Alvy finds her dragging her new partner to see his play *The Sorrow and the Pity*, a fact he considers a personal triumph.

Manhattan (1981). Inside the Guggenheim Museum.

In *Manhattan*, Isaac Davis is another Allen screen *alter ego*. Davis is a writer obsessed with New York City. The film begins with Isaac's struggle to begin a book which will glorify the city he loves:

Chapter One: he adored New York City, he idolized it out of proportion … make that … he, he romanticized it all out of proportion … better … to him, no matter what the season was, this was still a town that existed in black and white, and pulsated to the great tunes of George Gershwin ... uh, no let me start this over again ... Chapter One: he was too romantic about Manhattan, as he was about everything else. He thrived on the hustle bustle of the crowds and traffic. To him, New York meant beautiful women and street-smart guys who seemed to know all the angles ... no, too corny for my taste ... let me, let me ... Chapter One: he adored New York City. To him, it was a metaphor for the decay of culture; the same lack of independent integrity that had caused so many people to take the easy way out was rapidly turning the town of his dreams ... no, it will be too preachy. I want to sell some books here ... Chapter One: he adored New York City, although to him, it was a metaphor for the decay of culture; how hard it was to exist in a society desensitized by crime, TV, drugs, garbage ... too angry, I don't want to be angry ... Chapter One: he was as tough and romantic as the city he loved. Behind his black-rimmed glasses was the coiled sexual power of a jungle cat ... I love this ... New York was his town, and it always would be.[15]

Accompanying these nervous, muttering efforts at 'Chapter One' the audience hears Gershwin's symphonic work 'Rhapsody in Blue' and sees shots of historic and monumental sites in Manhattan. The music orchestrates the changing cityscape: lights flicker, traffic accelerates, buildings tower, and fireworks explode. These opening shots seem like the starry-eyed fantasy of a bedazzled spectator. Manhattan appears only to consist of luxury apartment blocks, fancy shops, art and history museums, exclusive restaurants, and beautiful people in Central Park. However, despite the triumphant visual and audio accompaniment, the audience senses this opening paragraph is about as far as Isaac will ever get with his novel.

Manhattan. Fireworks over Manahattan.

The major characters are next introduced as they eat at a typical New York diner: Isaac is accompanied by his much younger girlfriend, Tracy; and his friend, Yale, is accompanied by his wife. Isaac and Tracy discuss love in

Manhattan. New York City as the backdrop for romance.

Isaac's apartment. This scene has a particularly stage-like feel, as Isaac and Tracy are lit with a spotlight amidst a darkened background. However, we can see that his apartment is spacious, well furnished, and well maintained.

In the scenes that follow, Isaac and Tracy wander through elegant parts of the city, visiting the delicatessen Dean and Deluca; walking along clean sidewalks, and examining upscale stores. Together, they seem comfortable in these privileged spaces, walking slowly but with a sense of direction. And the camera seems to move at their pace. They are not jaded, but healthy and active. In the meantime, Isaac's friend Yale seems to be half-heartedly cheating on his wife with a new girlfriend Mary. Ironically, Isaac testifies to Yale that he should not cheat on his wife, because their marriage is the healthiest he has ever seen. But in his conversations with his wife, Yale simply seems bored.

While visiting a museum, Isaac and Tracy run into Yale and Mary. Immediately, Isaac and Mary display major character differences. Mary is well versed in art-historical jargon, but Isaac thinks she is snobbish, committed only to showing off unresearched opinions. Yale develops doubts about risking his marriage to continue his affair with Mary. He tries to set Mary up with Isaac to get out of dealing with the issue. Despite their differences, Mary and Isaac begin to take a liking to each other. They take walks together and visit various iconic New York sites: they visit historic locales, walk along the waterfront, go to the theatre. An unexpected rainfall that soaks them during a walk through Central Park symbolizes their romantic involvement. Again, the music of Gershwin follows along.

One day, however, Isaac receives a phone call from Mary, saying she is returning to Yale. Isaac and Mary meet for lunch at an upscale bar, but Isaac cannot convince her to do otherwise. Angry, Isaac takes a characteristic walk to exercise his body and clear his mind. He wonders to himself whether people he knows, and especially people in Manhattan, are just creating problems for

Manhattan. New York's turn-of-the-century and mid-century buildings are highlighted.

themselves to keep busy, to keep time moving, and to keep themselves from dealing with any real problems. He goes to his therapist where in a typical neurotic, stuttering manner, he tries to sort out his thoughts. It is during this meeting that he remembers his love for Tracy.

Soon after, Isaac confronts Yale about his anger concerning Mary. Yale offers no consolation. In a lunch meeting, Yale's wife also ironically blames Isaac for introducing Mary to Yale. In a final valiant effort to 'fix' this whole chain of events, Isaac runs to Tracy's apartment, where he finds her leaving for a year to join acting school in London – which is ironically what he had told her to do sometime before. He desperately tries to win her back, to convince her to stay, but he is too late. The final scene dispenses with all of these characters. The last shot is of *Manhattan*, reminiscent of old black-and-white photographs, showing a monumental landscape and very few people. The shots are accompanied again by the music of Gershwin. Despite this plot of decayed relationships, the orgasmic 'city symphony' plays on.[16]

If the New York of Manhattan is a forgiving place that enriches people's lives despite their personal failings, the New York of *Taxi Driver*, proposes an opposite view. This is a place of violence and cruelty that tears individuals apart. The film opens with views of the city as seen through the rain-tattered window of a taxicab. It is driven by Travis Bickle, a recently returned Vietnam veteran and the film's protagonist. The opening credits of *Taxi Driver* establish the scene as follows:

A rainy, slick, wet miserable night in Manhattan's theatre district … Cabs and umbrellas are congested everywhere; well-dressed pedestrians are pushing, running, waving down taxis. The high-class theatre patrons crowding out of the midtown shows are shocked to find that the same rain that falls on the poor and common is also falling on them. The unremitting sounds of honking and shouting play against the dull pitter-patter of rain. The glare of yellow, red and green lights reflect off the pavements and autos. 'When it rains, the boss of the city is the taxi driver' – so goes the cabbie's maxim, proven true by this particular night's activity. Only the taxis seem to rise above the situation: they glide effortlessly through the rain and traffic, picking up whom they choose, going where they please. Further uptown, the crowds are neither so frantic nor so glittering. The rain also falls on the street bums and aged poor. Junkies still stand around on rainy street corners, hookers still prowl rainy sidewalks. And the taxis service them too.[17]

Travis is unhappy and disillusioned with the meaning of his military service. He is lonely and obsessed with pornography and violence now that he has returned to civilian life. In his bare, destitute, and squalid apartment, he scribbles in his journal about how he detests the filth around him, and how he wishes for a 'rain' that 'would wash the whole thing clean'. One day, while driving his usual route, he catches a glimpse of Betsy (played by Cybill Shepherd), who is employed at the election headquarters of the politician Charles Palantine who is running for governor. Betsy, a Caucasian blonde, exudes perfection and purity. For Travis, Betsy becomes an almost religious

Taxi Driver (1978).
Film poster.

apparition of something right and true, something that can maybe fix all that has gone wrong with the city.

Travis makes a habit out of stopping his cab across from the campaign headquarters to peek at Betsy inside. He longs to make some sort of contact with her and one day, he goes and introduces himself. Intrigued by his approach, Betsy agrees to meet him for coffee. Their encounter reinforces Travis's uncomfortable and eccentric demeanour. Nevertheless, Betsy appears initially to be patient, and Travis tries to continue their unlikely romance by asking her to go on a date with him. On the date, however, Betsy is appalled when Travis takes her to a cheap pornographic theatre. Then when he tries to explain how he knows nothing about films, it only demonstrates to her how isolated and disturbed he is. He tries to apologize to Betsy for making her uncomfortable by sending her flowers, but she sends them back. He then hoards the flowers in his room until they begin to wilt. (In fact, he never gets rids of them for the entire film.) Angry and tormented, Travis begins to descend into the depths of his own paranoia.

Three incidents mark his increasing mental breakdown. One day, Betsy's boss, Charles Palantine, hops into Travis's cab. In the conversation that develops, Palantine encourages Travis to speak about his concerns as a voter. But Palantine is startled when Travis pours out his thoughts about the filth of New York. Then an incident occurs that solidifies Travis's rage towards the

Taxi Driver. Travis in the mean streets of New York.

city around him. While driving through a grimy section of the city, he pulls his cab over to a teenage prostitute who practically runs into the street to scramble in. Travis realizes she is attempting to flee from her pimp. But the pimp grabs the girl and pulls her back out of the cab and gives a $20 note to Travis telling him to 'forget about it'. For Travis, the young prostitute comes to symbolize the city, while her pimp becomes the evils that have besieged it. The third incident involves an otherwise 'normal' looking middle-aged upper-class man (played by Scorsese). As it turns out, the man is being cheated on by his wife, whose 'black' lover reflects the racial tensions in the city at the time. While the husband speaks in circles of his intent to murder his wife and her lover, and the weaponry he will use, Travis comes to realize he also needs to arm himself.

Travis enters the second stage of his descent when he decides that he needs to clean and reform himself before cleaning the city. In his cell-like apartment, he begins a training regimen of fanatic exercise, even though he is rapidly deteriorating into psychosis. He works out as though he is again preparing for battle. He purchases weapons, and practises firing them, in a violent effort to alleviate his anger over his failed relationship with Betsy and general hatred of the city.

In the third stage, Travis starts taking action. He speaks to the security personnel at Palantine's public appearance, and expresses a phoney desire

Taxi Driver. 'Be Alert! The sane driver is always ready for the unexpected!' Everybody is concerned with crime on the streets.

to join the Central Intelligence Bureau. Then, he focuses his attention on saving the young prostitute, Iris. He spots her on a tenement street, where she works guarded by her pimp, 'Sport', and arranges a trick with her. But in the sleazy room they go to Travis insists on having a heartfelt conversation, instead of sex. He then arranges to meet Iris for breakfast the next day. When they meet, Travis tries to convince her to leave her life as a prostitute, and her pimp, whom he calls the 'scum of the earth'. Travis believes she should have a quiet, domestic life suitable to her age. Iris defends Sport, but begins to crack and tells him she dreams of living in a commune in Vermont.

Convinced that Iris wants and deserves better, Travis decides vengeance. He shaves off his hair in a military style, which serves to demonstrate that he has gone completely 'insane'. After a failed attempt to assassinate Palantine, Travis turns once more to the case of the young prostitute. He finds the pimp Sport and shoots him. On his way to find Iris, he confronts the hotel manager and irrationally shoots the manager's hand off. A mad exchange of bullets ensues between Sport, Travis, and the hotel manager. Eventually, Travis manages to kill everyone and all in front of Iris. He then tries to kill himself too, but he is unsuccessful. The police arrive and Travis is hospitalized. As things turn out, Travis is hailed as a 'hero' by the newspapers. Iris is returned to her parents, who are grateful to Travis, and Travis returns to his normal life as a cabdriver. In the final scene, he picks up Betsy as a regular customer who is now content to ride in his cab. When she tries to pay him for the ride, he refuses to accept any money. In the brief conversation they have, Travis denies the importance of the recent events in his life. He then speeds off. Shots of the city from the perspective of the cabdriver end the film as they started it.

The Sophisticate versus the Misfit

The nature of space is so different in Allen and Scorsese's portrayals that it as though two different cities are being depicted. In Allen's films, the space presented is entirely bourgeois, the inhabitants are all modern *flâneurs* and, while gender differences play a crucial role in the narrative, class is assumed to be singular. He is a romantic wanderer who experiences a personalized, stylized, nostalgic vision of New York that is both modern and monumental and filled with nightclubs, trendy restaurants, and stimulating inhabitants. This is a city of celebratory consumption and his experience of the city is as a member of a privileged intellectual class.

Allen's glorification of New York gives the city an identity that is a sum of its bourgeois characters. Through scenes of glowing, monumental landscapes (synchronized with the Gershwin score in the case of *Manhattan*), the city emerges as its own confident, sexually explosive being, and at the ends of both *Manhattan* and *Annie Hall*, the viewer is left with the emotions of the characters materialized in a visual landscape.[18] The city remains eternal, uninterrupted by the petty-bourgeois squabbling of its citizens.

Both *Manhattan* and *Annie Hall* were written and directed by Allen and in both he plays the protagonist. An autobiographical influence is therefore undeniable, but its complexity and contradictions are worth investigating. The protagonist of both Allen's films is a self-conscious, sexually obsessed Jewish urbanite. And even if the details of the 'reel' lives of these characters differ from Allen's own, their strolls in the streets, meetings at restaurants, and chance encounters at hotels and museum offer an upscale vision that represents his nostalgia for the city of his dreams.[19] The shots of the landscape read like a tourist map: we see only the monuments, historic places, and cultural centres of the city. The New York scenes of *Annie Hall* and *Manhattan* are all shot in a manner that allows Allen to present the lived city of New York. But in this case, it is the city of intelligentsia and not simply a map used by a tourist. He packages it such that this is the New York that tourists aspire to and virtual New York becomes the one that everyone knows. Meanwhile for Allen, the 'other' kind of city is embodied by the dehumanized and indulgent Los Angeles.

In Kruth's opinion, Allen's protagonist can be described as an 'actor' well-suited to this particular Manhattan 'stage'.[20] He and the other characters are cosy and comfortable in the 'sheltering cocoon' of New York City. As Isaac Davis narrates in *Manhattan*: 'You're in the middle of New York City. This is your town. You're surrounded by people and traffic and restaurants'.[21] You can never be lost in Allen's Manhattan, and his narrative ponders the city via his relationships with his lovers and friends, as they attend films, performances, museums and dinners. Despite an analysis of masculinities and femininities, Allen's engagement of sexuality allows us to call to mind Butler's notions of 'performance' and the 'stage'-like presence of the city itself.

Allen creates this sense of 'stage' through many dimensions in his films. For example, he chooses tasteful jazz to score his story of Manhattan. In a way that is decidedly upper-class and nostalgic, the music always seems to guide the actors, their footsteps matching the beat of the drum, the draw of the violin bow. But the music seems to agree also with the pace of the entire city. Fireworks explode at the climax of the Gershwin symphony, and the streetlights flicker with the rhythm of the tune.[22] Another device Allen uses is a camera that travels with ease. It is smooth and direct, slow, but stable and patient. Even when Singer and Davis are emotionally perplexed, these contemplative protagonists walk through the streets guided by a camera that is purposeful, and that sympathizes with their emotions.[23] Allen's camera shots also invoke height and depth at view to portray certain urban qualities of New York City. As Patricia Kruth has explained, 'Allen uses rooftops as privileged settings for urban pastorals'.[24] In one scene atop the roof of Annie's West Side apartment building, Annie and Alvy have a superficial conversation, but their honest, inner thoughts are subtitled and revealed to the viewers. The sense of privilege in this scene is determined by both the location and the verbal exchange between the characters. Specifically, the characters are so fixated on their mutual flirtation that they hardly seem to notice the power of the backdrop. For Allen, Peter Conrad has suggested, the 'Impressionist city is a picnic site'.[25]

If New York is a tasteful city where humans can thrive, function, and belong, a city with a sense of accomplishment, cultural awareness, and history, Los Angeles, as seen in *Annie Hall*, provides a direct contrast. Los Angeles is a city in which the pedestrian is lost amidst interchangeable suburban mansions, a city in which light is so intense that it can only be unhealthy and decadent, a city in which moral corruption rules and vacant minds possess all power. Thus, through the eyes and words of Alvy Singer in *Annie Hall*, LA is so deeply saturated with sunshine that its inhabitants are nearly blinded. Alvy feels a passionate hatred toward this 'overexposed' city. For him, this 'pervasive, glaring sunlight' is symbolic of its vacancy.[26] Because the light is so blinding, it is misleading, unhealthy, and dangerous. Los Angeles lacks any character; its architecture is mismatched; its public spaces are privatized. At a house party, while Alvy and Annie are being given a tour of the house, they continuously interrupt the privacy of strangers. The guests of the party, who seem to represent all residents of Los Angeles, glare in their outfits[27] but are inwardly corrupted. Los Angeles is a superficial place that is 'less serene than gray-green New York'.[28] Thus, the roles of light and dark are 'expanded', exaggerated, and 'reversed'.[29]

Much of the scenographic effect of Allen films has to do with the fact that the protagonist (as a *flâneur* of twentieth-century New York and unlike the earlier *flâneur* of mid-nineteenth-century Paris) never wanders through anything besides an upper-class, ordered environment. As a male, he is also never harassed. Instead, we see him conversing in restaurants, shopping at fine stores, people watching in Central Park and visiting apartments with views. He never wanders into parts of town where streets are narrow and crowded with criminals or prostitutes. Allen's protagonist never wanders where parks are littered with trash, where flashing neon signs advertise pornography. The sense of this city was actually established by 1920s films of New York: 'the bridge, the kiss, the foghorn' were all part of the historical development of New York as a celluloid city.[30]

This is also a fully masculine city. In *Manhattan*, its skyscrapers shoot towards the sky framed by exploding fireworks just as Gershwin's symphony comes to its climax. In the narrative in this opening scene, Isaac Davis makes a connection between the sexual prowess of the main character of his book and the city's performance. 'Manhattan was his town'.[31] However, we see throughout the film that Isaac Davis, himself, cannot live up to the sexual dynamo of the city. Indeed, personal problems keep him from achieving his dream of sexual prowess. However, the sexual promise of Manhattan pulsates on, untouched by its insignificant inhabitants.

Annie Hall also ends with distant shots of characters, nearly hidden in the landscape of Manhattan. Despite both films' focus on the lives and troubles of several New Yorkers, the only thing that proves eternal and reliable, and the thing that is of real importance in the end, is the actual physical city itself. The gaze of Allen's *flâneur* is merely, and can only merely be a gaze. His city is too overpowering to ever really be penetrated by the personal and intellectual capabilities of his characters.

Unlike Allen's performative *flâneur*, Scorsese's protagonist is a disturbed, lower-class outcast whose internal traumas eventually lead him to a schizophrenic yearning to save the city by destroying it. Travis Bickle is at odds with the materialist city in which he lives.

Yet, the nature of the 'stage' where Scorsese sets his story also lacks spatial clarity, making the 'performance' he films dark and chaotic. In terms of editing, the second scene in *Taxi Driver* is demonstrative of the methods Scorsese uses to create this sense of dislocation. In it, the audience is shown Travis's squalid apartment: its bare light bulb, cracked paint, barren walls, junk-food wrappers and pornographic magazines. Scorsese uses triangles, circles, triangles within circles, rectangles, squares to frame shots or spatially enclose characters in order to illustrate the trapped effect that comes through in this film.[32] In the apartment, there is also a mirror hanging bleakly from the wall, that is its only decoration. His sole window to the outside world, the mirror merely reflects his own squalid life back at him. Kruth has suggested that the mirror is a physical manifestation of his split personality. Since he cannot make sense of the outside world, he retreats into his own consciousness, prisoner of his own psyche.[33]

When Travis is shown driving his cab, he also appears like a prisoner, isolated behind its windows that are smeared with filth from the city's streets. In these driving scenes, Travis is shown in medium close-up from all angles, and from front, side and back. His lack of education and manners prohibit him from interacting wtih his surroundings in a comfortable manner. Thus, his own private awkwardness is transformed onto the urban landscape, and the city becomes a metaphor for Travis' tormented personality. This visual fragmentation, Kruth has suggested, shows that Travis has no hand in his own destiny. Like the war he has just returned from, New York, Travis's cab, and Travis's mind will all eventually unravel into a senseless, directionless, purposeless welter of demons.[34]

Where Allen used New York's bright lights to create a celebratory effect, Scorsese uses them to signify approaching danger. Thus the fluorescent signs and streetlights are nightmarish and disturbing, revealing criminals who never rest. They shine down on passers-by cutting into their soulless insides. The city's colours are also washed-out by seemingly incessant rainfall. Travis wishes the rain would 'wash the city clean from its sins and corruption ... One day a real rain'll come and wash all the scum off the streets'.[35] As Travis drives, he makes judgements about the people he sees as though they were animals. The architecture of the streetscape seems like the skeleton of a dead city; it is an 'urban void', a black hole without vibrancy or purpose.[36] Yet even if Travis is angered by such a city, being a product of a specific urban class he remains seduced by its promise, and a prisoner of its reality.

Scorsese also shot his film in settings that show a different side of New York from Allen's. This life story provides insight into these choices of setting.[37] Unlike Allen, he did not grow up to view the city with a privileged position. And in *Taxi Driver*, he employs working-class motifs in neighbourhoods of all five boroughs from Harlem to Soho in Manhattan to the Bronx, Queens, Brooklyn, and Staten Island. He focuses particularly on Times Square and the avenues leading into and out of it, a key location for vice and crime in the New York of the 1970s. By contrast, Allen set most of his scenes in upper-class spaces such as Central Park and its surrounding neighbourhoods. Scorsese was born into a working-class family, and his film is both tainted and fascinated with this perspective. His sense of city space is far from the monumental skyline that is the hallmark of Allen's films. In fact, the only time we see a skyline in *Taxi Driver* is after Travis has purchased his weaponry to 'clean up the city'. From the window of the dingy Brook Heights hotel, the Manhattan skyline seems more like a target for one of Travis's gunshots.

While Allen's New York City is particular, Scorsese's may be considered a stand-in for all other large cities. Allen reinforces his definition of the city by using its cultural institutions and by contrasting with what he sees as their absence in Los Angeles. Scorsese, on the other hand, uses New York to talk about the urban experience of the metropolis of which New York's is the quintessential city.[38] The two directors create cities of juxtaposing but complex viewpoints about space and its production. The spaces are entered by a performance of the protagonist, a performance which is very much determined by upbringing and personal urban experience.

It would be a stretch to conclude by suggesting that the urban experience of the sophisticate or the misfit in the films discussed allows us to identify a unique modernity of class in the American metropolis of the 1970s. But there is no doubt that the political and cultural events that determined the American city in that time period, including the Vietnam War and economic crises, left their mark not only on the cities but also on how they were experienced as represented in both real and reel space. There is also no doubt that the emergence of the urban sophisticate and the urban outcast in the context of New York, in particular, may in and of itself be a product of a modernity unique to New York as it is to this specific historical period. It would not be a stretch to suggest that the duality and irreconcilability of Alvy Singer and Travis Bickle is precisely what characterizes the experience of modernity in urban America in the 1970s like the inner contradiction felt by Baudelaire's poet in the streets of Paris more than a hundred years earlier.

Notes

1   S. Hayward, 'Class', in *Cinema Studies: Key Concepts*. London: Routledge, 2000, pp. 59–61.
2   *Ibid.*
3   In Marx's original conceptualization, alienation occurs between the labouring body and the product of his labour. Lefebvre has argued that it is important to pay attention not just to industrial production but also to the production of space (for example, urban real estate becomes an important secondary circuit of capital producing surplus value). Taking this Marxist concept, Lefebvre locates alienation in everyday life but as this relates to the city, urban dwellers, by adopting urbanism, forget how space is produced. H. Lefebvre, *The Production of Space*, D. Nicholson-Smith (trans.). Oxford: Blackwell, 1991.
4   H. Lefebvre, *The Production of Space*.
5   J.P. Butler, *Gender Trouble: Feminism and the Subversion of Identity*. New York: Routledge, 1990. J.P. Butler, *Bodies That Matter: On the Discursive Limits of 'Sex'*. New York: Routledge, 1993.
6   J. P. Butler, *Gender Trouble*, p. 10.
7   E. Wilson, 'The Invisible *Flâneur*', in S. Watson and K. Gibson (eds.) *Postmodern Cities and Spaces*. Oxford: Blackwell, 1995, pp. 59–79.
8   Woody Allen (born Allan Stewart Konigsberg, 1935–) was born in the Bronx, NY., to a middle-class Jewish family. In the early 1950s, he briefly attended New York University to study film production. After a short episode in which he worked in Hollywood as a writer of comedy for a TV network, he returned to New York to pursue a career in writing and directing for both the stage and TV. In the 1960s, he made a reputation as a stand-up comedian. His first screenplay was *What's New, Pussycat?* (1965). Soon, he directed his first film, *Take the Money and Run* (1969). *Annie Hall* (1977) was based on a long-term relationship Allen had with its leading actress, Diane Keaton (1946–). The title, 'Annie Hall' was derived from Diane Keaton's nickname, 'Annie', and her original last name, 'Hall'. Viewed on 15 August 2005, on www.woodyallen.com.
9   Martin Scorsese (1942–) grew up in New York's Little Italy. He studied and later taught film at New York University. His first critical success came with the largely autobiographical *Mean Streets* (1973), which launched the acting careers of both Harvey Keitel and Robert De Niro. In subsequent films such as *Taxi Driver* (1976) and *Raging Bull* (1980), he continued to portray loners struggling with inner demons. Little Italy is cited as an influence on the director. It was a squalid and crime-ridden place where he later said only 'gangsters and priests were respected'. Scorsese rarely deals with Little Italy as a specific neighbourhood in any of his films. Yet, its nature, class background, criminal activity, and physical density and decay are themes he examines in all his New York films. Viewed on 15 August 2005, on www.imdb.com.

10 D. Albrecht, 'New York: Olde New York: The Rise and Fall of a Celluloid City', in Dietrich Neumann (ed.) *Film Architecture: Set Designs from Metropolis to Blade Runner*. Munich: Prestel, 1996, p. 39.

11 *Ibid.,* pp. 39–43.

12 *Ibid.*

13 *Ibid.*

14 P. Kruth, 'The Colour of New York: Places and Spaces in the Spaces of Martin Scorsese and Woody Allen', in F. Penz and M. Thomas (eds.) *Cinema and Architecture: Méliès, Mallet-Stevens, Multimedia*. London: British Film Institute, 1997, pp. 70-80. The reference is from page 70.

15 W. Allen, *'Manhattan Script',* Four Films of Woody Allen. New York: Random House, 1982.

16 *Ibid.*

17 P. Schrader, 'Taxi Driver' Script of Martin Scorsese's film (1976). Reprinted in A. Taubin, *Taxi Driver*. London: British Film Institute, 2000. In writing the screen play, Schrader used his personal experiences as well as drawing on the contemporary, real life story of Arthur Bremer's attempt to assassinate Alabama Governor George Wallace.

18 P. Kruth, 'The Colour of New York', p. 74.

19 *Ibid.*

20 *Ibid.*, pp. 72–73.

21 Quoted in *Ibid.*, p. 72.

22 P. Kruth, 'The Colour of New York', pp. 73–74.

23 *Ibid.*

24 P. Kruth, 'The Colour of New York', p. 75.

25 P. Conrad, quoted in *Ibid.*

26 *Ibid.*

27 L. Ford, 'Sunshine and Shadow', p. 129.

28 *Ibid.*

29 L. Ford, 'Sunshine and Shadow: Lighting and Color in the Depiction of Cities on Film', in S. Aitken and L. Zonn (eds.) *Place, Power, Situation and Spectacle: A Geography of Film*. Totowa, NJ: Rowan and Littlefield, 1994.

30 *Ibid.*, pp. 76–77.

31 W. Allen, *'Manhattan Script'*.

32 P. Kruth, 'The Colour of New York', pp. 70–71.

33 *Ibid.*, p. 72.

34 *Ibid.*

35 L. Ford, 'Sunshine and Shadow'.

36 *Ibid.*

37 E. Wilson, 'The Invisible *Flâneur*'.

38 P. Kruth, 'The Colour of New York'.

Chapter 8

An Alternate Modernity:
Race, Ethnicity and the
Urban Experience

It can be said that race[1] and ethnicity[2] have been insufficiently understood as essential mediators of the experience of modernity. While scholars continue to tackle new concepts with enthusiasm, much of the work has been limited to the frameworks of segregation and difference. Despite the absence of empirical evidence, the presence of so-called ethnic minorities in certain societies has often been attributed to migration, immigration and resettlement, gradual or sudden. It may be reasonable to suggest that all racial groups are, in a sense, ethnic groups. This however is not the position adopted in this chapter, which accepts that race and ethnicity as social categories are modern inventions produced primarily for political reasons and governance purposes. Hence, in this chapter we will invoke both concepts, often interchangeably, using the terminology applied by other authors to describe relevant commensurate cinematic or urban examples.

In urban studies, there has been very little attention given to the intersection of ethnic difference, modernity, and spatial geography. Following earlier sociological studies, race has only been analysed within the modern American and European city according to a rhetoric of crisis. This has limited its scope either to a study of the spaces of marginality or an exploration of the phenomenon of urban violence as a result of racial or ethnic tension.

The understanding of urban modernity itself leans heavily upon a particularly European experience that chooses the end of the nineteenth century as its originary moment.[3] Scholars such as Paul Gilroy have specifically critiqued these descriptions, and argued that such theoretical frameworks are overly influenced by the project of the European Enlightenment, which largely included ongoing brutality against blacks and other subject races during the colonial era.[4] In recent years, however, postcolonial and ethnic studies have attempted to adjust this model according to the notion of alternative modernities.[5] However, these effects have paid little attention to the intricacies of race and ethnicity as they play out in space, or as they constitute a politics of place. For example, more often than not, 'blackness' has been conflated with other forms of marginality, poverty, and disenfranchisement to provide a generalized Other to 'whiteness'. And when black identity in the contemporary city is analysed, it has been cast often only in terms of the black heterosexual male, avoiding a conversation of gender and race as disparate subject positions. Indeed, in analysing urban modernities in the context of race, the relationship between modernity and postmodernity is revealed to exist in a continuum; a tension depicted in the films used in this chapter. Though race and ethnicity are mediators through which the city is experienced, they unsettle critical assumptions of hybridity and struggles over the right to the city.

Unlike scholars of urbanism, scholars of cultural studies and sociology have long recognized the difficulties posed by racial identity. For example, as long ago as 1899 W.E.B. Du Bois argued that:

> Herein lie buried many things which if read with patience may show the strange meaning of being black here in the dawning of the Twentieth Century. This meaning is not without interest to you, Gentle Reader; for the problem of the Twentieth Century is the problem of the color-line.[6]

These words should be read by all who continue to evade the question of race in their understanding of the twentieth-century city. In particular, Du Bois's notion of black consciousness was tied to the African-American experience of being locked into a double-consciousness of being both black and American. Among other things, he saw this as creating an uncomfortable oscillation of identity that denied a confident or whole self-consciousness.[7] The time when Du Bois was writing was also when American cities were being restructured in terms of their racial composition due to the Great South–North Migration. As St. Clair Drake and Horace R. Cayton pointed out in *Black Metropolis* (1945), the influx of black workers into northern cities grew significantly during World Wars I and II, when labour shortages led recruiters to comb the South for workers, and transport blacks up north to serve as menial labourers.[8] However, while European immigrants had been absorbed into the city, proceeding through various urban zones, and moving from ethnically homogenous neighbourhoods to the 'melting-pot' suburbs, African-Americans remained confined to the inner city, to what Drake and Cayton call 'Black Metropolis'. The mechanisms of ethno-racial closure and control, including racial violence, technologies of city planning, and white flight, constitute what is the specific socio-spatial formation of the 'ghetto'.

In contrast to Du Bois's reading of black subjectivity in the US, Stuart

Hall has more recently attempted to address the notion of contemporary black and ethnic identity in the UK. Speaking from a postcolonial vantage point, Hall sees blackness as a broad historical, cultural and political category that was relentlessly produced, and doubtlessly resisted during the colonial era.[9] Hall has further echoed Gilroy's analysis of the centrality of race in a deeper understanding of modernity, arguing that the project of modernity has destabilized identity and the notion of historically continuous subject positions. According to Hall, '... this is the beginning of modernity as trouble. Not modernity as enlightenment and progress, but modernity as a problem'.[10]

Hall's idea of modernity as problematic and unsettling is further tied to the revision of older definitions of identity based on psychoanalysis and the construction of a distinct sense of Self and Other. Instead, Hall had envisioned a new subjectivity, one occasioned by the postcolonial moment, when the Self is reflected in the Other, and the Other is situated at the core of the Self. It is precisely this postmodern instability of identity that has allowed a reaffirmation of 'black identity' in Britain. Reacting to the particularly racist definitions of whiteness as national identity in the 1970s, Stuart Hall has argued that a diverse group of ethnicities (Bangladeshi, Indian, Pakistani, Jamaican, Caribbean, African) all situated themselves within the political category of black.[11] Thus, on one hand, Hall has proposed a model of blackness that is not unlike Du Bois's, in that it grows out of a double-consciousness. And yet, unlike Du Bois, he has looked at this double-consciousness as a strategic position, entered into as a deliberate act of agency, with the intent of subverting the mythical, stable core of white identity.[12] Such issues are central to the films examined in this chapter. If *My Beautiful Laundrette* elegantly captured the racial dimension of ethnic relations in the context of a liberalizing London during a conservative Tory regime, then no film better captures the American equivalent than Spike Lee's film, *Do the Right Thing* (1989), produced also during an equally conservative American regime.

Spike Lee's[13] film was conceived as a cinematic response to an incident in Howard Beach, Queens, NY in 1986 when a gang of white youths attacked three black men who were lost in the area, which is predominantly Italian and Jewish. One man was killed while attempting to escape.[14] The movie is not only powerful in its critique of racial tension and violence in the North American city,[15] but it was also prescient in that it was released two years before the LA riots,[16] sparked by the jury verdict in the Rodney King beating trial in 1991.[17] Stephen Frear's *My Beautiful Laundrette* (1984) is based in London at a time when the government of Margaret Thatcher was intent on eliminating most aspects of the former British welfare state and when virulent anti-immigration sentiments were becoming ingrained in the UK.[18]

It is based on a 1983 screenplay by Hanif Kureishi, a British author-director of Pakistani origin, renowned for tackling issues of race, nationalism and sexuality.[19] Each of these films attempts to expose ambivalent spaces of an urban modernity and postmodernity characterized by changing notions of race and ethnicity.

Brooklyn of the *Do the Right Thing*

The setting for *Do the Right Thing* is in the Bedford-Stuyvesant area of Brooklyn, New York (often referred to as Bed-Stuy). The film opens with a shot of the inside of the local radio DJ's tiny cubicle. The DJ, Senor Love Daddy, broadcasts that it will be the hottest day of the year, and as the day's events unfold, the social climate will parallel the weather, finally exploding. From this opening claustrophobic space, the camera pans out to the larger context of the street, where the story will take place. There, it follows the chief protagonist, Mookie (played by Spike Lee himself), as he goes about his morning routine.

Spike Lee chooses the street as his *mise-en-scène*, and a large part of the film revolves around its culture. On this hot day, when almost all of the block's residents must come out of doors because they have no air-conditioning, the street itself becomes the main arena of social interaction. The one block where the film takes place includes Love Daddy's radio cubicle, Sal's pizzeria, a grocery store run by Korean immigrants, and the flats rented by Mookie's sister and girlfriend. The film is animated with a host of colourful characters. These include Sal and his sons, Vito and Pino,

Do the Right Thing (1989). The 'Bed-Stuy – Do or Die' mural.

the neighbourhood matriarch, Mother Sister; the local wino, Da Mayor, who mutters words of wisdom; Radio-Raheem, a bulky young black man who carries an oversized boom box that plays 'Fight the Power' (by Public Enemy); Smiley, who is retarded and carries around black-and-white photos of Malcolm X with Martin Luther King; Buggin' Out, a young black man who seems to be in a constant state of rage; the police officers who patrol the streets and survey the block; and the Corner Men – ML, Sweet Dick Willie, and Coconut Sid – who appear throughout like a Greek chorus commenting on their surroundings. With its black, white, Puerto Rican, Italian-American, Korean immigrants, and Caribbean-black residents, the block appears at first a caricaturized US melting pot. Yet it is clear from the beginning that the politics of race simmer just below the surface. The cracks between races and ethnicities are indeed deep, and they are soon exposed.

An important theme that runs through the film is how people identify themselves with the neighbourhood. In various ways, they see their presence there as expressing a fundamental right to the city. Thus, even as the Corner Men and Buggin' Out appear to have neither homes nor jobs on the block, they refer to it as 'their neighbourhood'. The Corner Men, who sit around all day and don't work, look at the Koreans with envy and loathing because they've been off the boat for less than a year, and yet are already doing great business in 'our' neighbourhood. Ironically, the person who presses these charges most loudly speaks with a Caribbean accent, and is duly reminded that he has not been in the country that long himself. For his part, Sal sees the neighbourhood as his territory because it is where he has owned a business for decades.

As the film begins, Mookie is shown diligently and patiently counting a

Do the Right Thing. The three black men sitting at the street corner.

wad of money in his sister's apartment. The scene then shifts to Sal's pizzeria, the central space of the film. Sal (played by Danny Aiello) gets by with help from his two sons, Pino and Vito, while Mookie serves as their delivery boy. Except for Mookie, the black characters are shown to do nothing to make a living though they are fully cognizant that it is they who keep establishments such as Sal's running. With this recognition, and a communitarian sense of ownership, Buggin' Out asks Sal to put some pictures of 'black brothers' up on his walls. Sal refuses, citing notions of private property. In the past he has always been able to buy off racial trouble by slipping a few dollars to Da Mayor or Smiley or Mookie.

Do the Right Thing. Mookie delivers pizza while everyone hangs out on their stoops.

A memorable fragment of the film features a quick-cutting montage of various characters (black Mookie, Italian-American Pino, Latino Stevie, white police officer Long, and the Korean store owner) as they spew hate-speech based on racial stereotypes. The montage follows a particularly intense back and forth between Pino and Mookie, when the former is irritated because he believes that Mookie is lazing about on the job. In order to get back at Pino, Mookie cleverly turns the tables on him by simply asking him who his favourite basketball player, movie star, and rock star are. Pino innocently answers the first two questions by naming black Americans. But he stops before the third, as he recognizes the trap that Mookie has led him into. 'Prince', Vito answers on his behalf. Pino then defends his choices by arguing that those celebrities he has named are not 'really' black. The tension that arises between the two characters leads into the name-calling montage,

Do the Right Thing. Mookie and Sal argue in front of the 'Wall of Fame'.

but just as this choreography of racism reaches its crescendo, the scene cuts to Senor Love Daddy, who acts as the voice of reason and advises everyone to chill out.

In the final part of the movie, an argument in Sal's pizzeria between Sal and Radio Raheem, who refuses to turn down his music, escalates first into racial name-calling and then a full-scale brawl. The policemen who arrive use excessive force and end up strangling Radio Raheem to death. As they drag the dead body away, an angry crowd gathers. The crowd holds

Do the Right Thing. A riot breaks out in front of the pizzeria.

Sal and his two sons responsible for the death of Raheem. Da Mayor tries to protect them from further violence, but Mookie makes the decision to smash the pizzeria's front window. As all hell breaks loose, the establishment is first vandalized, and set ablaze. As the fire burns, Smiley is seen pinning his photos of Malcolm X and Martin Luther King, Jr. up on Sal's Italian-American wall of fame. The irony is that neither the pizzeria nor the wall will survive.

A particularly poignant moment in the film comes just after Radio Raheem's death. The mob gathered outside Sal's turns on the Korean couple making them the new targets of their rage. The Korean shopkeeper flails a broomstick, desperately trying to protect his store from the destruction that has just been wreaked on Sal's. In an attempt to protect himself, the Korean cries out in broken English that he is also black. Even though the crowd initially mocks him, some begin to feel for him. Oscillating between hate and love, violence and peace, rivalry and brotherhood, the 'right thing to do' becomes less and less clear as the movie progresses.[20]

Do the Right Thing. The Korean shop owner tries to protect his store from the mob.

The London of *My Beautiful Laundrette*

My Beautiful Laundrette deals with many of these same issues of ethnicity and race but in a European context. Its characters are similarly challenged by social tensions, and they vacillate about the right thing to do. The story hinges on the chance encounter of two young Londoners, Johnny (played by Daniel Day-Lewis) and Omar (played by Gordon Warnecke), who happen to be ex-schoolmates and ex-lovers. It develops around their resumed relationship and collaboration to revamp a run-down South London launderette. But as Johnny and Omar become increasingly successful, their ethnic and social backgrounds catch up with them. Johnny is a working-class white with friends in the British National Party (BNP), a fascist group whose members take pride in bashing immigrants. Omar is a second-generation Pakistani living with his alcoholic, ex-journalist father, Ali, and working for his entrepreneur uncle Nasser. Omar's father and uncle are antithetical characters. While the father, a one-time 'leftist-communist/socialist-news-writer', wants Omar to get an education, his uncle prioritizes making money. It is the uncle who eventually provides the more powerful role model for Omar within the context of Thatcherite Britain.

The film opens to a scene of race role reversal, as a couple of young white squatters are being evicted by Asians and blacks. As it turns out, it is Johnny and a friend who are being thrown out of a run-down and dilapidated South London flat. The film then switches to the interior of Omar's small council flat, which he shares with his father, Ali. This tiny space is constantly filled by the din of trains, and at night their lights shine through its windows. Omar has just had a lucky break, since uncle Nasser, who owns a chain of parking garages and storefront retail shops, has just hired him to wash cars.

As the film progresses, Omar begins his job at the garage as a rather reluctant understudy. But he quickly realizes that, despite what his intellectual father has told him, such jobs will be his only route upward. At the garage, Omar soon meets Nasser's white mistress, Rachel, and his business

My Beautiful Laundrette (1985). The view from Omar's flat in South London consists of railway viaducts and the abandoned Battersea Power Station.

partner, Salim. He also meets Nasser's family, including his daughter, Tania – who may one day be his bride. Nasser has a luxurious home and a wife and kids who provide him dignity in his ethnic community. Nasser and Rachel socialize at white establishments that might otherwise be out of Nasser's reach as a 'Paki'. Rachel comes from a working-class background, but like Nasser, she dreams of an upper-class life. So, in effect, the extramarital relationship has benefit for her as well. This is made clear at the grand opening of Omar and Johnny's laundry, when Rachel and Nasser's wife encounter each other for the first time. Rachel argues that her relationship with Nasser is her only chance in life to exceed her class position. Meanwhile, she points out that Nasser's family members are all upwardly mobile and their lives are full of prospects. Later, however, Rachel decides to leave Nasser, when she falls ill with a skin rash apparently caused by the magical powers of Nasser's wife. And toward the end of the film, Nasser's Westernized daughter Tania also leaves him. Bored with her role in traditional family life, Tania first approaches Omar, and then Johnny, without realizing they are homosexual. She then runs away from home.

Both Salim and Nasser, have managed to buy their way out of the slums of South London with their quasi-legal businesses and quick-money schemes. But Salim is the more corrupt of the two. He traffics drugs and hires Omar to deliver them. He also tells Omar, when he starts to work for them that, 'Your uncle can't pay you much. But you'll be able to afford a decent shirt, and you'll be with your own people. Not in a dole queue. Mrs. Thatcher will be pleased with me'.[21] Salim is not critical of Thatcher's policies. In fact, he and the other entrepreneurial Pakistanis shown in the film take pride in their

My Beautiful Laundrette. The revamped launderette is a huge success.

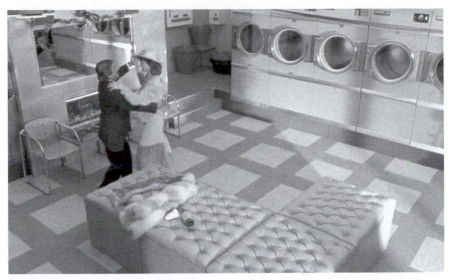

My Beautiful Laundrette. Nasser and Rachel dance in the recently opened launderette.

independence from previous British social-welfare policies. In general, they support the Thatcher government despite the fact that some of its polices have racist underpinnings that harm their own communities.

After years apart, Omar and Johnny come across each other again when the former is taking Salim and his wife home from a Pakistani soiree. At a stoplight by some railway viaducts, a bunch of skinheads surround their car and begin to bully them. Omar recognizes Johnny and reintroduces himself. At the time, Johnny is unemployed and embarrassed by the implied associations with a Paki and the fact that Omar appears much better off than him. But when Omar offers Johnny a job in his new launderette, the latter sees it as a way to make a new start. But Johnny's low-class identity and skinhead background soon cause Omar and Nasser to call on him to throw people out of the launderette, evict 'bastard' tenants, and run drugs, despite his repeated protestations that he 'don't do anything rough no more'.[22] As Omar and Johnny renovate their run-down launderette, Johnny's former skinhead friends also try to intimidate him into returning to their life of vandalism. The 'own people' dialogue comes to a head when Johnny's skinhead friends show up and try to wreck the launderette. They tell Johnny that the Pakis were brought over to England to work for them, and that Johnny shouldn't forget his own people. In the end, everyone has to belong, they say. Nevertheless, Johnny defends his choice and continues to invest his labour in rebuilding the launderette.

On the opening day of the chic new launderette, renamed 'Powders', Johnny's skinhead friends wreck Salim's car, to get back at him for injuring their friend. At first, Johnny stands back and watches, a bit reluctant to save

My Beautiful Laundrette. Omar and Johnny repair the launderette.

Salim, whom he despises, but eventually he joins the fight and ends up being beaten up by his former friends. Clearly, he is torn between his racial and class identity, as a white, unemployed youth in South London and his love for Omar and the upward mobility that his job at the launderette provides him. As the laundry is transformed from its decrepit state to a clean, flashy space with neon lights, its customers too change. The teenage punks who used to hang out there are replaced by working people impatient to get their laundry done.

Race, Ethnicity, Entrepreneurship, and Urban Identity

To assess the thread of racial anger that runs through these two films, we must first return to Du Bois's notion of double-consciousness. Particularly in *Do the Right Thing*, we see how accepted measures of success, fame, wealth, beauty, cultural supremacy, and intelligence are all established against a dominant ideal of whiteness. However, while these are set as a benchmark of aspirations for black Americans, it is understood blacks will never be able to reach them. It is in this regard that more recent scholars of black identity such as Cornel West have argued that it is the 'amused contempt and pity' with which white America looks down at its black population that fuels black rage.[23]

The spectral impossibility of blacks achieving any form of acceptance in a world organized by whites is made clear in *Do the Right Thing* when Pino declares that popular icons like Prince are not black: 'It's different. Magic, Eddie, Prince are not niggers, I mean, are not black. I mean, they're black

My Beautiful Laundrette. Thugs smash the launderette's window.

but not really black. They're more than black'. The reputation of the blacks Pino names goes beyond their blackness. Pino's statements are a reminder to Mookie (and others) that once black people reach a level of fame and success in a 'white' world, they escape their racial identity. More importantly they cease being black in a way in which people like Mookie can continue to relate. By contrast Sal, Pino and Vito can still relate to the Italian-Americans which include names like Frank Sinatra, Al Pacino, Liza Minnelli, Sylvester Stallone, and Luciano Pavarotti on the pizzeria's wall of fame.

To understand the trope of black rage portrayed in the film, it is important to understand the differences in views of the two historical figures of black identity who appear in it. The vastly different political ideologies of Malcolm X and Martin Luther King are captured both in the photographs of them which Smiley carries around, and in the long quotes that appear at the end of the movie.[24] Specifically, unlike King, Malcolm X came to embrace the reality of rage as an important avenue for black consciousness, because it freed black people from passive acceptance of their 'double-consciousness' and helped overturn their feelings of powerlessness and take control of their place in American society. Cornel West has summarized this point as follows:

> Malcolm believed that if black people felt the love that motivated the rage, the love would produce a psychic conversion in black people; they would affirm themselves as human beings, no longer viewing their bodies, minds, and souls through white lenses, and believing themselves capable of taking control of their own destinies.[25]

Of course, these racial issues have played out differently in the cities of the UK, unlike the US. Slavery was not the overt source of race problems that are the subject of *My Beautiful Laundrette*.[26] Rather, they emerged from the legacy of colonialism and the desire of former colonial subjects to immigrate to the UK to seek better lives for themselves and their families. It is in this sense that a dialogue over 'true' British identity has since developed and has involved racist notions and anti-immigrant sentiment. Ironically, however, the same Thatcher conservative government that established quotas on immigration from former colonial regions has pointed to the very entrepreneurial vigour of these immigrants as evidence of the new social climate it hoped to establish.

As part of this social revolution, Adrian Kearns has remarked that the British Conservative government developed the concept of active citizenship as a way to facilitate the dismantling of welfare government services.[27] Active citizenship would transfer the burden of providing such services to charity organizations, the family, and community groups. The decreasing role of the state was to be thus matched by individual citizens acting via an increased sense of moral obligation. However, as Kearns pointed out, this re-definition of individual and state relationships that was sold as diminishing paternalistic state power only served to substitute other forms of patriarchy for centralized state power.[28]

In *My Beautiful Laundrette*, the relationship between Omar and his uncle Nasser falls into precisely this patriarchal contract of needy recipient and wealthy benefactor. Thus, even though Omar is less than thrilled about his job cleaning cars, it is his only way to avoid going to the dole. It is important, however to read properly the motivations of individual characters in this particular equation. Salim and Nasser are both well aware of their 'constructive' roles in providing employment for Omar. But Omar exercises agency via his role as a beneficiary of the system. While Kearns has said that active citizenship reduced recipients to passive agents of charity, Omar seizes the opportunity provided by Nasser to create his own set of personal opportunities.

The idea of dependence on an individual benefactor also emerges in the character of Sal, the pizzeria owner in *Do the Right Thing*. He and his business are presented as the economical pivot around which the neighbourhood functions. It is through his munificence that Da Mayor is able to sweep the street corner and make the few dollars that will get him his next bottle of beer. Similarly Mookie's relationship with Sal echoes that between Omar and uncle Nasser. Mookie and Omar are both aware they are being exploited, but they are lured into their respective social transactions by a prospect of wealth. A new kind of social contract is presented here, where Mookie and Omar's circumstances are a product of state policies, yet their everyday life is controlled by a patriarch whose position derives from the absence of a state presence in the community.

Both movies also offer insights into the production of gender as a result of these intricate dependent relationships. In *Learning to Labour* (1977), Paul Willis wrote about the construction of masculinity as a sign of counter-culture among high school students in England. In particular, he examined the formation of social cliques around expressing resistance to normalized patterns of authority. In *My Beautiful Laundrette*, Johnny's friends fall into the category Willis called 'lads', those who see working for wages as a sign of conformity. However, it is interesting to note that in *My Beautiful Laundrette*, the anger of Johnny's BNP thug-friends does not find a specific 'establishment' target. There are no signs of patrolling cops or any other formalized means of state control. And in the absence of a centralized state apparatus the BNP lads direct their anger towards the only visible forms of social order in their urban milieu, in this case run by South Asian immigrants.[29]

Thatcherite ideas of entrepreneurialism also have a double meaning in terms of ethnic identity. In the film, Nasser is portrayed as having escaped the limits of race by buying into a supposedly 'colour-blind' capitalism. Thus, the scenes showing Johnny being evicted from his apartment are repeated in a curious manner when the one-time squatter himself helps Nasser evict a poor, black poet. During this second eviction, Johnny comments that it doesn't look good for a Pakistani to evict his own kind – i.e., another coloured person. But Nasser replies that he is a professional businessman and not a professional Paki, and that there is no question of race in new enterprise culture.[30] Nasser's view of Thatcherite politics is not negative because he wants to belong to the dominant society so much that he regards his own exclusion as a personal failing and tries to fill the gap with visible symbols of a white, middle-class lifestyle. Besides the cars and suburban house he can afford to provide for his family, this yearning for social mobility is best defined by his white mistress, Rachel, who he dresses in furs, and who escorts him to fancy bars.

Yet, class relations in this multicultural society are complex. At the end of the film it is revealed that Rachel comes from a working-class background. And when Nasser's daughter Tania accuses her of being a parasite, Rachel reminds Tania that they are of different classes and generations. Everything is available for Tania, but the only thing that was ever available for her was Nasser. Associating herself with a rich, albeit coloured, man has allowed Rachel to transcend class boundaries in much the same way that Johnny's association with Omar has lifted him out of his own low-class background. But even as the film holds out wealth as a great social leveller (since it can buy class, racial ambiguity, and even culture – as seen in Salim's apartment, which is decorated with elegant paintings by the well-known Indian artist M.F. Hussain), it only provides agency and inclusion within certain spheres. In particular, it cannot buy political agency. Indeed, the education and social awareness possessed by Omar's father Ali prove grave liabilities that exclude him from an active part in Thatcherite society. Thus, even as active citizenship appears to hold the promise of influence and power, clear boundaries still protect the monopoly of the state over other important areas of British life.

Race, Urban Space and the Displacement of Community

What does *My Beautiful Laundrette* tell us about London? What is the sense of urban modernity related through this film? Not once in the film does the audience see any traditional images of the city. In fact, its absence is enough for some to ask if the movie is not really based in some other blighted English town. Frears deliberately bypasses the usual urban symbols of London (for example, the dome of St. Paul's, Trafalgar Square, Docklands) to present the city as composed of derelict council houses, grimy car garages, defunct laundromats, and the spaces underneath train viaducts. *My Beautiful Laundrette*'s London is precariously perched at the intersection of multiple ends – the end of empire (represented by the spaces of deprivation); the end of socialism (embodied by the isolated father Ali); the end of the myth of an ethnically pure and properly gendered Britain (Johnny and Omar's relationship that is taboo for reasons beyond homosexuality). Accompanying this city of endings are the continually transgressive identities of its main characters: Johnny is white by race, black by class; Omar is black by race, but white by class in relation to Johnny and his BNP friends. Johnny becomes the thug who is called on to beat up vagrants; Omar never declines the proposal to marry Tania. Yet, they easily slip out of these transitional masculine roles to be tender with one another. Class, gender, race are constantly mediating one another to provide this slippage. Who is the black person or the poor person at the end of the film – Johnny, Omar, or Nasser?

As the main characters in *My Beautiful Laundrette* slip between identities, the past is always present in the idea of 'home', here used to reference Pakistan. Salim's wife, Cherry, is the only person who emphatically claims her Pakistani identity, even as she tells Omar she is 'sick of hearing about these in-betweens', in reference to him never having been to Karachi. But Omar's nostalgia for countries where he has never been is evident in the interest he expresses in knowing about 'Juhu beach' or the 'house in Lahore'. Like an exile, he sets up the place of his origin as an imaginary geography shaped largely through nostalgia.[31] Ali (Omar's father), on the other hand, has a different nostalgia for Pakistan. He says he wants to go 'home' so that he will be free to think, write, and express his political thoughts – which he is unable to do in Britain. But Nasser disabuses him of this optimism when he argues 'that country has been sodomized by religion, which interferes with the making of money'.

By leaving the usual symbols of London out of the film, *My Beautiful Laundrette* also presents London as a decidedly postcolonial city. In *Edge of Empire*, Jane M. Jacobs tried to define London according to spatial and temporal geographies of empire.[32] According to some, London is post-imperial because imperialism is over. However, Jacobs maintains that imperialism, as ideology, is ever present under the guise of globalization and neoliberalism. As a result, Jacob prefers to designate London a postcolonial city because local articulations of imperialism's heritage are reconstituted on a daily basis in the heart of the empire.[33] Indeed if nineteenth-century notions of racism based on the denigration of the colonial other have been discounted, it does not mean that racism has disappeared. Along with the new form of imperialism, the terms of racism are complicated by different positions based on axes of class and race. Here race is seen as a culture, rather than a skin colour.[34] In this sense, Anne Marie Smith has explained how in the context of Thatcherite Britain 'tolerance' came to be seen as a way to denigrate others who were thought to belong elsewhere. Smith also pointed to the conflation of racism and homophobia during the Thatcher years as potential threats to the idea of a properly Christian Anglo-Saxon nation.[35] Against such a political background at the centre of *My Beautiful Laundrette*, the interracial relationship between two gay men is doubly problematic. The film affirms Michael J. Watts's assertion that 'Difference and identity is produced and reproduced within a field of power relations rooted in interconnected spaces linked by political and economic relations'.[36]

Such a society exists in the slippage of identities where no one is fixed in a position of simply black or simply white. In this alternate urban modernity, hegemony is produced by some groups through the playing off of differences that subvert collective will or choice. Here, Nasser's triumphant assertion that in the new entrepreneurial culture, there is no room for race serves to uphold the very structures that marginalize his own ethnic group as it mandates the production of consent. The racism in *Do the Right Thing* is constructed as a historic and social category. Thus, the harder the characters try to escape their racial confines, the more they are locked into it. It thus shows how blackness is produced as a social category with little regard for the physicality of race.[37]

In the first part of *Do the Right Thing*, Lee emphasizes the modern melting-pot sense of community among the people of this block. When Pino pleads with Sal to consider moving to their 'own' neighbourhood (Little Italy), he replies that he identifies with the people on the block because they grew up eating his food. In another scene, a couple of black kids open up a fire hydrant so that everyone can enjoy some respite from the heat. A little girl draws a house and a sun with a 'smiley' face on the street. Thus the film sets up a seductive, romanticized version of community, which it then purposefully destroys. What starts out as a display of hybridity, as various and complex identities living together, soon degenerates into hateful and narrow descriptions of the Other in a landscape where everyone is the Other.

Do the Right Thing attempts to challenge the simplistic binary opposition used to describe the modern African-American cultural experience. Contemporary commentators like Cornel West have perceived such ideas as Du Bois's notion of 'double-consciousness' or the 'double personality' portrayed by James Weldon Johnson as a crisis of identity by anxiety-ridden middle-class intellectuals.[38] The film rises to West's challenge to deconstruct the early 'modern black strategies of identity formation'. Instead, it constructs an alternate modern or possible postmodern 'multivalent and multidimensional response to the diversity of black practices in the current global era'.[39] Hence, the film does not offer a simple closure, not even the promise of one. Similarly, Henry Louis Gates has not seen the outcome of the film as predestined. Rather he has argued that the different characters' choices shape its complex outcome.[40] He has further argued that the film consists of dynamic and indeterministic relationships in which meaning and truth remain multiple and non-fixed.[41] Likewise, the somewhat sympathetic portrayal of Italian-Americans complicates the story and supports Lee's position that 'everybody's right. And everybody's wrong. And nobody's a hero'.[42]

According to J.C. McKelly, 'The dramatic structure of *Do the Right Thing* situates Mookie, the film's protagonist played by Lee himself, in the midst of this architecture of polarities constructed around the cultural logic of "two-ness"'.[43] As he has further argued, Mookie is 'Henry Louis Gates's *homo rhetoricus Africanus*' who moves freely between 'two discursive universes'.[44] Radkte has suggested that this non-participatory centrality in the film emerges from his showing us around his neighbourhood.[45] 'He is a pair of eyes on feet who we can see through out into the community … His motives, intentions and desires are not revealed'.[46] He is in a sense the racialized and ethicized *blasé*-cum-*flâneur* whose disengagement, while wilful, is partly a product of his race. He represents a type of late-twentieth-century modernity, which is urban in nature but neighbourhood-based in scale. As Linda Hutcheon has argued, the neighbourhood, in this case Bed-Stuy, becomes an 'assertion not of centralized sameness but of decentralized community'.[47]

McKelly's use of Mikhail Bakhtin's work on Dostoevski is further help in explaining Mookie's experience in Bed-Stuy. According to McKelly, 'Mookie's eyes become a medium for the "unification" of all of the neighborhood's "incompatible" elements'. As in Bakhtin's analysis of

Dostoyevski's novels, the plurality of consciousness cannot be 'reduced to a single ideological common denominator'.[48] 'The only unification offered by Bed-Stuy is the unity of place: Simultaneity, coexistence, and interaction'.[49] The neighbourhood then becomes a symbolic modern space in which the unresolved ambivalences about race and ethnicity leads to its polarization and its emergence as a place of discursive ambiguity. As an alternative modern protagonist whose principle identification is his race, Mookie becomes:

> a walking synecdoche for his neighborhood's dialogical assimilation of a plurality of cultural signifiers … he becomes what Bakhtin calls 'an internal dialogic' character containing … a cacophony of autonomous irreconcilable significations in conflict each reflecting a persistence of double-consciousness: Sal/Bugging Out, Pino/Vito, Da Major/Mother Sister,…Cool/Heat, Love/Hate, Right thing/wrong thing'.[50]

As a modern protagonist who accepts the economic realities of the modern capitalist structure in which he lives, Mookie offers a model not for an integral and stable resolution of his inherent doubleness but for the refusal to abide by its 'schizophrenic cultural logic'.[51]

Omar and Mookie emerge as the new figures of an alternate modernity of race and ethnicity within Europe and America. Their presence in the urban scene is not new. Rather their engagement with dominant society within the urban spaces of the twentieth century requires us to recalibrate our understanding of both modernity and postmodernity. There is here continuity with the urban modernity of the nineteenth century where encounters between classes revealed a transient and contingent quality to urban life. This continues to have some validity throughout the twentieth century. However, the situatedness of Omar and Mookie poses a series of challenges to this well-established frame of reference. Indeed, the twentieth century has witnessed the rise of substantial ethnic communities in the many cities of the First World demanding a redefinition of the urban experience that not only encompasses race but also problematizes it in the same way that early nineteenth-century modernity articulated class. Moreover, the late twentieth-century modernity of class and ethnicity is equally transient and contingent, and ephemeral. As the new ethnic protagonist forces his way into the hybrid postmodern spaces of the city based on new axes of identity and encounters of difference, we must remember that hybrid spaces do not always encourage the celebratory pluralistic tendencies or multicultural practices synonymous with globalization. Equally true is that hybrid places do not always accommodate hybrid people, just as hybrid people do not always create hybrid places.[52]

Notes

1   Race came into common use in the English language around the sixteenth century as a category that designates differences amongst groups of people according to real or perceived physical and biological characteristics. Although these differences between races arose as a result of mutation, selection and adaptation, the category of race has not disappeared in common culture. R. Williams, *Keywords*. Oxford: Oxford University Press, 1976, p. 248.

2   Ethnicity has been in the English language since the fourteenth century when it was originally used to designate 'heathen and pagan cultural groups', but it emerged in the mid-twentieth century to designate distinct categories of national or local populations whose culture and physical appearance is different from the dominant majority. *Ibid.*, p. 119.

3   M. Berman, *All That is Solid Melts into Air*. New York: Viking, 1988.

4   P. Gilroy, *The Black Atlantic: Modernity and Double Consciousness*. Cambridge, MA: Harvard University Press, 1993.

5   D. P. Gaonkar (ed.) *Alternative Modernities*. Durham, NC: Duke University Press, 2001.

6   W.E.B. Du Bois, *The Souls of Black Folk* (1903). New York: Penguin, 1989, p. 1.

7   *Ibid.*, p. 5.

8   St. C. Drake and H.R. Cayton, *Black Metropolis: A Study of Negro Life in a Northern City*. Chicago: University of Chicago, 1993.

9   S. Hall, 'Old and New Identities, Old and New Ethnicities', in Anthony D. King (ed.) *Culture, Globalization and the World-System: Contemporary Conditions for the Representation of Identity*. London: Macmillan, 1991, p. 53.

10   *Ibid.*, p. 44.

11   *Ibid.*, p. 55.

12   'Third generation young black men and women know they come from the Caribbean, know that they are black, know that they are British. They want to speak from all three identities. They are not prepared to give up any one of them. They will contest the Thatcherite notion of Englishness, because they say this Englishness is black'. *Ibid.*, p. 59.

13   Spike Lee (1957–) was born in Atlanta, Georgia, and raised in Brooklyn, NY. He studied at traditionally black Morehouse College and later attended New York University's well-known Tisch School of The Arts, where his master's thesis project (*Joe's Bed-Stuy Barber Shop: We Cut Heads*, 1983) brought him early recognition (Student Director Oscar, 1986). *Do the Right Thing* (1989) brought him national, and *Malcolm X* (1992) international fame. He has directed films engaging a variety of topics, but all are 'black stories'. In his press profile, he advocated making 'black films' using not only black stories but also black crews, as a form of resistance to the white dominated Hollywood studio system. 'Spike Lee', in H.L. Gates Jr. and C. West (eds.) *The African-American Century: How Black Americans Have Shaped Our Century*. New York: Simon and Schuster, 2002, pp. 359–361.

14   S. Lee, in S. Lee and L. Jones (eds.) *Do the Right Thing: A Spike Lee Joint*. New York: Fireside, 1989, p. 118.

15   Some have argued that Lee's films prepared the ground for the reception of other black films (e.g., *Boyz in the Hood, New Jack City, Straight Out of Brooklyn, Juice*). W. Lane, 'No Accident: From Black Power to Black Box Office', *African American Review,* vol. 34, no. 1, 2000, pp. 39–59. The reference is from p. 47.

16   D. Muzzio, '"Decent People Shouldn't Live Here": The American City in Cinema', *Journal of Urban Affairs*, no. 18, pp. 189–215, cited in N. AlSayyad, 'The Cinematic City: Between Modernist Utopia and Postmodernist Dystopia', *Built Environment,* vol. 26, no. 4, p. 274.

17   The LA riots erupted at the intersection of the Pico Union, South Central and Koreatown districts of Los Angeles. This occurred after the police, accused of beating Rodney

King, were acquitted. The trial had been held in Simi Valley, a predominantly white Republican stronghold, despite the fact that the incident took place in Los Angeles.

18 Stephen Frears (1941–) began a career in television in the 1960s. He directed his first television film, *Gumshoe*, in 1972. He directed *My Beautiful Laundrette* for Channel 4 as a TV production. It was subsequently released in cinemas and led Frears to direct other successful films in the UK as well as in Hollywood.

19 Kureishi grew up in the suburbs of London. He describes his London as follows: '… for me, London became a kind of inferno of pleasure and madness… And so I would go up to the King's Road and just see these incredible people, and the shops, and all of that. And just think, and think; you know, I just wasn't to be here with these people. And then, at the end of the day, you'd have to go home [to Bromley] and it was rather disappointing. So London was always a place that I imagined… So you know my London isn't going to be like anybody else's London. It's a playground, it's a place where I can imagine, where I can play'. C. MacCabe, 'Interview: Hanif Kureishi on London', *Critical Quarterly*, vol. 41, no. 3, 1999, pp. 37–56.

20 Mookie's action has caused much debate in film criticism. For example, W.J.T. Mitchell has argued that Mookie indeed did do the 'right thing' by directing anger from Sal and his sons to their property. W.J.T. Mitchell, 'The Violence of Public Art: *Do the Right Thing*', *Critical Inquiry*, no. 16, 1990, pp. 880–99. As cited in W. Lane, 'No Accident', p. 48.

21 H. Kureishi, *Collected Screenplays*. London: Faber and Faber, 2002, p. 10.

22 *Ibid.*, p.43.

23 C. West, *Race Matters*. New York: Vintage Books, 1994, p.138.

24 'The greatest miracle Christianity has achieved in America is that the black man in white Christian hands has not grown violent. It is a miracle that 22 million black people have not risen up against their oppressors – in which they would have been justified by all moral criteria, and even by the democratic tradition! It is a miracle that a nation of black people has so fervently continued to believe in a turn-the-other-cheek and heaven-for-you-after-you-die philosophy! It is a miracle that the American black people have remained a peaceful people, while catching all the centuries of hell that they have caught, here in white man's heaven! The miracle is that the white man's puppet Negro "leaders", his preachers and the educated Negroes laden with degrees, and others who have been allowed to wax fat off their black poor brothers, have been able to hold the black masses quiet until now'. *The Autobiography of Malcolm X as told to Alex Haley*. New York: Ballantine Books, 1999.

25 C. West, *Race Matters*.

26 In the UK, the Tory candidate, Peter Griffiths, gained notoriety for having said, 'If you want a nigger for a neighbour, vote Labour', quoted in 'Cry Nigger: Playing the Race Card in British Politics', *The Journal of Blacks in Higher Education*, no. 32, 2001, pp. 69–70.

27 A. Kearns, 'Active Citizenship and Urban Governance', *Transactions of the Institute of British Geographers*, vol. 17, no. 1, 1992, pp. 20–34.

28 It bears noting here that the concept of active citizenship came about in reaction to the public censure that Thatcher's government received in its first two terms due to what was seen as a shameless promotion of greed and selfishness. This was characterized best by Thatcher's own statements such as, 'There is no such thing as society'. Active citizenship was seen then as the tonic that would both counter such allegations through its emphasis on Christian morality, while providing a justification for the decrease in social services provided by the state. *Ibid*.

29 In *Do the Right Thing*, his sons criticize Sal for recruiting local blacks as a form of charity. Pino goes as far as to scold, 'We runnin' welfare or somethin'?'. Although Pino himself is living off his father's good will, in his understanding, his familial tie supersedes the business. Sal is both encouraged and disturbed by his own son's aggressive attitude, which verges on racism. He tries to protect Mookie – at times

treating him as a son, but at others as merely a dispensable employee. Sal's relationship to Mookie, as well as the black community that constitutes his clientele, is situational. If they are good customers, Sal treats them well. If they create problems, Sal does not refrain from violence. Then he bashes Radio Raheem's boom box with his bat. According to the black community in the vicinity, the film suggests it is Sal who 'receives'. According to Sal, however, it is him who 'provides'.

30 H. Kureishi, *Collected Screenplays*, p. 50.

31 S. Rushdie, *Imaginary Homelands: Essays and Criticism 1981–1991*. London, Granta and Penguin, 1991.

32 J.M. Jacobs, *Edge of Empire: Postcolonialism and the City*. London: Routledge, 1996.

33 Despite the ambivalence Jacobs has expressed about the designation of 'postcolonial' at the time of writing her book, it seems that the term is gaining acceptance in London. How London's socio-political demography is related to and constructed by diverse cultures has become of increasing interest to mainstream intellectual debate in the city from the Architectural Association's 1999 conference and accompanying photographic competition, 'London: Postcolonial City' (12–13 March 1999), to the series of Hanif Kureishi's films at the National Film Theatre. M. Cousins, *Critical Quarterly*, vol. 41, no. 3, 1999, p. 36. A recent publication that reflects this trend is McLeod's *Postcolonial London*. J. McLeod, *Postcolonial London: Rewriting the Metropolis*. London: Routledge, 2004.

34 A.M. Smith, 'The Imaginary Inclusion of the Assimilable "Good Homosexual": The British New Right's Representations of Sexuality and Race', *Diacritics*, vol. 24, no. 2/3, 1994, pp. 58–70.

35 *Ibid.*

36 M.J. Watts, 'Mapping Meaning, Denoting Difference, Imagining Identity: Dialectical Images and Postmodern Geographies', *Geografiska Annaler*, vol. 73, no. 1, 1991, pp. 7–16. The quote is from page 14.

37 S. Hall, 'Old and New Identities'.

38 J.W. Johnson, *Autobiography of an Ex-Coloured Man,* New York: A. Knopf, 1927, p. 72.

39 J.C. McKelly, 'The Double Truth, Ruth: "Do the Right Thing" and the Culture of Ambiguity', *African American Review*, vol. 32, no. 2, Summer 1998, pp. 215–228. The reference is from page 12.

40 H.L. Gates, *The Signifying Monkey*. Oxford: Oxford University Press, 1988, p. 48.

41 *Ibid.*, p. 25.

42 As cited in J. Radtke, 'Do The Right Thing in Black and White: Spike Lee's Bi-Cultural Method', *The Midwest Quarterly*, vol. 41, no. 2, 2000, pp. 208–228.

43 J.C. McKelly, 'The Double Truth, Ruth:…'.

44 *Ibid.*

45 J. Radtke, 'Do The Right Thing in Black and White…'.

46 *Ibid.* The full quote is as follows: 'He is a pair of eyes on feet who we can see through out into the community, not a hero or anti-hero who we can see inside and line up behind or against. His motives, intention, desires are not revealed'.

47 L. Hutcheon, p. 18, quoted in J.C. McKelly, p. 9. In L. Hutcheon, 'Beginning to Theorize the Postmodern', *Textual Practice,* no. 25, 1987, pp. 10–31.

48 M. Bakhtin as cited in J.C. McKelly. M. Bakhtin, *Problems of Dostoevski's Poetics,* C. Emerson (trans.). Minneapolis: University of Minnesota Press, 1984, p. 17.

49 J. C. McKelly, 'The Double Truth, Ruth:…'.

50 *Ibid.*, p. 32.

51 *Ibid.*, p.12.

52 For a more detailed discussion of the relationships between ethnic minorities and dominant societies, as such relationships are articulated in urban space, refer to my book N. AlSayyad (ed.), *Hybrid Urbanism: On the Identity Discourse and the Built Environment*. Westport, CT: Praeger, 2001.

Chapter 9

Exurban Postmodernity: Utopia, Simulacra and Hyperreality

This book began with a discussion of urbanization and industrialization and their effect on small-town life, particularly in America. It is befitting to end, then, with a return to the small town in the postindustrial era. The small town thrived as the symbolic centre of American life until the 1940s.[1] In the late 1970s urban planners again took interest in small towns, particularly the vernacular architecture of their Main Streets, and a movement began to preserve their historic neighbourhoods and downtowns.[2] The preservation movement revolted against both big-city urban renewal and ubiquitous suburban development, citing the failures of Modernist utopian visions. Instead the outlines of a new utopia began to develop, one that looked backward rather than forward. This alternative ideal, which crystallized a particular form of postmodernity in America, is today best exemplified by the urban design movement known as New Urbanism.

New Urbanism emerged in the US in the 1980s, came to prominence in the 1990s, and has flourished since then. Typically, most New Urbanist developments are described as 'towns', a term that carefully avoids the negative social and environmental connotations of suburban development (which are seen as unsustainable in the long term) and the images of social disorder associated with the city. As planned settlements, they aim to provide the diverse amenities of the city, the pastoral beauty of the suburbs, and the social integration of the traditional small town. Although most New Urbanist developments occupy somewhat isolated suburban sites, or are new towns, altogether, their designers define them as urban because they incorporate such urban characteristics as pedestrian scale, public space, and bounded neighbourhoods.

New Urbanist towns differ from older urban areas and suburban settlements not only in planning principles, but also in the design of their residential and civic architecture. In particular, their designers aim to create a neotraditional feel by emulating features of historic American vernacular architecture. Thus, most New Urbanist communities are based on design codes that require homes to conform to certain patterns, such that they include porches, or that a particular roof pitch be used to emulate a local tradition.[3] Advocates argue that such codes help to ensure both harmony and diversity in design, which are otherwise difficult to achieve without the benefit of centuries of established building practice.[4] However, New Urbanist designers do not want to merely re-create the small town in spatial form and scale, but also as a social structure. Their designs are thus predicated on the idea that 'design affects behaviour'. In order to create the functions of community, they believe the town should play 'host to its social and political structures'.[5] In other words, design and planning should be concerned with increasing opportunities for social interaction in order to foster a more integrated community.

With the establishment of the Congress of New Urbanism (CNU), in the 1990s, the number of New Urbanist settlements expanded. One of the earliest was Seaside, Florida, an exclusive second-home community designed by architects Andres Duany and Elizabeth Plater-Zyberk in 1981. Another highly publicized development was Celebration, Florida, built by the Disney Corporation in 1997. Like Seaside, Celebration took shape on a remote 'greenfield' location. But its vision for an experimental ideal community on the edges of its Disney World property was far more comprehensive. Walt Disney, founder of Disney, had actually once proposed a similar project in the 1950s. Known as EPCOT (Experimental Prototype Community of Tomorrow), he imagined a community in which to house his workers while simultaneously demonstrating a 'living blueprint of the future'.[6] This utopian idea was revived thirty years later at Celebration, where the Disney Corporation aimed to create 'not just a housing development, but a community'.[7] In line with New Urbanist ideas, neotraditional aesthetics would provide an important part of this community's identity. Thus, all buildings in Celebration would be regulated by a 'Pattern Book', and protected by codes, covenants and restrictions (CC&Rs).[8]

These examples provide a brief glimpse of the way in which the architecture and social structure of the traditional small town were revived by the New Urbanists in the 1990s. Using cinematic representations of two such neotraditional towns, this chapter will argue that these nostalgic simulations now indicate the ascendancy of a new anti-urban utopia. Such nostalgia for small-town life is the dominating force in American urbanism at the beginning of the twenty-first century.

With regard to this change from modernist urbanity to postmodernist nostalgia, French philosopher Jean Baudrillard has commented that the ideal of the city has been replaced by that of the 'cosy nook'. He has further argued that the new anti-urban urban utopian vision implies the replacement of public spaces by 'idealized', 'naturalized' spaces, which are the 'epitome of all that is beautiful', but which negate the possibility of public assembly.[9] In 'See You in Disneyland', American architectural critic Michael Sorkin has similarly suggested that pseudo-public spaces such as those at Disneyland have now been accepted as a solution to the dissipation of public identity in cities like Los Angeles.[10] Sorkin has critiqued the way that 'a simplified, sanitized experience stands in for the undisciplined complexities of the city'.[11] According to this view, active civic participation in urban life is being replaced by passive consumerism in carefully controlled private landscapes. Indeed, Don Mitchell has differentiated between these private landscapes, 'where one basks in the leisure of a well-ordered scene', and public spaces, which engender 'inclusiveness and unmediated interaction'.[12]

Places such as Disneyland which idealize urban spaces into replicas such as 'Main Street, USA' become truly public because they create landscapes outside of time where the idea of community is naturalized and political history is erased. According to Sorkin, by idealizing and sanitizing everyday places, Disney creates a landscape that 'inscribes utopia on the terrain of the familiar'.[13] The effect is to hide or repress the normal social conflict and political struggle that take place in the public sphere. Thus, in spaces like Celebration, new forms of 'utopian subjectivity' imply a 'homogenized, under-dimensioned citizenship', where residents are downgraded to mere consumers.[14] Such a neoliberal vision today fills the void left by the collapse of the welfare state and the ideal of universal citizenship, giving rise to a different articulation of postmodern space.

In order to understand these unique conditions of postmodernity in America at the turn of the twenty-first century, this chapter will examine the nostalgia for and re-creation of the traditional small town in Garry Ross's[15] *Pleasantville* (1998) and Peter Weir's[16] *The Truman Show* (1998). These films capture two different aspects of 1990s anti-urban utopia.[17] The narrative in *Pleasantville* builds on the longing for an ideal American life outside the messy realities of geography or history. As Baudrillard has argued, 'America is neither dream nor reality. It is hyperreality … it is a utopia which has behaved from the very beginning as though it were already achieved'.[18] Thus, *Pleasantville* attempts to depict the utopian image of American small-town life, and then questions the implications of this ideal. *The Truman Show*, on the other hand, takes place not in an imaginary space, but in a simulacrum, a deliberately fake space modelled on the small town, but existing only as the set of a television show. The film articulates Sorkin's idea of the paranormal, where the stage set of the small-town is 'just like the real thing, only better'.[19]

Simulation and Hyperreality as Urban Attributes

Before discussing these two films in detail it is necessary to articulate further some important ideas related to simulated spaces and hyperreality. Because late capitalism is based on producing ever greater differentiation of taste and then creating the means to fulfil those appetites, it has rendered the ideals of Fordism obsolete. In such a social and economic milieu, the postmodern city itself becomes a simulacrum, created by competing signs and simulations. Baudrillard believes that this indicated that our current age of the hyperreal is based on little more than simulations that engender further simulation. The resulting interplay of signs and symbols[20] establishes new rules of economic and cultural exchange.[21]

If high modernism has been blamed for the destruction of the fabric of the traditional city in the hands of authoritarian ideologues, postmodernism has created a new urban vision based on a populism of highly differentiated signs and symbols.[22] In the production of such an urban symbolism, vernacular traditions and the local history of any place can be readily mined and combined with other elements of a global stylistic eclecticism.[23] Thus the adapted traditions often became associated with media images to take on meanings beyond their former or immediate social or economic context.[24] David Harvey has further related these ideas to the form that the postmodern city takes under a regime of flexible accumulation/symbolic capitalism, as discussed earlier.[25] In particular, in order to become successful simulacra, postmodern spaces must be disengaged from the decaying modernist landscapes that surround them. New Urbanist small towns are an excellent example of this disengagement.

Baudrillard has outlined a progression by which this disengagement occurs, and by which a disassociation between representation and reality is produced. He has argued it begins with a representation that is a reflection of reality; moves on to the perversion of that reality when the original is no longer present, and finally ends with the simulacrum, a form of representation with no further relationship to the original.[26] Baudrillard has gone even further to describe a hyperreal condition brought about by the 'meticulous reproduction of the real, preferably through another reproductive medium such as advertising or photography, and that during their multiple medium reproductions, reality itself became unstable and hence hyperreal'.[27]

Pleasantville and America:
Nostalgia for Another Time and Place

Pleasantville contrasts the idyllic all-American lifestyle of the small town as portrayed in a fictional 1950s television show with a real vision of troubled society in the 1990s. The main characters, Jennifer (played by Reese Witherspoon) and David (played by Tobey Maguire), live in a Southern California suburb with their divorced mother. Although Jennifer is content

Pleasantville (1998). The schoolteacher describes the key features of the town.

in this environment, David is not. In particular, he is nostalgic for the imagined happier times portrayed in the TV show, 'Pleasantville', and he often escapes into its black-and-white world to avoid the conflict between his feuding, divorced parents.

David has an opportunity to experience this idyllic small-town life when he and Jennifer are mysteriously transported into the show. An anachronistic television repairman, who claims to be a fellow fan of 'Pleasantville', presents David with a peculiar remote control. While fighting over the remote, Jennifer and David are transformed into Bud and Mary Sue, the teenager stars of the show. At first, David uses his vast knowledge of 'Pleasantville' trivia to try to fit in and preserve the show's harmonious character. However, Jennifer, who is less than thrilled to be stuck in the show, tries to create excitement by challenging the *status quo* of the town. Ultimately, however, both David and Jennifer introduce outside behaviours, values, and knowledge that destabilize the equilibrium of the formerly closed community, and slowly transform it. For instance, when they first arrive, the owner of the soda shop, Mr. Johnson, must complete all of his work tasks in a specific order. However, when David shows up late to work one day, Mr. Johnson expresses pleasure in the spontaneity he experiences. This leads him to question the carefully scripted responsibilities and codes of behaviour to which he had formerly conformed. And ultimately, he experiences an existential dilemma, and begins to dream of transcending his role as a hamburger maker, to pursue a fantasy of becoming an artist.

More importantly, Jennifer transgresses the town's gender norms by introducing sexuality to Pleasantville. Her flirtations and sexual encounters with Skip Martin offer an alternative to the town's sweet and well-mannered courting rituals. As a result of her prodding, public displays of affection

Pleasantville. The Soda Shop.

no longer involve the formal pinning ceremony and going steady; instead, couples kiss in public and frequent Lover's Lane to explore their sexuality. Jennifer also introduces her 'mother' Betty to sexual pleasure, allowing her to develop an identity beyond that of a wife and mother. As the citizens of the black-and-white Pleasantville, particularly the youth, begin to discover their sexuality, their bodies, clothes, and familiar objects around them begin to turn to colour. Some of the characters even turn completely 'coloured', a term that is used in the dialogue very carefully to underline its double meaning. These transformations are presented as occurring when individuals experience authentic emotions.

But the transformations brought by the presence of David and Jennifer are not only sexual. Before Jennifer and David came to this virtual town, all its books were blank, and residents had no knowledge of the outside world. However, David and Jennifer's memory of the plots of books allow their pages to be filled in, introducing knowledge of different social orders. Hereafter, reading becomes a subversive act in Pleasantville. Jennifer herself turns coloured one night when she abandons her usual exploits to stay up reading, something she was unaccustomed to doing in her real life. David, on the other hand, changes to colour when he defends Betty from being harassed by a black-and-white boy. Thus, the change to 'coloured' can also be caused by deviating from community-imposed norms to discover one's own individuality.

The changes taking place in Pleasantville are not approved of by all the residents. Those in danger of losing power and prestige, such as the men of the Chamber of Commerce, are anxious to preserve and regain the 'pleasant' values of the past. But despite their efforts, the town erupts into violence as its citizens become divided into factions – the 'coloureds', and those still in

Pleasantville. The Chamber of Commerce doubles as the town hall.

black-and-white, Mr. Johnson's soda shop becomes a site of conflict, after it is vandalized by a mob of black-and-whites when he paints a nude portrait of Betty on its window. The Chamber of Commerce tries to respond to these events by creating a Code of Conduct to suppress rebellious behaviour and restore order. However, Bud and Mr. Johnson decide to challenge the new rules by painting a mural depicting the recent events in the town. At their trial for misconduct, Bud tries to convince Bob, the head of the Chamber of Commerce, that change is a positive and inevitable force, and that individuals need to express their true character. As tempers flare, and the town is forced to confront the changes occurring, even Bob, in a fit of anger, is enraged into colour. The film ends after the whole black-and-white town turns coloured, and Pleasantville ceases to be a utopian social space.

At the end of the film, both of the main characters are also changed

Pleasantville. The Soda Shop becomes the object of rage, as it becomes coloured.

by their experiences. Jennifer chooses to remain in Pleasantville to attend college, thus exploring an undeveloped side of her personality and taking advantage of a lifestyle unavailable to her in the 1990s. David, on the other hand, returns wilfully to the 1990s. Cured of his nostalgia, he embraces the uncertainty and freedom of real life.

The *Truman Show* and the Neotraditional Small Town

The Truman Show's protagonist Truman Burbank (played by Jim Carrey) believes he is living an ordinary life in the small island town of Seahaven. He has a perky wife, a cosy home, friendly neighbours, and a boring job in insurance sales. Truman, however, is not just another man. Adopted at birth by a corporation at the instigation of a television producer, Christof, he is the unwitting star of a top-grossing reality television show. Since birth, Truman has lived in a studio set that functions like a real town, from which his every move is broadcast around the world to millions of viewers, twenty-four hours a day. At the beginning of the film, Truman has no idea that he is being watched, or that all the people around him, including his family and friends, are actors. And he has no idea that the show is financed through advertisements worked into his day. Indeed, everything around him, from hot chocolate to kitchen appliances, is for sale. Truman's longing for adventure is ignited by bits of knowledge about the outside world presented to him in a filtered manner. And then he is confronted by a series of strange occurrences. One day a light fixture falls from the sky. Then he hears a radio broadcast reporting his every move. Finally the appearance of his deceased father causes him to doubt the reality of the world around him.

The Truman Show (1998). Truman is under constant surveillance.

As the film progresses Truman gradually develops a paranoia that he is being watched, and begins to distrust and withdraw from the people around him. He becomes particularly suspicious of his wife Meryl, whose ill-timed product placements contribute to his sense of estrangement. The only person Truman continues to trust is his best friend Marlon, to whom he expresses his suspicions. 'Maybe I'm losing my mind', Truman says. 'But … it's like the whole world revolves around me somehow … everybody seems to be in on it'. To this Marlon responds, as if with perfect candour: 'The last thing I would ever do … is lie to you'. As Christof feeds him lines through an earpiece, Marlon continues, 'I mean, think about it, Truman. If everybody's in on it, I'd hafta' be in on it, too'.[28]

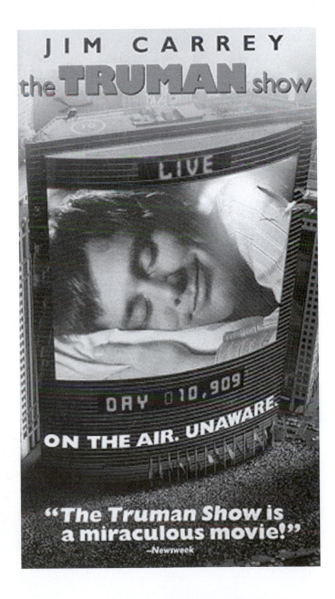

The Truman Show.
Film poster.

As Truman's suspicions mount, he begins to test his environment, spontaneously exploring places off his normal route. Departing from his normal behaviour, he eventually discovers a 'backstage' area where an elevator should be. However, the greatest obstacle he faces is a deep-seated fear of water that inhibits him from crossing the bridge to leave the island. In fact, flashbacks reveal, Christof has manufactured many ways to keep Truman on the island. He even developed an episode in which Truman's father died in a tragic boating accident in order to programme Truman psychologically to fear the ocean. This fear is further fed through continual suggestions, including newspaper articles, radio dialogue, and advertisements that proclaim the dangers of travel.

On a real radio programme Christof is questioned by a caller, who turns out to be Sylvia, a rebellious member of the cast. Christof justifies his refusal to free Truman from the confines of the show by arguing that if Truman really wanted to leave Seahaven, he could. Yet, all the while, Christof has managed to exploit Truman's longing for a larger world, staging and reshaping his emotional turmoil to create a gripping story line. For example, one of Truman's greatest motivations for leaving Seaside is to search for his lost high school sweetheart. This character was played by Sylvia, who was kicked off the show after she tried to tell Truman the truth about his world. Truman dreams of flying to Bali, where 'Sylvia's' family supposedly moved to cure her 'mental illness'. Christof further sells this story component by including clips of the episodes in which it played out on a best-hits tape, and by piecing flashbacks to it in later shows to explain Truman's behaviour. Christof also manages to manipulate the unexpected return of Truman's father, who breaks into the set with the hope of seeing his 'son' again by

The Truman Show. The downtown seaside is entirely fabricated as the town of Seahaven.

The Truman Show. Truman's neighbourhood in the film is a real site – Seaside, Florida.

writing the father back into the show in a dramatic scene where they are reunited.

Despite the manipulations of Christof, whose name alludes to his position as God in Truman's life, Truman becomes increasingly determined to find out the truth and escape from the island. After a failed escape attempt when he succeeds in crossing to the mainland but is apprehended by police at a suspicious roadblock, Truman pretends to settle back into routine. However, one night he evades detection by the hundreds of cameras that monitor him pretending to be asleep in his basement and tries to sail away. Yet even as Truman is finally escaping across the 'ocean' toward the edge of the set in a small sailboat, Christof still tries to remain in control. To find Truman, he transgresses the seeming rules of nature, first turning the moon into a searchlight and then deciding to 'cue the sun' in the middle of the night. He even has all the actors from the show walk in lock step through the town searching for Truman. In this scene the cast is depicted as a unified entity, obedient to the corporation and programmed toward a single purpose of keeping Truman in Seahaven.

When Truman is finally located, in a sailboat, Christof creates a dangerous and possibly deadly storm in his attempt to stop him from sailing to the edge of his world. However, Truman does finally reach the horizon and his sailboat punctures the painted wall of the studio. As Truman hesitates in front of the studio exit, Christof amplifies his voice from the sky and introduces himself as 'the creator ... of a television show that gives hope and joy and inspiration to millions'.[29] He implores Truman to stay; however, in the end Truman walks out the studio door in search of an authentic life.

The Truman Show. Seaside as the set of Seahaven.

Pleasantville and Seahaven: Hyperreality and Simulacra

The towns portrayed in these films tell us a lot about late-twentieth-century American notions of urbanism. As portrayed in film, Pleasantville seems to have only a commercial Main Street and a residential Elm Street. Its downtown is similar to that of many Midwestern towns where a business district grew cumulatively at the intersection of two important streets.[30] Where the two streets cross, there is a town square, a town hall and a public library. Otherwise, the architecture of Pleasantville depicts an idealized American small town in the 1950s. Its public spaces are surrounded by neoclassical civic architecture, while its houses are primarily neocolonial, featuring central entrance halls and symmetrical flanking wings.

Beyond this image of small town perfection, however, the town has no physical or social connections to other places. It is an imaginary place, outside of time and space, where the roads go in circles, and there is no possibility for change. Indeed, when Jennifer, posing as Mary Sue, asks, 'What's outside of Pleasantville?' she is confronted by blank stares. There is no concept of outside, let alone access to it. And when she persists, asking, 'What's at the end of Main Street?' the teacher only laughs and replies, 'You should know the answer to that … the end of Main Street is just the beginning again'. Here Main Street is not only the 'moral centre'[31] or the 'lifeblood of the town',[32] but a veritable axis mundi of existence.

In contrast to this perfect image of 1950s America, the 1990s are represented as embodying only suburbs without a past – or a future. David and Jennifer live in a neighbourhood where rows of dreary stucco houses protrude from a smoggy asphalt desert. At school, teachers proclaim the lack of opportunities for their students in a world of disease, economic decline, and environmental decay.

This pessimistic view is directly contrasted with the optimism of the small town in the 'Pleasantville' TV show with which David is infatuated. In Pleasantville, none of the societal problems of the 1990s is present – but nor are the societal cleavages of the 1950s. For example, the population of Pleasantville is entirely white and middle class, and everyone behaves in a 'courteous and pleasant manner', according to unquestioned communally-held norms. Politics and dispute are similarly absent, and authority, according to tradition, remains in the hands of prominent men. Although Pleasantville has a 'Town Hall', its government is not democratically elected. Instead, it is run by the Chamber of Commerce, an oligarchic committee of self-appointed male business owners. It is interesting to note an emblem of two white hands shaking represents this organization. This logo is strikingly similar to that of the US Agency for International Development (USAID), a government agency that provides economic 'assistance' to countries in order to encourage the development of capitalist enterprise, particularly in the global South. USAID, like the Chamber of Commerce, often uses undemocratic economic pressures to coerce the countries it assists into adopting American values and business practices. Here, decisions in Pleasantville are made not through democratic voting, but through business committee decisions, providing an interesting analogy.

Before David and Jennifer came to Pleasantville, the closed nature of this society precluded any conflict or change. However, when Jennifer and David are zapped into the television show, the outside influences they bring cause Mr. Johnson, Betty, and the town's youth to challenge the codes of acceptable behaviour and the perceived proper ways to use public space. In particular, prior to their arrival, the town has been spatially ordered according to gender divisions of labour and recreation. However, as Pleasantville changes, so too do the meanings of its previously gendered spaces. Thus the kitchen and bathroom become places where Betty can re-imagine the bounds of her identity, rather than conform to norms of domesticity. And the bowling alley and the barbershop are transformed from confident bastions of male dominance, to places of escape from the disorder of changing social relations. Ultimately, when Betty leaves George, she also challenges the sanctity of the space of the home, and the social ordering of the entire town based upon the needs of the nuclear family.

Levy has argued that in the films of the 1950s, generally, small-town life was depicted as 'emotionally stifling, intellectually suffocating, and sexually repressive'.[33] In Pleasantville such constrictive norms are challenged after the arrival of David and Jennifer by its youth, who introduce sex, literature, art, and rock and roll music. Eventually, such public spaces as the soda shop and the library become places for innovation and rebellion. In addition, Lover's Lane becomes a place where they can evade the town's repressive sexual codes. Levy has written that in 1950s films such places were often depicted as natural places of 'uninhibited life', where protagonists could escape the constrictions of society.[34] However, Lover's Lane in Pleasantville also becomes a place of rebellion, an Eden where the characters taste the forbidden fruits of sexual experience. Along with the soda shop, it is one of the first places that turns to colour. These are places where the awakened youth resist the dominant social order of Pleasantville.

In Pleasantville, the main symbol of authority of this dominant social order is the Town Hall. However, this building remains little more than a symbol, albeit a powerful one, until it is forced into use in an effort to stem the unprecedented changes ongoing in the town, and the violent reactions to them by some of the town's people. Toward the film's end, the Town Hall becomes a meeting place where the citizens of Pleasantville discuss the changing social order. And it serves as a courthouse where the Chamber of Commerce announces its new rules, and attempts to punish offenders. In these meetings and trials, Bob, the head of the Chamber of Commerce, plays mayor and judge, standing front and centre, flanked by the all black-and-white male members of the Code of Conduct Committee. During the final pivotal trial, the citizens of the town are depicted as seated in two tiers in this building; the black-and-white citizens in the main area below, while the 'coloured' characters sit in the balcony above. This division recalls the segregation of public spaces under the Jim Crow laws in the South during the first half of the twentieth century. Similarly trial scenes were used to demonstrate 'communal pride', acting to reinforce the order of the town's 'moral centre' after an outbreak of deviant behaviour.[35]

In the film, this reinforcement is ultimately unsuccessful, as the 'coloured' deviants finally manage to convert all the town's black-and-white residents. Nevertheless, after its transformation, Pleasantville retains its small-town character – but with greater social liberty. The roads now connect to other towns, residents have access to higher education, and people may come and go freely. The opening of this closed social space at the end of the film signifies the relaxation of traditional norms of behaviour, allowing a freedom similar to that enjoyed by David and Jennifer in their real former suburban life.

Unlike *Pleasantville*, which begins as an imaginary ideal space, *The Truman Show* takes place in a real fake space created in a large domed studio. This environment is complete with an artificial sun, computerized weather systems, and a horizon. In the moon room, the director and video technicians watch over the set using a system of five hundred cameras. The fictional world created is Seahaven, an island off the Florida coast. The 'sets' emulate a commercial centre with a flourishing street life, quaint neotraditional homes, and pristine public spaces.

As in *Pleasantville*, therefore, much of *The Truman Show*'s plot takes place in a virtual space where the characters' actions are scripted, and their lives are broadcast to the world. In this world, buildings act as stand-ins, evoking a certain public or private institution or agency that one might expect in a small town, without actually filling those functions. However, unlike in Pleasantville, Seahaven is not an imaginary space, but a real stage set inhabited by actors. Its façades thus do not hide absences as in Pleasantville, but backstage areas occupied by the real community that supports the television show.

Both the real environment and fictional geography represented in *The Truman Show* are islands, isolated from the influence of the outside world. Thus the domed studio delineates a space outside 'the real world'. So too does the setting of Seahaven on a small island off the coast of Florida. One can only reach the mainland by crossing a small channel by a bridge or a ferry. Despite the effectiveness of this barrier in keeping Truman from discovering the true limits of his world, knowledge of the 'outside' is not erased, only filtered. Truman thus learns of other places and times, and is given manufactured memories of travels he never took to distant places. However, the images are always hazy, and they are always accompanied by discouraging commentary. The outside world is normally portrayed as a scary place, that is out of control and where lethal accidents are common.

On the other hand Seahaven is carefully scripted as a nurturing environment where friendly neighbours are always smiling. As in Pleasantville, all the residents of Seahaven are middle class – even if they are not all white. Thus where Pleasantville represents nostalgia for the past, Seahaven represents the transplanting of a politically correct version of that nostalgic past into the present. On the set of Seahaven, a cast of thousands takes their places each morning to create the illusion of a thriving small town. Yet, the only real action taking place there is the creation of a television show. The extras repeat scripted loops of behaviour on foot or bicycles only occasionally being called upon to improvise to control Truman's increasingly erratic behaviour.

In this place there is no real division of public and private space. Although traditionally, the home is a sphere where an individual can act outside public view, Truman does not have this luxury. His every move is captured on camera and the directors determine what of it to broadcast. Home is also normally a place where family members can behave intimately with each other. However, Truman's wife Meryl is too busy spouting advertisements to really see or hear Truman. As an actor, she believes, '... there is no difference between a private life and a public life. My life is my life; my life is *The*

Truman Show'.[36] On the other hand, Truman, despite being an unwittingly permanent public figure, is a very private person, and he often tries to find secluded spaces where he can engage his repressed fantasies. In the basement, he stores mementos of his father and high school sweetheart Sylvia out of sight of his wife, family and friends. He is unaware that millions of viewers watch him during these moments and believe they are sharing them with him. Indeed, Truman's most private moments are what make him valuable as a public commodity.

The Changing Neotraditional Town

In their own ways, each of these films critiques the contemporary American desire to reconstruct urban experience to achieve an ideal past, as represented by the small-town life of the 1950s. In *Pleasantville*, this nostalgia crystallizes in the longing for a fantasy of supposed normality based on harmonious social and physical environments. *The Truman Show* goes further to depict the re-creation of this past in a specially made neotraditional town whose residents' scripted behaviour is then broadcast as a TV show. Both films thus embody 'real' utopias, where the 'real' past has been free from a physical decay and social unrest.

Baudrillard has likewise argued that America is currently engaged in a vast 'clean-up operation', 'getting rid of rubbish, and patina, getting back to an original state of cleanliness'.[37] Thus nostalgic neotraditional environments now exist not only in the space of film but in the actual restored environments of the preservation movement and in the developments of New Urbanism. And the designers of many New Urbanist projects in particular may aspire to re-create not only the real social institutions and physical spaces of the traditional American small town, but idealized versions of them as constituted in film and on television. Thus, today's neotraditional town may actually be 'a copy without an original', a simulacrum once removed from the object it tries to reproduce.

In *Pleasantville*, this American utopia is daily modelled on the physical and social condition in such television shows as 'Leave it to Beaver', which represented the traditional family values and behaviours supposedly typical of small-town life.[38] However, these types of shows depicted a purified vision of small-town life that erased signs of struggle and nonconformity.[39] Thus, many of these shows manufactured a picture of the 1950s that was cleansed of political, economic, or racial difference. In the film, the 'Pleasantville' television show is depicted as just such a utopian construction broadcast for consumption by the masses. However, Gary Ross critiques it by showing how the introduction of outside characters subverts its black-and-white representations, and 'colours' its world according to the conflicts of real life.

The Truman Show depicts not a return to a fictional past, but an attempt to re-create it in the present. Like the modern-day developer, Christof creates an entire fake neotraditional town in which to set the actions of an 'everyman'. He claims this has 'given Truman a chance to live a normal life', one he never could have lived in the turmoil of the real world. According to Christof, 'The world … is the sick place, Seahaven is the way the world should be'.[40] But this stage set really only acts as a paranormal space, according to Sorkin, because it is 'just like the real thing, only better'.[41] And Truman is ultimately also unaware that his entire universe is a commercial construction and that everything around him is for sale.

Commenting on the California landscape, Baudrillard has similarly argued that 'everything is destined to reappear as simulation … you wonder if the world itself isn't advertising a copy for some other world'.[42] And he has argued that such present-day environments, characterized by an obsession with cleanliness and the desire to 'withdraw into some protective bubble' are predicated upon a fear of death, and a struggle for survival.[43] Sorkin further believes that such spaces mimic the theme park experience, where cleanliness and friendliness serve as a 'redemption of the industrial metropolis'.[44] By contrast in both these films, the main character subverts behavioural norms and achieves the freedom of authentic experience.

Many of the characters in both films, including Christof and the television repairman, represent those sectors of society which believe in an integrated *Gesselschaft* form of community that existed in the premodern small town. But these idealized images ignore many negative aspects of the premodern world, such as its isolation, authoritarianism, and ignorance. Many urban theorists, like Tönnies, have lamented the loss of rural forms of community. And New Urbanists have tried to re-create this 'lost' form by re-creating the physical and social infrastructure of the small town. Thus Peter Katz has stated that New Urbanism 'addresses many of the ills of our current sprawl development pattern while returning to a cherished American icon: that of a compact and close-knit community'.[45] New Urbanists assume that by simulating the forms of the small town, they can engineer a rebirth of a past way of life, erased by the onset of modernity. It is not surprising therefore that The Truman Show was filmed at Seaside, Florida, one of the earliest New Urbanist developments.

In both *Pleasantville* and *The Truman Show*, the equilibrium of such small-town utopia is upset by outside influences that challenge the *status quo*. In *Pleasantville* this is the appearance of David and Jennifer from the real world of the 1990s. In *The Truman Show*, it is the reappearance of Truman's presumably dead father, and a series of technical malfunctions and clumsy script improvisations. In both instances, the outside forces cause the residents of these perfect worlds to ask questions about themselves. Such a search is personally liberating, as it opens the door to real 'social' problems incompatible with the utopian small-town vision.

Both Sorkin and Michael Pollan have addressed how the Disney Company faced similar problems when it tried to create its New Urbanist community at Celebration. Sorkin observed that when such utopian ideals are put into practice, the resulting settlements quickly develop urban problems.[46] Disney had earlier been frustrated that its iconic Disneyland was surrounded by uncontrolled development at its 'undisciplined periphery'. But at Celebration, it faced even greater challenges. Pollan has argued that 'real community is messy, ever changing, and inevitably political... At Celebration, Disney has set in motion an experiment that it can only partially control'.[47]

Disney has, of course, tried to retain this control by maintaining political and economic jurisdiction over the town. Thus, the unpredictability of democratic government and political conflict was replaced by the more even-tempered authority of a company-appointed town manager. And in Celebration, there is supposedly no need for debate, because the rules and procedures are all clearly outlined in codes, covenants and restrictions. Indeed the very purpose of Celebration is to avoid change in political, economic, or aesthetic terms. According to Pollan, its master planner, Robert Stern, even 'spoke of time leaving its mark, not people'.[48] Thus codes require residents to maintain their homes according to standards which range from prescribing acceptable exterior paint colours to prohibiting red curtains. Stern has defended the rules, stating, 'In a freewheeling capitalist society, you need controls – you can't have community without them... I am convinced that these controls are actually liberating to people. It makes them feel their investment is safe'.[49] But such comments underscore the reality that in communities like Celebration, freedom is defined economically, rather than socially or politically. In Celebration residents do not have the freedom to challenge town policy, or to make their own aesthetic choices. Instead they have freedom 'from': freedom from the fear of losing their investment, of encountering strangers in their midst, or of having to see the 'icky' red curtains in their neighbour's window.[50]

Celebration's codes of conduct, regarding both aesthetics and behaviour, are similar to those of Pleasantville. At the beginning of the film, the town is dominated by a strong set of unwritten, unquestioned beliefs and behavioural norms. These maintain gender divisions of space and labour; prohibit violence, sexuality and politics; and enforce an overall pleasant mode of social interaction. It is only when this closed social space is threatened by outside values and behaviours that these norms need to be codified. Thus the codes of conduct signal not harmony, but the need for new forms of discipline. Such legal codifications of unwritten traditions frequently signal the tensions between the premodern world and modern forms of governance. And it is in this context that New Urbanists argue that codes help create a balance between collective norms and individual diversity typical of towns developed over decades or centuries.[51] However, a common theme in small-town films of the 1950s, according to Levy, is the stifling effect of such norms on individuality.[52] According to Ross, by trying to speed up the historical circumstances that create local character, and by replacing the unwritten transmission of tradition with elaborate forms of regulation, New Urbanist communities risk institutionalizing social norms to a point where they oppress residents' freedom.[53]

In both the films and towns discussed in this chapter, the quest to avoid change creates an environment in which individual ideas, rights, or concerns are subordinated to those of the community. In *Pleasantville*, when the 'coloureds' threaten the town's way of life, they come to be seen less as people with their own rights than as a negative collective force. In the real town of Celebration, Pollan has reported that politics is similarly equated with 'divisiveness'.[54] In Celebration, the first great challenge to community harmony was a debate over teaching strategies at the local public school. When a group of parents organized to challenge the curriculum, they were blamed for creating negative publicity, which company executives claimed, 'galvanized the whole community'.[55] One resident subsequently complained: 'I knew Celebration was going to be a controlled situation … but as soon as you run into a problem, you find that there is no mechanism to change things'.[56]

In *The Truman Show*, this situation is even more extreme, since most characters are scripted to preserve the illusion that Seahaven is a real town. Any character who acts spontaneously or expresses opposition to this scripted world is simply fired. As in Seahaven, individual political views pose social and economic risks in Celebration. Residents are bound to contribute to the success of the town socially if they are to protect their economic investment. Thus if a resident disagrees with Disney policies or is unwilling to live by the local standards, that person must either repress their opposition or move.

In Celebration, as in Pleasantville, architectural symbols of democracy also substitute for truly democratic institutions. Both towns showcase a town hall as an emblem of this small-town democratic structure. However, in Celebration, the Philip Johnson-designed structure is not only a stylistic perversion of Beaux-Arts traditions but serves only as an office building for a privatized government that offers 'one stop shopping for services'.[57] Thus, at Celebration public functions are privatized, and citizens become consumers.

As in *Pleasantville*, there were no elections for leadership positions in Celebration as a development. According to Pollan, the Disney-appointed town manager acts only as a 'sort of mayor', who 'sees running Celebration not as a matter of politics but as consensus building'.[58] Like the figure of 'Big Bob' in *Pleasantville*, the Celebration manager's primary responsibility is to avoid any social conflict that might degrade its commercial values. Neither figure is accountable to the members of the community as a whole – only to the elite groups that appoint them. In *Pleasantville*, 'Big Bob' represents the white, male business owners; in Celebration the manager enforces the codes stipulated by the Disney Corporation. These figures do not rule with the iron fist but rather through uncompromising coercion – what Pollan has called 'Big Brother with a smiley face'.[59] For example, Celebration's manager may arrange 'focus groups' to discuss problems as they arise, a tactic that allows residents the satisfaction of being heard without actually being able to make political demands. According to Ross, the residents of Celebration have responded favourably to this government form, believing that a 'benevolent dictator' can more efficiently respond to their needs than typical city officials.[60] They see Celebration as an ideal state where bureaucracy is avoided, and where 'community' is instead created 'without government layers of elected officials to stifle the process of self-determination'.[61] Disney has thus developed a new form of democracy, one no longer defined in 'terms of power and voting, rights and self-rule', but rather according to a 'responsive government' of 'being listened to'.[62] And he has pointed out that such authoritarianism can only claim the garb of democracy in a place where town officials relate to residents as consumers, rather than through the 'republican principle of citizenship'.[63]

The Inverted Panopticon

In *The Truman Show*, Seahaven is an enclosed environment where Truman's every move is filmed by hundreds of cameras. He is thus the prisoner of a panopticon; however, this device acts very differently from that described by Foucault. Foucault's panopticon aimed to control and punish by subjecting prisoners to constant surveillance by a single central viewing authority. Here the prisoner is unaware of his surveillance, and is subject to view not by a central authority but by the entire world. *The Truman Show* thus, in a sense, inverts the diagram of the Panopticon.

The creators of *The Truman Show* justify the construction of this world, citing the supposed benefits it produces: these include the quality of Truman's life in Seahaven and the joy that watching him brings to his audience. Baudrillard has argued that such environments of 'natural and social over-protectedness' usually create all the 'agonies of the carceral universe'.[64] Sylvia criticizes the show claiming, 'He's not a performer. He's a prisoner'. To this, Christof responds 'What distresses you, really, caller, is that ultimately, Truman prefers his "cell", as you call it'.[65] Sorkin has commented on what he sees as the evolution of this panoptic idea, noting the growing 'willingness of its subjects to participate'.[66] He pointed out that in the 1990s, many people began to choose freely to live in prison-like suburban enclaves, since the residents of gated communities 'submit to an elaborate system of surveillance with the ultimate rationale of self-protection'.[67]

The panopticon presented in *The Truman Show*, however, is actually a hybrid between the centrally controlled surveillance of the modernist utopia, as seen in *Brazil*, and the voyeurism depicted in *Sliver*. In *Brazil*, surveillance through ubiquitous television monitors allowed an urban world to be controlled by a powerful central authority. In *The Truman Show*, Christof plays a similar role, and the panopticon he operates allows a powerful corporation to produce the Truman television show. Thus, when Truman begins to act erratically, such as when he threatens Meryl, the producers can use its powerful apparatus to intervene in the 'scene' and correct his behaviour. The producers are also able to use the information they glean from surveillance to mould the course of Truman's life.

Commenting on the postmodern nature of such a condition, Norman Denzin has stated that the 'real in its plentitude can be captured if only the right camera angle and shot can be found'.[68] In this sense, Truman is the 'real' that Christof is trying to capture. He even states that 'While the world he inhabits is in some respects counterfeit, there's nothing fake about Truman himself. No scripts, no cue cards ... It isn't always Shakespeare but it's genuine'.[69] However, Christof pursues his objective of depicting Truman's humanity without reflecting on the ethics of his own position and is ultimately willing to take any action to preserve the television show. Denzin has noted that ethnographers have developed various ethics for their methods of observation. The most lenient, known as the conflict/deception model, 'endorses voyeurism in the name of science, truth and understanding... [I]n this model the researcher uses any method necessary to obtain greater and deeper understanding ... telling lies, deliberately misrepresenting the self, duping others ...'.[70] This is the approach that Christof takes in pursuit of his belief that 'true stories can be told'. Thus, he commodifies Truman's life, turning it into a series of episodes for public consumption.[71]

Like the main characters in *Rear Window* and *Sliver*, the public that watches the Truman television show is hungry for images of life and starved for real social relationships. Thus, the camera is not only a tool of control but also a source of truth and meaning which is absent in the real. At the end of the movie, when Truman discovers he was a character in a television show, he asks, 'Was nothing real?' To this Christof responds: 'You were real. That's what made you so good to watch'.[72] The public, although not directly responsible for Truman's incarceration, is nevertheless complicit in it by serving as willing 'consumers' of the spectacle of his life.

A further irony evident in *The Truman Show* concerns the interdependence of the sense of reality it creates and that of the real town of Seaside in which it was filmed. New Urbanist communities are in some respects designed to emulate an ideal of small-town life as promoted by TV. But *The Truman Show* has now been used to promote Seaside despite the fact that the film ultimately questions the sustainability of such artificial environments.

In this regard, the staged town of *The Truman Show* also evokes a central aspect of postmodernist thought. Stuart Aitken and Leo Zonn have described this as a convergence between the real and the image of the real.[73] Like Truman, there is no guarantee in the postmodern world that what we experience is, in fact, reality. Reality depends on one's point of view – one person's reality may not be the same as another's.[74] The real must also be understood in relation to its representation. Thus *The Truman Show* ultimately does depict a reality beyond the fake stage set. And, Truman gradually comes to understand what exists beyond his immediate environment.

Within the film, these conditions are symbolized by the establishment of two public spaces. The first is the fake town square of Seahaven – the public space as experienced by Truman within the virtual city. The second is the 'virtual' public space of Truman's life as it is made accessible through television to millions of viewers. It is in the town square that Truman comes to suspect that the world he occupies is not as real as it seems, but is indeed a tightly controlled theatrical production.

But at the film's end, Christof alludes to the importance of the second form of public space when he tells Truman of the community of viewers who have shared his life. Paul Adams has discussed this phenomenon of a television community and the way it affects people's sense of reality.[75] He has even argued that TV spaces are no different from real spaces in their ability to construct meaning, provide social context, and serve as gathering places. Indeed, in *The Truman Show*, the TV show becomes just such a 'virtual' public space that it sustains public debate over the ethical and moral identity of the society that has constructed it.

Such 'virtual' public space, however, differs significantly from real space in the way it is experienced. As well as the events within it, one's view of this type of public space is always controlled and mediated by those who create it. Thus just as the camera subjugates Truman, it also subjugates the perceptions of those who view him. According to Friedberg, this involves 'a received perception mediated through representation'.[76] Eventually, exposure to this 'mediated gaze' may reach such levels that we begin to see everything with a 'virtual gaze' – as though it were nothing more than a TV show. Similarly, by bringing its 'public' space into the private homes of viewers, television blurs the boundary between public and the private. But, in the 'public space' of television, just like Truman, viewers lack the freedom to 'see and be seen'.[77]

In this blurred public/private space of the virtual, Truman lacks the freedom to withdraw from the public gaze, just as his television viewers may lack the freedom to both enter or escape this virtual space.

The question raised by these two films requires us to rethink whether the real Seaside or Celebration serve as the model for the reel Seahaven or Pleasantville. Instead, in the current era of globalization, it is increasingly becoming clear that the opposite is true, in that real cities are now often imagined, built, and articulated based on reel experiences. In some sense, we have now returned full circle to Walter Benjamin's seminal work in which he argued, 'Even the most perfect reproduction of a work of art is lacking one element; its presence in time and space, its unique existence at the place where it happens to be'.[78] Through the movie camera, the spatial distance diminishes between the subject who is seeing and the object being seen.[79] In continuing Benjamin's project, Jean Baudrillard has suggested that the dislocation between representation and reality has produced 'the generation by models of a real without origin or reality: a hyperreal'.[80] The progression from representation to simulation is important here. In the former, reality still exists as a frame of reference; in the latter, the connection between reality and the simulacrum is totally severed. Umberto Eco, also continuing in this conceptual framework, has suggested that in America, in particular, things that look real become real even if they never existed.[81] Hence, Disneyland – a physical articulation of fantasy – not only produces illusion but stimulates the desire for it. As a result, the copy becomes far more interesting, compelling or enjoyable than the original, and the original simply ceases to be of any interest or significance altogether. This is indeed the case with both Seahaven and Pleasantville's hyperreal environments – products of a virtual gaze – that find their potential in the postmodern condition of the ex-urban spaces of America at the beginning of the twenty-first century.

Notes

1   R. Lingeman, *Small Town America: A Narrative History 1620–Present*. New York: G.P. Putnam's Sons, 1980, p. 471.
2   *Ibid.*
3   For a detailed survey of New Urbanism, refer to P. Katz, *The New Urbanism*. New York: McGraw Hill, 1994, p. xxxv.
4   A. Duany and E. Plater-Zyberk, *Towns and Town Making Principles*. New York: Rizzoli, 1991, p. 22.
5   *Ibid.*, p. 13
6   M. Sorkin, 'See You in Disneyland', *Variations on a Theme Park*. New York: Hill and Wang, 1992, p. 224.
7   M. Pollan, 'Town Building is No Mickey Mouse Operation', *New York Times Magazine*, 14 December, 1997, p. 57.
8   A. Ross, *The Celebration Chronicles*. New York: Ballantine Books, 1999, p. 88.
9   J. Baudrillard, *America*. London: Verso, 1988, p. 44.

10 M. Sorkin, 'See You in Disneyland', p. 218.

11 *Ibid*., p. 208.

12 D. Mitchell, *Cultural Geography: A Critical Introduction*, Oxford: Blackwell 2000, p. 136.

13 M. Sorkin, 'See You in Disneyland', p. 226.

14 *Ibid.,* p. 231.

15 Garry Ross (1956–) is the son of black-listed scriptwriter Arthur Ross. He studied at the University of Pennsylvania. After a brief career as a novelist, he was recruited by Paramount Pictures as a writer. Since his screenplay 'Big' (1988) brought him national acclaim, he has written and directed films with stories on mistaken identities and subversion of the *status quo*. Viewed on 23 August 2005, on http://movies2.nytimes.com.

16 Peter Weir (1944–) was born in Australia, the son of a real estate agent. After travelling around Europe, he returned to Australia to work for the Commonwealth Film Unit. He directed his first film in 1971 (*Three to Go*), but it was *Gallipoli* (1981) that brought him – and its star, Mel Gibson – international recognition. Soon, Weir moved to the US to work in Hollywood. Viewed on August 23, 2005, on http://movies2.nytimes.com.

17 *Pleasantville* and *The Truman Show* are both 'suburban-centred' in the words of Douglas Muzzio and Thomas Halper. For a concise analysis of suburbia in movies – and particularly on 'how films have influenced and reflected public discourse on suburbs', see: D. Muzzio and T. Halper, 'Pleasantville? The Suburb and Its representation in American Movies', *Urban Affairs Review,* vol. 37, no. 4, 2002, pp. 543–574.

18 J. Baudrillard, *America*, p. 28.

19 M. Sorkin, 'See You in Disneyland', p. 226.

20 J. Baudrillard, *Simulacra and Simulation*, Sheila Faria Glaser (trans.). Ann Arbor, MI: University of Michigan Press, 1994, p. 2.

21 *Ibid.*

22 F. Jameson, *Postmodernism, or the Cultural Logic of Late Capitalism*. Durham, NC: Duke University Press, 1991, p. 2.

23 D. Harvey, 'Flexible Accumulation through Urbanization: Reflections on "Postmodernism" in the American City', in Ash Amin (ed.) *Post-Fordism: A Reader*. Oxford: Blackwell, 1994, p. 363.

24 M. Featherstone, 'City Cultures and Postmodern Lifestyles', in Ash Amin (ed.), *Post-Fordism: A Reader*. Oxford: Blackwell, 1994, p. 392.

25 D. Harvey, 'Flexible Accumulation…', p.374.

26 J. Baudrillard, *Simulacra and Simulation*, p. 16.

27 *Ibid*., p. 19

28 A. Niccol, 'Truman Show Script'. Viewed on 23 August 2005, on http://www.un-official.com/Truman/TrumanShow.html.

29 *Ibid.*

30 R. Lingeman, *Small Town America*, p. 116.

31 E. Levy, *Small Town America in Film: The Decline and Fall of Community*. New York: Continuum, 1991.

32 R. Lingeman, *Small Town America*, p. 295.

33 E. Levy, *Small Town America in Film*, p. 256.

34 *Ibid.*, p. 295

35 *Ibid.*, p. 144.

36 A. Niccol, 'Truman Show Script'.

37 J. Baudrillard, *America*, p. 33.

38 G. Ross, 'Pleasantville'. Viewed on 23 August 2005 on http://www.hundland.com/scripts/Pleasantville.htm.

39 E. Levy, *Small Town America in Film,* p. 143.

40   A. Niccol, 'Truman Show'.
41   M. Sorkin, 'See You in Disneyland', p. 226.
42   J. Baudrillard, *America*, p. 12.
43   *Ibid.*, p. 43.
44   M. Sorkin, 'See You in Disneyland', p. 228.
45   P. Katz, *The New Urbanism: Toward an Architecture of Community*. New York: McGraw Hill, 1994, p. ix.
46   M. Sorkin, 'See You in Disneyland', p. 210.
47   M. Pollan, 'Town Building …', p. 58.
48   *Ibid.*, p. 62.
49   *Ibid.*, p. 66.
50   *Ibid.*, p. 66.
51   A. Duany, and E. Plater-Zyberk, *Towns and Town Making Principles*, p. 22.
52   E. Levy, *Small Town America in Film*, p. 260.
53   A. Ross, *The Celebration Chronicles*, p. 44.
54   M. Pollan, 'Town Building …', p. 66.
55   *Ibid.*, p. 63
56   *Ibid.*
57   *Ibid.*, p. 65.
58   *Ibid.*
59   *Ibid.,* p. 66.
60   A. Ross, *The Celebration Chronicles*, p. 310.
61   *Ibid.*, p. 236.
62   M. Pollan, 'Town Building …', p. 66.
63   *Ibid.,* p. 66.
64   J. Baudrillard, *America*, p. 45.
65   A. Niccol, 'Truman Show Script'.
66   M. Sorkin, 'See You in Disneyland', p. 222.
67   *Ibid.*
68   N.K. Denzin, *The Cinematic Society: The Voyeur's Gaze*. London: Sage, 1995, p. 198.
69   A. Niccol, 'Truman Show Script'.
70   N. K. Denzin, *The Cinematic Society*, p. 205.
71   *Ibid.*, p. 210
72   A. Niccol, 'Truman Show Script'.
73   S. Aitken and L. Zonn, 'Representing the Place Pastiche', in S. Aiken and L. Zonn (eds.) *Place, Power and Spectacle*. Lanham, MD: Rowman and Littlefield, 1994, pp. 3–25.
74   Many of these ideas came up in discussions with Larissa Hinde. Detailed discussions can be found in her unpublished Master's thesis 'The Virtual City', Spring 2001, University of California at Berkeley.
75   P. Adams, 'Television as a Gathering Place', *Annals of the Association of American Geographers*, vol. 82, no. 1, 1992, pp. 117–135.
76   A. Freidberg, *Window Shopping: Cinema and the Postmodern*. Berkeley, CA: University of California Press, 1993, p. 17.
77   *Ibid.*, p. 19.
78   W. Benjamin, 'A Work of Art in the Age of Mechanical Reproduction', in *Illuminations*, London: Fontana, 1974, p. 16.
79   L. Manovich, *The Language of New Media*. Cambridge, MA: MIT Press, 2001, p. 174.
80   J. Baudrillard, *Simulations*. New York: Semiotext(e), 1983, p. 2.
81   U. Eco, *Travel in Hyperreality: Essays*. London: Picador-Pan, 1987.

Epilogue

The American TV series 'Sex and the City' has been very popular at the beginning of the twenty-first century. The show attempts to capture the urban experience of four single women, friends pursuing different careers, as they navigate New York City's cultural scene. Its success has brought many tourists to places in the city where its episodes have been taped. Through a travel agency providing specialty tours to the New York of 'Sex and the City', many have come to visit the cafés, restaurants, and even apartment buildings inhabited by the fictional characters of the show, including the narrator and protagonist Carrie Bradshaw. (In a twist of irony, though the actress Sarah Jessica Parker who plays Carrie in the show lives close by, her apartment does not attract any serious attention.). When the residents of Perry Street – the real neighbourhood in which the show was taped – became fed up with the onslaught of visitors, they struck a deal with the tour agency to cash in on the tourist gaze. The agency must now pay a monthly user fee, taken from its earnings from these tours, to assist in neighbourhood upkeep and infrastructure improvement. This has included upgrading the neighbourhood with street details, such as lampposts, similar to those in the show.[1]

The story of 'Sex and the City' brings us back, full circle, to the anecdote of my five-year old nephew who invoked the reel medium as a frame of reference to understand, or comprehend the real city, and possibly to act in it. Indeed, this book has shown how the relationship between the real and reel city is unstable, volatile and changing, leading us to conclude that perhaps, like other forms of urban modernity, cinematic modernity is also transient, contingent and ephemeral.

Works discussed in the early chapters of this book, including the films *Berlin* and *Modern Times*, demonstrated how film was originally used to document, record or capture the city. In this generation of films, the real was simply recorded on celluloid. In subsequent chapters, which look at the modernity of the first half of the twentieth century, films such as *Cinema Paradiso* and *It's a Wonderful Life* portray modern life as rife with problems, but also possibilities. Here the reel is still presented as the real, but with a touch of realism – or in the case of *Mon Oncle* and *Playtime*, coupled with irony or cynicism. Other films, however, depicted dystopian modernity. For example, in *Metropolis* and *Brazil*, the reel emerges as a critique of the real, warning how an imagined dystopian future may one day turn into a present-day reality. Similarly, films that investigate postmodern urban conditions (*Blade Runner*, *Falling Down*, *Sliver*, and *The End of Violence*) become predictive treatises about the real, assigning the reel the principal function of anticipating changes in real space. Finally, in films dealing with the simulacra of post-traditional environments (*The Truman Show* and *Pleasantville*), the reel emerges as the main frame of reference, where the copy replaces the original – and even negates its relevance. Here the reel becomes the only reality that is left.

As we traverse the modernity – postmodernity axis and intersect it with the utopia–dystopia continuum, we need to reflect on the different cinematic tropes encountered in our journey. What emerges as a trope of industrial modernity in Chapter 1 is the character of a naïve individual who struggles to understand his position in society. Unlike the *flâneur*, who is detached through a leisurely and unhurried mode of observation, the tramp is the man in the crowd, motivated by the desire to join the urban masses and immerse himself in the urban experience of the city. The trope of an urbanizing modernity that emerges from the loss of small-town life is one of a *blasé*, an individual so hardened by the brutality of the metropolis that he must deaden his senses. Under this condition, he becomes a consumer of the city who equally retreats, avoids and confronts some of its more unpleasant encounters. The rendezvous, hence, develops as a specifically sociological form that signifies both the encounter with what is desired as well as its location in space. The trope of Orwellian modernity is that of the human being turned by the bureaucracy into a machine. Each individual must accept the role assigned to him – a robot-like figure invented by the social welfare state or capital to enhance the Fordist mode of production synonymous with this absolute modernity. The trope of the modernity of urban renewal is the character of the cynic, whose experience makes him part *flâneur*, part *blasé*, and part tramp, unable to relate to his modern surroundings. As we move to a postindustrial and post-Fordist system, the trope of this postmodern condition is the cyborg or replicant. Designed as the slave of off-world colonies, he must replace the everyman and the colonized Third World man, both of whom are being put out of work by an economy based on outsourcing. The trope of the modernity of surveillance is represented by the voyeur, an urban figure empowered by technology and his invisibility, and seduced by access to the private space of others. However, the logical end of voyeurism demonstrates a shift in scale, from the practice of the individual to that of the state, which turns entertainment into a dictatorship of empty images. Finally, the trope of the postmodern ex-urban condition is the inverted panopticon, which lies at the centre of simulacra. This is a new world where the reel has become the real and where the observed have entered the camera itself, reprojected on the screen not as themselves but as larger models that transcend the spatial-virtual divide.

It is this changing relationship between the real and the reel that starts to distinguish modernity from postmodernity, along a simple continuum. In the cinematic realm, modernity and postmodernity are not historical periods, but different political articulations of the relationship between the urban experience and its artistic representations. While modernity attempted to reconcile these two forms of cognition, postmodernity accepted their disjunction while allowing each to challenge the other. Ultimately, however modernity and postmodernity are states of mind that must constantly adapt to an ever-changing urban condition.

Illustration Sources and Credits

The publisher and author would like to thank the following for providing the images and films stills in this book and for permission to reproduce copyright material. While every effort has been made to trace and acknowledge all copyright holders, we would like to apologize should there have been any errors of omissions.

Columbia Pictures; Friedrich-Wilhelm-Murnau-Stiftung; Le Studio Canal+; Les Films de Mon Oncle; MGM CLIP + STILL; Miramax Films; New Line Productions, Inc.; Paramount Pictures; Regency Enterprises V.O.F; Eva Riehl; Roy Export Company Establishment; Transit Film GmbH; UCB Architecture Slide Library; Universal Studios Licensing LLLP; Warner Bros., Production Limited.

Credits for individual illustrations are listed below.

Cover
Playtime (1966). © 1967 Les Films de Mon Oncle

Chapter 1
page 24: *Modern Times* (1936). Film poster. By courtesy of the UCB Architecture Slide Library
page 25: *Berlin: Symphony of a Big City* (1927). The collage represents the city. © Eva Riehl
page 26: *Berlin: Symphony of a Big City*. The train arrives in the city. © Eva Riehl
page 27: *Berlin: Symphony of a Big City*. Morning scene: A shopkeeper cleans up before beginning the day. © Eva Riehl
page 28: *Berlin: Symphony of a Big City*. A restaurant during weekday lunchtime. © Eva Riehl
page 29: *Berlin: Symphony of a Big City*. Pedestrians, horse charts and trams share the street. © Eva Riehl
page 30: *Modern Times*. The Capitalist behind the production line. © Roy Export Company Establishment

page 31: *Modern Times*. 'Scientific management' applied to eating. © Roy Export Company Establishment

page 32: *Modern Times*. The tramp as part of the machinery of production. © Roy Export Company Establishment

Chapter 2

page 49: *Cinema Paradiso* (1989). Film poster. By courtesy of the UCB Architecture Slide Library

page 50: *Cinema Paradiso*. Giancaldo's main square becomes animated with cinema-goers.© 1989 Miramax Films

page 51: *Cinema Paradiso*. The main square from the projection booth. © 1989 Miramax Films

page 51: *Cinema Paradiso*. Alfredo projects the film out onto the façade of a building across the square. © 1989 Miramax Films

page 53: *Cinema Paradiso*. The town's crowd waits for the demolition of Cinema Paradiso. © 1989 Miramax Films

page 54: *It's a Wonderful Life* (1946). Film poster. By courtesy of the UCB Architecture Slide Library

page 55: *It's a Wonderful Life*. The Bailey Building and Loan's motto: 'Build your own home'. © Paramount Pictures. All Rights Reserved

page 55: *It's a Wonderful Life*. A suburban development like Bailey Park, built by Bailey Building and Loan – a place for families and children. By courtesy of the UCB Architecture Slide Library

page 57: *It's a Wonderful Life*. Bailey Park's antithesis is 'Pottersville'. By courtesy of Wesleyan University Cinema Archives.

Chapter 3

page 75: *Metropolis* (1926). Film poster. By courtesy of the UCB Architecture Slide Library

page 76: *Metropolis*. The master of the Metropolis and the scientist Rotwang deliberate over the robot in the making. © Friedrich-Wilhelm-Murnau-Stiftung. By courtesy of Transit Film GmbH

page 77: *Metropolis*. When their shifts are over, workers descend down to their underground city. © Friedrich-Wilhelm-Murnau-Stiftung. By courtesy of Transit Film GmbH

page 78: *Metropolis*. Workers operate the 'Moloch' machine. © Friedrich-Wilhelm-Murnau-Stiftung. By courtesy of Transit Film GmbH

page 79: *Metropolis*. Multi-levelled traffic flows in this city of the future. © Friedrich-Wilhelm-Murnau-Stiftung. By courtesy of Transit Film GmbH

page 80: *Brazil* (1985). Film poster. By courtesy of the UCB Architecture Slide Library

page 81: *Brazil*. Sam and Tuttle, the alleged terrorist outside of Sam's apartment. © 1985 Embassy International Pictures, N.V. By courtesy of Universal Studios Licensing LLLP

page 82: *Brazil*. The security apparatus at the reception of the Ministry of Information puts Jill on display next to herself. © 1985 Embassy International Pictures, N.V. By courtesy of Universal Studios Licensing LLLP

page 83: *Brazil*. Clerks hurry about in the Department of Records. When the boss disappears, they tune their TV screens to watch an old western. © 1985 Embassy International Pictures, N.V. By courtesy of Universal Studios Licensing LLLP

page 83: *Brazil*. Sam and Jill drive on a highway lined with commercial ads that block out the grey, polluted industrial landscape. © 1985 Embassy International Pictures, N.V. By courtesy of Universal Studios Licensing LLLP

page 84: *Brazil*. Inside the torture chamber, a microcosm of the whole city and nation. © 1985 Embassy International Pictures, N.V. By courtesy of Universal Studios Licensing LLLP

Chapter 4

page 102: *Mon Oncle* (1958). Monsieur Hulot lives in a ramshackle apartment building that creates the backdrop for his nostalgia. © 1958 Les Films de Mon Oncle

page 103: *Mon Oncle*. In Monsieur Hulot's imagined 'old Paris', neighbours use public spaces actively. © 1958 Les Films de Mon Oncle

page 105: *Mon Oncle*. Only Monsieur Hulot appears not to recognize the importance of the car as the icon of postwar modernity. © 1958 Les Films de Mon Oncle

page 106: *Mon Oncle*. The Arpels organize a garden party. © 1958 Les Films de Mon Oncle

page 107: *Mon Oncle*. Monsieur Arpel's home is a cubist villa, a stage for modern life; one that is uncomfortable. © 1958 Les Films de Mon Oncle

page 110: *Playtime* (1966). Modernist apartments become television screens stacked on top of each other for Tati's camera. © 1967 Les Films de Mon Oncle

page 111: *Playtime*. Monsieur Hulot is disoriented when he finds himself in a modern office space with identical cubicles. © 1967 Les Films de Mon Oncle

page 114: *Playtime*. Monsieur Hulot's inadvertent destruction of the restaurant set encourages spontaneity. © 1967 Les Films de Mon Oncle

page 115: *Playtime*. A round-about in the modernist city: congestion leading to nowhere. © 1967 Les Films de Mon Oncle

Chapter 5

page 128: *Blade Runner* (1982). 'Off world' colonies are advertised with the slogan: 'Live Clean'. Website image. By courtesy of UCB Architecture Slide Library.

page 129: *Blade Runner* The Tyrell Corporation. Website image. By courtesy of UCB Architecture Slide Library

page 129: *Blade Runner*. Inside the Tyrell Corporation. Website image. By courtesy of UCB Architecture Slide Library.

page 131: *Falling Down* (1993). Film poster. By courtesy of the UCB Architecture Slide Library

page 131: *Falling Down*. Los Angeles as a dysfunctional city: traffic jam on the highway. © 1993 Warner Bros., Production Limited, Regency Enterprises V.O.F. and Le Studio Canal+. All Rights Reserved

page 132: *Falling Down*. Foster on the 'turf' of Chicano youths. © 1993 Warner Bros., Production Limited, Regency Enterprises V.O.F. and Le Studio Canal+. All Rights Reserved

page 133: *Falling Down*. Foster smashes the grocery store owned by the Korean. © 1993 Warner Bros., Production Limited, Regency Enterprises V.O.F. and Le Studio Canal+. All Rights Reserved

page 134: *Falling Down*. Foster walking through Los Angeles. By courtesy of UCB Slide Library

Chapter 6

page 150: *Rear Window* (1954). Film poster. By courtesy of the UCB Architecture Slide Library

page 150: *Rear Window*. Jeff is able to see what others cannot. By courtesy of the UCB Architecture Slide Library

page 152: *Rear Window*. The courtyard view from Jeff's apartment. By courtesy of the UCB Architecture Slide Library

page 152: *Rear Window*. The courtyard reflected in Jeff's lens. By courtesy of the UCB Architecture Slide Library

page 153: *Rear Window*. Viewing the neighbours' private lives through the windows. By courtesy of the UCB Architecture Slide Library

page 155: *Sliver*. Carly is seduced by the equipment of voyeurism. © Paramount Pictures. All Rights Reserved

page 157: *The End of Violence*. Ray in the control room. © 1997 MGM Distribution Co. All Rights Reserved

page 158: *The End of Violence*. Surveillance cameras watch over the city. © 1997 MGM Distribution Co. All Rights Reserved

page 159: *The End of Violence* (1997). Looking over the city from the observatory. © 1997 MGM Distribution Co. All Rights Reserved

page 160: *The End of Violence*. Security men look over the highways. © 1997 MGM Distribution Co. All Rights Reserved

Chapter 7

page 173: *Annie Hall* (1977). Alvy and Annie on the rooftop. © 1977 Metro-Goldwyn-Mayer Studios Inc. All Rights Reserved

page 174: *Annie Hall*. Christmas in Los Angeles. © 1977 Metro-Goldwyn-Mayer Studios Inc. All Rights Reserved

page 175: *Manhattan* (1981). Inside the Guggenheim Museum. ©1979 Metro-Goldwyn-Mayer Studios Inc. All Rights Reserved

page 176: *Manhattan* Fireworks over Manhattan. © 1979 Metro-Goldwyn-Mayer Studios Inc. All Rights Reserved

page 177: *Manhattan*. New York City as the backdrop for romance. © 1979 Metro-Goldwyn-Mayer Studios Inc. All Rights Reserved

page 178: *Manhattan* New York's turn-of-the-century and mid-century buildings are highlighted. © 1979 Metro-Goldwyn-Mayer Studios Inc. All Rights Reserved.

page 179: *Taxi Driver* (1978). Film poster. By courtesy of the UCB Architecture Slide Library

page 180: *Taxi Driver*. Travis in the mean streets of New York. © 1976, renewed 2004 Columbia Pictures Industries, Inc. All Rights Reserved

page 181: *Taxi Driver*. 'Be Alert! The sane driver is always ready for the unexpected!' Everybody is concerned with crime on the streets. © 1976, renewed 2004 Columbia Pictures Industries, Inc. All Rights Reserved

Chapter 8

page 192: *Do the Right Thing* (1989). The 'Bed-Stuy Do-or-Die' mural. © 1989 Universal City Studios, Inc. By courtesy of Universal Studios Licensing LLLP

page 193: *Do the Right Thing*. The three black men sitting at the street corner. © 1989 Universal City Studios, Inc. By courtesy of Universal Studios Licensing LLLP

page 194: *Do the Right Thing*. Mookie delivers pizza while everyone hangs out on their stoops. © 1989 Universal City Studios, Inc. By courtesy of Universal Studios Licensing LLLP

page 195: *Do the Right Thing*. Mookie and Sal argue in front of the 'Wall of Fame'. © 1989 Universal City Studios, Inc. By courtesy of Universal Studios Licensing LLLP

page 195: *Do the Right Thing*. A Riot breaks in front of the pizzeria. © 1989 Universal City Studios, Inc. By courtesy of Universal Studios Licensing LLLP

page 196: *Do the Right Thing*. The Korean shopowner tries to protect his store from the mob. © 1989 Universal City Studios, Inc. By courtesy of Universal Studios Licensing LLLP

page 197: *My Beautiful Laundrette* (1985). The view from Omar's flat in

South London consists of railway viaducts and the abandoned Battersea Power Station. © 1985 Channel Four Television Company, Ltd. All Rights Reserved

page 198: *My Beautiful Laundrette*. The revamped launderette is a huge success. ©1985 Channel Four Television Company, Ltd. All Rights Reserved

page 199: *My Beautiful Laundrette*. Nasser and Rachel dance in the recently opened launderette. ©1985 Channel Four Television Company, Ltd. All Rights Reserved

page 200: *My Beautiful Laundrette*. Omar and Johnny repair the launderette. ©1985 Channel Four Television Company, Ltd. All Rights Reserved

page 201: *My Beautiful Laundrette*. Thugs smash the launderette's window. ©1985 Channel Four Television Company, Ltd. All Rights Reserved

Chapter 9

page 215: *Pleasantville* (1998). The schoolteacher describes the key features of the town. ©1998 New Line Productions, Inc. All Rights Reserved. Photo by Ralph Nelson. By courtesy of New Line Productions, Inc

page 216: *Pleasantville*. The Soda Shop. © 1998 New Line Productions, Inc. All Rights Reserved. Photo by Ralph Nelson. By courtesy of New Line Productions, Inc

page 217: *Pleasantville*. The Chamber of Commerce doubles as the town hall. © 1998 New Line Productions, Inc. All Rights Reserved. Photo by Ralph Nelson. By courtesy of New Line Productions, Inc

page 217: *Pleasantville*. The Soda Shop becomes the object of rage, as it becomes coloured. © 1998 New Line Productions, Inc. All Rights Reserved. Photo by Ralph Nelson. By courtesy of New Line Productions, Inc

page 218: *The Truman Show* (1998). Truman is under constant surveillance. © Paramount Pictures. All Rights Reserved.

page 219: *The Truman Show*. Film poster. By courtesy of the UCB Architecture Slide Library

page 220: *The Truman Show*. The downtown of Seaside is entirely fabricated as the town of Seahaven. By courtesy of the UCB Architecture Slide Library

page 221: *The Truman Show*. Truman's neighbourhood in the film is a real site – Seaside, Florida. By courtesy of the UCB Architecture Slide Library

page 222: *The Truman Show*. Seaside as the set of Seahaven. By courtesy of the UCB Architecture Slide Library

Selected Bibliography

Aitken, Stuart and Zonn, Leo (eds.) (1994) *Place, Power, Situation and Spectacle: A Geography of Film*. Lanham, MD: Rowman and Littlefield.

AlSayyad, Nezar (2001) *Consuming Tradition, Manufacturing Heritage: Global Norms and Urban Forms in the Age of Tourism*. London: Routledge.

Baudrillard, Jean (1988) *America*. London: Verso.

Baudrillard, Jean (1994) *Simulacra and Simulation*. Ann Arbor, MI: University of Michigan Press.

Berman, Marshall (1982) *All That Is Solid Melts Into Air*. New York: Simon and Schuster.

Clarke, David (ed.) (1997) *The Cinematic City*. London: Routledge.

Clarke, David (2003) *The Consumer Society and the Postmodern City*. London: Routledge.

Davis, Mike (1992) *City of Quartz: Excavating the Future in Los Angeles*. New York: Vintage Books.

Debord, Guy (1967) *The Society of the Spectacle*. New York: Zone Books.

Denzin, Norman (1995) *The Cinematic Society: The Voyeur's Gaze*. Thousand Oaks, CA: Sage.

Gray, Chris (2001) *Cyborg Citizen: Politics in the Posthuman Age*. New York: Routledge.

Harding, James (1984) *Jacques Tati: Frame by Frame*: London: Secker & Warburg.

Harvey, David (1989) *The Condition of Postmodernity: An Enquiry into the Origins of Cultural Change*, Oxford: Blackwell.

Hunter, Ian (ed.) (1999) *British Science Fiction Cinema*. London: Routledge.

Jameson, Fredric (1991) *Postmodernism, or, the Decline and Fall of Community*. Durham, NC: Duke University Press.

Lamster, Mark (ed.) (2000) *Architecture and Film*. New York: Princeton Architectural Press.

Lefebvre, Henri (1991) *The Production of Space*. Oxford: Blackwell.

Levy, Emanuel (1990) *Small-Town America in Film: The Decline and Fall of Community*. New York: Continuum.

MacKinnon, Kenneth (1984) *Hollywood's Small Towns: An Introduction to the American Small-Town Movie*. Metuchen, NJ: Scarecrow Press.

Minden, Michael and Bachmann, Holger (eds.) (2000) *Fritz Lang's Metropolis: Cinematic Visions of Technology and Fear*. Rochester, NY: Camden House.

Maddock, Brent (1977) *The Films of Jacques Tati*. Metuchen, NJ: Scarecrow Press.

Neumann, Dietrich (ed.) *Film Architecture: Set Designs from Metropolis to Blade Runner*. Munich: Prestel.

Penz, François and Thomas, Maureen (eds.) (1997) *Cinema and Architecture: Méliès, Mallet-Stevens, Multimedia*. London. British Film Institute.

Shiel, Mark and Fitzmaurice, Tony (eds.) (2001) *Cinema and the City: Film and Urban Societies in a Global Context*. Oxford: Blackwell.

Sorkin, Michael (1992) *Variations on a Theme Park: The New American City and the End of Public Space*. New York: Hill and Wang.

Virilio, Paul (1991) *The Aesthetics of Disappearance*. Brooklyn, NY: Semiotext(e).

Index

Note: illustrations are indicated by *italic page numbers*, notes by suffix 'n' (e.g. '187n8' means page 187, note 8); main entry for each film shown by **emboldened page numbers**